BAGHDAD OPERATORS

BAGHDAD OPERATORS

EX SPECIAL FORCES IN IRAQ

James Glasse

with

Andrew Rawson

Pen & Sword
MILITARY

956.704438

First published in Great Britain in 2013 by
Pen & Sword Military
An imprint of
Pen & Sword Books Ltd
47 Church Street
Barnsley
South Yorkshire
S70 2AS

ISBN 9781781593653

A CIP catalogue record for this book is
available from the British Library

Typeset in 10 pt Palatino by Faction Press
Printed and bound in India by
Replika Press Pvt. Ltd.

Pen & Sword Books Ltd incorporates the Imprints of Pen & Sword Aviation,
Pen & Sword Family History, Pen & Sword Maritime, Pen & Sword Military, Wharncliffe
Local History, Wharncliffe True Crime, Wharncliffe Transport
Pen & Sword Select, Pen & Sword Military Classics, Leo Cooper, The Praetorian Press
Remember When, Seaforth Publishing and Frontline Publishing
Claymore Press

For a complete list of Pen & Sword titles please contact
PEN & SWORD BOOKS LIMITED
47 Church Street, Barnsley, South Yorkshire, S70 2AS, England
E-mail: enquiries@pen-and-sword.co.uk
Website: www.pen-and-sword.co.uk

Contents

Preface

The world changed on 9/11 2001, when four planes were hi-jacked in the skies over the United States and flown into the World Trade Centre and the Pentagon. Then came the war in Afghanistan, a war which is still going on in 2013. In March 2003, ten years before this book was published, the invasion of Iraq, Operation Iraqi Freedom began. It did not take long to topple Saddam Hussein's regime and President George W. Bush was soon announcing 'Mission Accomplished'. But the mission was far from accomplished...

While battles were still being fought around Baghdad a team of five British ex-Special Forces began work escorting a client around Iraq's electricity grid, as part of the reconstruction plan for the country. What was a 'one-off' job turned into a business as the construction work snowballed and the need to protect the contractors increased. Before long the five man team had over 200 employees, many of them ex-Special Forces from around the world, working for them.

Follow the highs and lows of working in the security industry as the security teams came to terms with the chaos on Baghdad's streets, where dickers, snipers, carbombs, and IEDs were constant hazards. Discover how the men used their military skills to survive and how they constantly changed their operating procedures to try and keep one step ahead of the bad guys. And find out what happened when it went badly wrong.

The company expanded from the Basra oilfields into the Baghdad area, where life in the Green Zone evolved in complete contrast to that of the civilians living in the Red Zone. As work mushroomed, so did the dangers. But without their security teams, contractors could not function and the Coalition Provisional Authority could not fulfil its promises. Eventually the work expanded into the desolate country of Kurdistan, a fiercely independent area where everyone was viewed with suspicion.

The battles fought across Iraq were well documented by news teams and the casualties are remembered with honour. However, few know the details about the private wars fought to rebuild and protect Iraq's infrastructure while the fallen and the injured are only remembered by their families and their mates.

While some called them mercenaries, they called themselves 'Operators'.

Introduction

Army Days

I WENT TO SCHOOL in Yorkshire in the 1970s but I turned away from studies when it was time to leave. I was mixing with the wrong crowd and believed it was unfashionable to study; all I wanted to do was join the army. So, it was off to join the Paras and the harsh environment that brought, but I thrived on the discipline and knew I could become somebody in the army. It was during that time that I first came across the Special Forces when one of their guys walked through our lines, said "alright lads" and headed towards the enemy looking to fight his own war. We were amazed because we needed so much backup and all our mates to fight our war. The image of him walking alone into enemy territory never left me.

Having done all my courses and with no conflicts on the horizon, I applied for Special Forces and after a long wait was accepted onto Selection. Weeks of gruelling exercises followed in the Welsh hills, the Borneo jungle and the Scottish mountains. The selection process whittled the numbers down from over 250 to a handful but I made it and a personal greeting from the colonel welcomed us into Regiment. But that was only the start.

Over the next ten years I had many adventures all around the world but little did I know that the skills we were acquiring were also preparing me for a career after I left the services. Time spent on the streets of Northern Ireland trained us how to move covertly in potentially hostile urban environments. It also taught us the many ways of intelligence gathering when facing paramilitaries and the importance of understanding information. Then there was two years looking after a communications expert across a variety of terrains, ranging from the arctic to the arid and from mountains to desert. Little did I know the skills acquired working with a close protection team would serve me well years later.

Because in the 1990s the global security industry was tiny compared to the multi-billion dollar industry it is today. No one back then knew how the world was about to change in the aftermath of 9/11 and the wars in Afghanistan and Iraq. So when I retired in the spring of 2001, I was left wondering what I would do next: global terrorism had not been heard of. It was soon to change, but first I had to carry out one last operation.

Chapter One

One Last Operation

WHEN YOU LEAVE THE REGIMENT it does not leave you. The military exploits of the Special Forces are often in the public domain, either through the media, books or documentaries. People come to think of you as some sort of super hero, either jumping out of planes or jumping into embassies. But a lot of operations are non-military in nature and while it is in the national interest to carry them out, it is not in the national interest for them to be scrutinized by the media. After all we do not want the bad guys knowing what we get up to, do we?

Today the focus of national security is terrorist groups, such as those affiliated to al-Qaeda, and stopping them carrying out attacks. During my service a lot of our work was in Northern Ireland and what happened there will never be forgotten by some. Problems would develop if you spoke freely about your past adventures to the wrong people on civvy street. And, believe it or not, someone could pay you a visit and remind you to keep your mouth shut.

After leaving the army in April 2001 I was free to do what I wanted, and the first thing I wanted to do was move overseas. My wife and I had always been attracted to living abroad and now we had the money and the children were old enough, we decided to make the move. We decided to relocate to a favourite destination of many holiday makers and ex-pats alike: Mallorca, one of Spain's Mediterranean islands.

We looked forward to the warm climate, the laid back lifestyle and had good recommendations for local schools. While my family settled into the life, I could continue in the security business and hop on a flight to London any time; after all it was only two hours away.

Like everyone, I had built up a collection of papers relating to my work throughout my career. Some of them were training records and certificates while others related to jobs I had been involved in. While we were not officially supposed to keep anything relating to operations, I had kept copies of documents and photographs in case any court cases were brought about later. Investigations about incidents in the Troubles are still going on in Northern Ireland and you never knew when you might be called as a witness. In short I was covering my backside.

I had also acquired a haul of souvenirs and mementoes of jobs I had been on; again against official procedures. Some might say they were the spoils of war or trophies. The random mixture of items included clothing, gadgets, a few bits of military hardware and general bits and pieces. While I should have disposed of some of the items, I had never got round to it.

I had always stored my collection in two rented steel containers, the sort you see on ships, and they were kept in a local hire company compound where I could get to them anytime. Having made the decision to leave for Mallorca, I had to move the items as well; a pretty straight forward task you might think. I contacted a courier to move everything to Mallorca and he reckoned it would take two large vans. I also arranged for a mate of mine to take the military contraband off my hands and he would lose them in an army stores. The rest of the stuff could be disposed of. With everything in place, I headed to the Mediterranean while a friend supervised the move. So, as I sat back on the plane, I was confident that my stuff was on the road.

I had only been a few days in Mallorca when the courier rang me on the Saturday morning and told me he had bad news; one of their vans had been stolen. I immediately assumed they had stolen the one carrying my motorbike. But no such luck, the stolen van had been the one loaded with my paperwork and mementoes. Twenty years of documents relating to my life had gone in a flash. Although the courier offered his condolences and asked if I could fly over to sort out the details, I was in shock. After putting the phone down I sat down and tried to remember what had gone missing. There were literally hundreds of highly sensitive papers. And then the situation went from bad to worse.

Two hours later I received a call from a senior officer in my local police force back in England. He also had bad news. While the stolen van had been found on waste ground only a few miles from the compound, it was completely empty and there was no sign of the boxes; not a single piece of paper. Now I knew they were too heavy for one person to carry far and they would have had to have a getaway car. And yet a quick look in any of the boxes would have proved there was nothing of monetary value inside.

While my head span with the information, the police officer was far more interested in the full container. During the investigation the courier driver had reported seeing rifles inside the container from which the cargo had come; which was news to me. The officer was really on my case about the unauthorized firearms and demanded that I opened the container straight away and hand them over. While I tried to explain that I was in Spain, he countered that he would obtain a warrant as soon as the Magistrates Court opened on Monday morning and break it open. He also advised me to move fast unless I wanted to face a serious charge.

A quick call to the courier confirmed the details of the robbery but they did not add up. To begin with, the thieves had climbed into a secure courier compound when they could have taken any vehicle they wanted off the street. They then decided on the vehicle loaded with my stuff even though it was in the middle of dozens of similar vans of all shapes and sizes. After hot-wiring the vehicle, they did not check out to see if there was anything valuable in the back. They then drove out of the secure compound without being stopped by security. It did not help when the courier company told me the driver who had loaded the van and who had spoken to the police did not work for the company any more. He had only been a short-term driver and they could not find his contract details. Now if that all sounds strange to you, it did to me too. And then the penny dropped; I was a victim of our own system.

I did not sleep much that night because I kept going over what was missing in my head. I needed advice and fast. Systems had been put in place for such circumstances, and anyone who had retired from the Special Forces could call a handler 24/7 if they encountered a difficult situation in civvy street. Normally a call would be put in if someone started asking unusual questions or if we felt we were under surveillance. However, my situation was an unusual one. I explained the robbery to my handler and asked him to look into the consequences. He replied quickly, telling me that he believed it was an opportunist thief who had dumped the material; well at least that was the official line. While I thought differently, there was no way of proving it.

Something was very wrong and while I suspected what had happened, I did not have time to ponder over it, I needed to head off the police. After all what if the courier driver had been right? If the 'thieves' had the balls to spirit away a van, they would have the balls to plant unauthorized firearms in my container. If they had then I had a big problem. It was the classic diversionary tactic, dating back to Sun Tzu's 2,500 year old 'Art of War'; confuse your enemy at the same time as you attack.

With no time to lose, I contacted an old mate of mine in the North of England who was still serving in the military and explained the problem. The long and short of it was I wanted him to empty the container before I met the police on Monday morning. We did not discuss how he would do it; I just told him where to find it.

Early on the Sunday morning he called with good news; the job was done; I was in the clear. So how had he done it? Well he needed to find a way into the compound without raising suspicion. After emptying the container he needed to escape with everything, again without drawing attention. So it was time for a lot of lateral thinking and a bit of stealth.

He started by contacting a mate who worked for a company which supplied the construction industry with accommodation. On the Saturday evening a lorry carrying five porta-loos pulled up outside the container yard; only there was a man inside each loo. My mate blagged his way past security, telling him he was there to change the site toilets and apologized for the late hour which had resulted from a breakdown. The security guard felt sorry for him and let the wagon inside. My mate quickly located the container, picked the lock and the guys emerged to empty the contents into the porta-loos. After locking the container the five guys hid on the floor of the cab as the driver drove back to the gate. He explained that he had the wrong address and drove off leaving the security guard to watch his television, unaware that he had just been scammed. Job sorted.

My mate also confirmed that there were no high velocity weapons inside, just a couple of old air rifles. They had been planted and I guess to the untrained eye they looked like rifles in the back of a dark container. Either way they provided the police with an excuse to break open the container and cause me a whole load of grief.

I was happy that one mystery had been cleared up and caught the early flight to England, driving at top speed from the airport to the container site. All well and good you might think but when I reached the container yard on that wet Monday morning, there was mayhem. The police officer was there but so were another dozen and they had brought an armed response unit with them. It was like a scene from a highly charged cop movie; only it was about to turn into a scene from the Keystone Cops. As a crowbar was produced, I made it clear I had the key, but they took no notice; they had a point to make. I held my breath as the padlock was snapped off and the doors were pulled open. I then stifled a laugh as everyone peered inside and realized what I had known all along... there was nothing inside.

Of course all eyes turned on me and it was suggested that I had removed the contents. I countered with my plane ticket and hire car receipt. They proved I had stepped off the plane only a couple of hours earlier, leaving only enough time to drive straight to the compound. After all, the container was inside a secure compound watched by a vigilant security guard...

Of course I knew my legitimate belongings were already on their way to Mallorca in another van. I also knew my next stop was to pick up the dodgy ordnance so I could deliver them to my mate. But there was still no trace of my missing boxes.

To this day, ten years later, not a single piece of paper has been found. Although the police told me to claim on my insurance there was nothing of financial value, just sentimental value and – of course – operationally sensitive material.

My whole life in the services had disappeared in that van. Everything from my service beret and belt to photographs and certificates, from training notes to my law degree papers. Apart from a handful of copies of photographs, I had nothing but memories.

A couple of years later I was discussing my work in Iraq with my handler when he posed a question; off the record... He asked me to think if I would have been able to leave for Spain with the boxes? I did not have to think about the question for long; of course not. And it was impossible to cherry pick sensitive papers from the boxes; it would have made me even more suspicious about the robbery than I already was.

But any time I brought the question up, the official line was still that the robbery had been carried out by an opportunist thief who had got it wrong. At one point the police even suggested that a couple of drunkards had stolen the van on the way home from the pub. Although I later asked if I could at least get some photographs and my degree qualifications back, I was still met with a wall of silence.

So there you had it and in hindsight it was exactly how I would have carried out a similar job. Think about this. Rather than me leaving for Spain with boxes of mementoes, what if it had been a suspected terrorist leaving the country with boxes of notes and drawings relating to potential targets. While you want to follow the suspect to find out where he was heading and who he was meeting, you could not let the paperwork out of the country.

Now consider what happened to me and my paperwork... And you can see how I was both victim and instigator of my last operation.

Chapter Two

Back in The Mob

SO AFTER MANY YEARS in the army it was time to leave. After so long in the forces I wanted to forget about the army and go and do something completely different. I had always fancied the warm Mediterranean climate and my favourite place was the Spanish island of Mallorca. It also allowed me time to think about what I wanted to do next. And I was doing just that when, like everyone else, I was glued to the television on 11 September when terrorists struck in the United States. They flew two hi-jacked planes into the World Trade Centre in New York, while a third hit the Pentagon in Washington D.C. A fourth plane, probably destined for the State Capitol building in D.C., crashed in Pennsylvania after passengers fought with the hijackers. Over 3,000 people died in the attacks and the world changed that day; my life was also about to change.

I was still on the Army reserve list and I soon received a call from my headquarters. There were plans afoot to send troops to Taliban controlled Afghanistan where it was believed that al-Qaeda had bases. I was given a simple choice. Did I want to volunteer immediately or did I want to wait until I was issued with a compulsory call up. It was also suggested that there could be future opportunities in Afghanistan, and those who volunteered would have first call on what was referred to as a bit of icing on the cake.

I was not told what these opportunities would be and it did not matter, I was a Special Forces soldier and I volunteered straight away. I was packing my bag, the moment the call ended. I was looking forward to getting back with the lads once again and off I went, not knowing where I was heading or when I might return.

As I flew back to England and reported to headquarters, events around the world were changing rapidly. Within a week of the attacks, the United States President, George W. Bush Jr., had announced that Osama Bin Laden had been behind them and that he was hiding out in Afghanistan. I was immersed in training and briefings while the calls for the Taliban to hand over Bin Laden and his lieutenants were rejected. Bush's ultimatum on 20 September 2001 to close down terrorist camps in the Afghan mountains was also ignored. The Taliban's offer to try Bin Laden in an Islamic Court on 7 October was in turn rejected and an intensive United States and British bombing campaign began immediately.

I was already on my way into hostile territory with my detachment when it began. So what were we going to be doing? While we were too old for strenuous active service in the mountains of Afghanistan, we had something the younger guys did not; combat experience.

Ten years had passed since the Regiment had been involved in a major conflict, in Iraq back in 1991. Many operations had been in the country's Western Desert where teams had slipped behind enemy lines and set up observation posts overlooking the Iraqi Army's main supply routes, or MSR's. Convoys were reported and important targets were located so that airstrikes could be called in. The Regiment was doing what it did best, using stealth to pave the way for the battle ahead by creating mayhem and confusion behind the Iraqi lines. I was personally involved in dealing with air crashes and the rescue of pilots, the recovery of black boxes and the destruction or booby trapping of plane debris.

By December there were reports that al-Qaeda were holding out in the mountainous region known as Tora Bora, or Black Cave, near the Pakistan border; Bin Laden was also reported to be hiding there. Our guys were joining the combined Allied assault on the caves, using stealth to locate the caves used by al-Qaeda and then called in air strikes. It was a difficult task and while the younger guys had the training and the fitness, they did not have experience of full scale combat. So we older guys passed on our experience of working in inhospitable areas, advising our younger comrades about the problems they might face.

The battle did not last long. Al-Qaeda had not had the time nor resources to build extensive fortifications in Tora Bora. By mid December the area was clear and while many of the caves were demolished or blocked, garrisons were overrun in others. The only problem was, Osama bin Laden and the al-Qaeda leadership were missing.

Once the Taliban had been toppled, the military side of Afghan operations was scaled down and reservists like myself were due to be released from duties. After three months in Afghanistan, my army service was once again coming to an end. However, as I prepared to demobilize, the question was put to me if I was interested in staying in Kabul to do something a little different.

The United Nations Security Council established the International Security Assistance Force (ISAF) on 20 December to coordinate the activities of all the military forces in Afghanistan. Over 40 countries had troops in the country with over half of them from the United States. The ISAF had to restore order across the country so that a Presidency and a government could be installed. Security trained personnel were needed to protect the president's staff and government officials and I was asked if I wanted to stay on and train Afghan soldiers to do the work.

The world of personal protection and security was only a small industry before 9/11. Many ex-Special Forces guys worked in Third World countries, protecting important people and assets while training the local military and militias to do the work. While a lot of my comrades had worked in the business, I had never planned to do so.

I was told that I would be employed by the United States Department of Defense rather than the British military. I also learnt I would be working with a small group of like minded guys and the work was not too taxing or dangerous. What could go wrong? There was good money on offer, money which would supplement my army pension. It was a short-term private contract and I would soon be back home in Mallorca. I did not have to think about the offer for long; it was time for me to enter the world of private security.

Virtually overnight I converted from a military capacity into a private capacity and I hardly noticed the difference. I was getting orders from a new organization and while the money was much better, the work was easier and safer. I joined a team of around sixty advisors, the majority of them from the U.S. Special Forces, in the Afghanistan capital Kabul and we quickly immersed ourselves in our new work.

Steps were being taken to install a new administration and we had the task of training 60 bodyguards to protect senior officials. We started by pooling our skills to organize a training programme covering both security and private protection work. I got to know my American counterparts well and during the course of conversations it became clear that something was afoot in Iraq. Everyone knew about the weapons inspectors searching for the weapons of mass destruction across Iraq but the operations were highly secret. There were also rumours that units from the Joint Special Operations Command were preparing the way for conventional warfare.

We continued our work in Kabul while the United States and Great Britain called for action against Iraq and we concentrated on our training while the United Nations Security Council and other NATO countries refused to support action and anti-war groups protested. However, we took note of the rumours about troops moving into Saudi Arabia and the reconnaissance missions along the Iraqi border; they all pointed to an impending invasion.

As the world waited to see if diplomacy would prevent a war, talk in our group began to revolve around our own futures. Our work was coming to an end in Kabul but we had all learned a lot about the business of private security. Surely if there was an invasion, it would be over soon like Operation Desert Storm in 1991. On that occasion the criticism had been that the U.S. military had withdrawn too soon and allowed Saddam Hussein to reassert his power.

Our employers suggested that once Iraq had been conquered there could be a mass of work rebuilding the country's infrastructure and oilfields. Engineers and technicians working for foreign contractors, particularly United States companies, would need personal protection in such a hostile environment. Oil fields, power stations and government buildings would also need protecting. While it sounded plausible, I thought the military would do it.

The U.S. military launched Operation Iraqi Liberation (later named Iraqi Freedom) on 20 March, crossing the Kuwaiti border and advancing rapidly northwest. The British also launched Operation Tulec, and their objectives included the city of Basra, the surrounding oilfields and the port of Umm Qasr. As I watched the air strikes and rocket attacks on the television, I wondered what my mates were up to as I remembered my time in Iraq.

Most Iraqi units fled the Allied onslaught and the only major battle took place around Nasiriyah, where Route 1 crossed the Euphrates River and the Saddam Canal, halfway to Baghdad. On 9 April, the leading elements of the United States forces entered the capital and symbolically marked the end of Saddam Hussein's reign by tearing down his huge statue in Firdos Square. Troops also occupied the palaces and ministries on the west bank of the River Tigris.

Although the conventional war was over, civil order quickly broke down and the capital was subjected to widespread looting while the U.S. military's stretched lines of communications came under attack. The war officially came to an end on 15 April when U.S. Marines captured Tirkit, Saddam Hussein's home town 100 miles northwest of Baghdad. Two weeks later President Bush famously declared that it was "Mission Accomplished" to soldiers and sailors on the aircraft carrier U.S.S. *Abraham Lincoln*. Little did he or the servicemen gathered on the flight deck know that there was still a lot of work to be done. Meanwhile, I was wondering when was it time to go home.

Once the U.S. military had completed the objectives set them, it was time to install an interim government to replace Saddam's regime. The Coalition Forces established the Coalition Provisional Authority (C.P.A.) on 21 April as a division of the United States Department of Defence. In Baghdad its offices were installed in Saddam Hussein's palaces, in the area which would become known as the Green Zone. The governor and his group of the administrators then set about restoring life to normal in Iraq.

The C.P.A.'s first order ordered the de-Ba'athification of Iraqi society, removing all supporters of Hussein's regime from positions of power. The second order disbanded the Iraqi Armed Forces. In hindsight the two orders were the start of Iraq's problems. In its first month in power the C.P.A. had put tens of thousands of young men out of work and left them with no alternative means of income, at least no legitimate means. But while they had no money, they did know where hundreds of arms dumps had been set up ahead of the Allied invasion.

While the C.P.A. set to work restoring order in Iraq, I was only concerned with my own future. My work was coming to an end in Afghanistan and although there was talk of security work up for grabs in Iraq, none was coming my way. Many of the Americans I was working with were being offered new contracts but so far the Brits I had worked with had not been offered any.

By the time my contract was up, we had a fully trained group of security personnel. My time was over in Kabul and I packed up and headed back to England where I could demobilize for a second time. Once again I joined my family in Mallorca and for the next two weeks we slipped back into the gentle Mediterranean way of life. And then the telephone rang. Apparently my work in Kabul had been appreciated and my name had been noted for future reference. The C.P.A. was inviting companies into Iraq so they could bid for infrastructure contracts. I was asked if I was interested in getting together a small close protection team which could escort a senior businessman around Iraq. Yet again it was tabled as a short-term contract with good pay. I had not had time to organize any other work so I agreed and prepared to say goodbye once more to my family. Only this time I was going to be working as a private contractor. I was about to become an operator.

Chapter Three

A One-off Job

POST WAR IRAQ was suffering from years of neglect, financial cutbacks and embargoes on foreign goods. Over half a million tonnes of high explosive had been dropped on the country by the Allied Air Forces, leaving the country's infrastructure in a terrible state. Everything we take for granted in the Western World needed attending to; roads, bridges, buildings, power plants, water plants and sewerage plants to name but a few. Iraq was going to become one massive building site and companies from around the world, but particularly from the United States, were eager to have a share of the work.

One area the C.P.A. was keen to restore to normality was the Basra area in the southeast corner of Iraq. This area had been captured by the British after heavy fighting and the local population had welcomed the end of the Hussein regime and the dreaded Ba'ath party. The people in the area were Shi'ites, opponents of the Sunnis who supported Saddam Hussein, and they had risen against his regime during the 1991 invasion. He responded violently when the Allied forces withdrew, ordering executions and the destruction of many buildings. A second uprising in 1999 resulted in more mass reprisals.

The port of Umm Qasr, where the Euphrates and the Tigris met to become the Shatt Al-Arab River and flowed into the Persian Gulf, was now Iraq's gateway to the world. Huge amounts of humanitarian aid were being delivered to the port and then taken by road to the cities across the country. While thousands of barrels of oil a day could be delivered to the port from the oilfields around Basra, electricity was needed to extract the oil. But the war had left the electricity situation across the oilfields in a sorry state and plenty of work had to be carried out before they would be producing again.

A United States company had been invited to tender for work in the Basra oilfields and a senior executive of the company had to assess the current installations around the oilfields before heading to Baghdad to negotiate the contracts with the C.P.A. The protection team I had been asked to put together would look after him while he travelled around the country.

I called up four mates I had known for years, all British guys with long careers in the Regular Army and the Special Forces and they agreed to join the team. We had all reached around the same rank and had similar experience but the main thing was that we could all trust each other. The chance of a bit of excitement with a wedge of money at the end appealed to us all. We would be back with our families in a couple of weeks and able to clear a few bills.

Our outline plan was to establish an operating base in Kuwait City, so we had a place to sleep and organize ourselves. We could then collect the client, take him across the border into Iraq and drive around the oilfields and Umm Qasr port. The area was under the control of the British military and there was a good chance we might bump into a few old mates. There was also a good chance we could pull a few strings along the way to ease our journey.

So all five of us flew into Kuwait City and rented two cars from one of the desks in the airport, the same as you would when you go on holiday. We hired two Mitsubishi Pajeros, normal 4x4 vehicles that any family would drive around Kuwait City in. We paid up front in cash, much to the hire company's delight; cash is king in the Middle East and paying with U.S. dollars helps you avoid awkward questions. We did not mention we were crossing the border into Iraq; at best it would have bumped up the insurance premium considerably; at worst they would have refused to hire us the cars.

We planned to be as covert as possible when we drove around, so we did not attract attention to ourselves. There was a large military presence in the Basra area and reports indicated that while the locals were suffering from the lack of food and water, they were not directing their frustrations against the new regime; they still blamed their problems on Saddam Hussein's regime.

Next stop was a drive to our hotel to meet our client. From a Brit's point of view he was a typical American, if there is such a thing, being larger than life in more ways than one. We got on well and the initial meeting was businesslike but light hearted, ideal for what we had to get through over the next two weeks. He gave us the itinerary of what he had to accomplish, where he had to visit and how long he expected to spend at each site. We were allowed a couple of days to plan the journey and after booking ourselves into the hotel, we settled down to study our new assignment.

Each team member was allocated a list of tasks and everyone reported back at the end of each day to talk over progress. New problems were discussed, broken down into new tasks and then delegated. Planning is everything when you undertake a job like this and while you cannot cover every eventuality, the team's experience and knowledge help you to anticipate many problems. Emergency procedures also had to be agreed, so we were ready to deal with the unexpected.

Two of the guys studied our routes into Iraq and around the Basra area, making relevant notes on landmarks, useful places and areas to avoid; they were also getting the maps inside their heads so that the chances of getting lost were reduced to a minimum.

Two of the guys were tasked with sorting out the logistics for the trip. We had to consider food, water, first aid and medicines for ourselves. The cars also needed fuel, spare tyres and our team mechanic collected tools and parts so he could carry out road side maintenance. Arrangements also had to be made for weapons and ammunition and while the military would not allow us to take any guns across the Kuwait border, there was no way we were going to travel around Iraq unarmed. Although the country was relatively safe, we would still be vulnerable to car-jacking and armed robbers looking for cash. For now all we could take were pistols which we had to conceal.

We also had to arrange clearance with the British military authorities in the Basra area and their United States counterparts in Baghdad. We could not just drive around freely because we were entering a war zone where military operations were still going on. Our client's company had obtained a visa and other papers from the United States Department of Defence allowing us to enter Iraq on business. People in the C.P.A. were pushing for the work to start and the paperwork had been rushed through so that our client could meet his deadlines. The main thing was the visa would allow us across the border while other papers would get us through military checkpoints.

We did not get involved in what our client's company was going to do in Iraq, but the ultimate objective was to restore electricity across the country. Government buildings, hospitals, schools, industry and commerce needed a regular electricity supply for machinery, lighting and computers. Families needed it to cook their food and light their houses; air conditioning was a big thing in the hot summer months. Many things we take for granted need electricity; everything from refrigerators for food storage, water pumps for clean water, pumps to remove sewerage, street lighting and even traffic lights. Without it the country was going nowhere and the people were going to get frustrated. Our client had a full schedule of refineries, generators and power stations to visit and he had to assess if they could be repaired or if they needed to be replaced.

Before leaving Kuwait, we had to brief our client what to expect when we were on the road. Although he told us where we had to be, when we had to be there and for how long; how we got there and what we did on route was up to us. The deal was he always followed our instructions without question. If we told him to get down in the car, he had to do so; if he was pushed to the ground or dragged behind cover, he had to do so. Security can involve manhandling without warning and our client had to agree to it before we set off. We were his guardians, watching all angles for threats. We had to assess each threat and then immediately act on it.

There was no time for arguments; the questions and answers would be dealt with later when it was safe to do so. It is the same in any close protection or Special Forces role. The client decides the itinerary and we decide the safest way to carry it out. We needed a mutual respect for each other's job and a trust in each other's professionalism for it to work. Without that the contract was off, whatever money was on offer.

In the years to come hundreds of Private Security Details, or PSDs, would be working across Iraq for over twenty different companies, including Blackwater, ArmorGroup, Edinburgh Risk and Sabre to name but a few. However, in the spring of 2003, as President Bush declared Mission Accomplished, war was over, there were hardly any security teams in the country. The multi-million dollar business of security was all in the future and we were just one of a handful of teams who had been asked to enter the country. What we were about to embark on was new to us and the client.

With everything in place, we picked up the client and drove the 100 kilometres north up the coast road. Stopping just short of the border, we filled up with petrol, not knowing where the next fuel point would be and gave the cars a final look over. "Have you got a Leatherman", I enquired as I knelt behind the car. "Yeah sure, here you go", said my mate, handing me the multi-head tool. Our client watched as I unscrewed the number plates and threw them in the boot. "What are you doing that for?" he asked. "We do not want anyone to know this car comes from Kuwait, there would be too many awkward questions" I replied. I could see the client's eyes widening as I spoke; the enormity of the adventure we were about to embark on had just hit him. He did not say anything else and we were soon on our way.

Kuwaiti plates singled our cars out to anyone who was interested, be it the military, armed robbers or disgruntled locals. We did not want to draw attention from anyone, and our experience told us that no plates were better than foreign plates. We were preparing to enter a war zone and no one knew what to expect; particularly our client.

Further up the road the British troops at the checkpoint made us stop and show our visa and papers. After a quick look over, we were through and on our way. Although I had been into Iraq, many years before, this time I was going in as part of a PSD. There was no organized back up and no fire support on the end of a radio call if we ran into trouble. There would be no emergency extraction by helicopter either if any of us were injured. All we had with us were concealed pistols in case we ran into trouble. However, we were never going to be far away from British troops and Basra was the safest area in Iraq.

We had followed the coast road through Kuwait heading for the Umm Qasr border crossing. It took us out of our way, but the border crossing at Safwan, on the main road between Kuwait City and Basra, was only open to military personnel at this time. We headed for the military base in the port where the personnel were trying to make sense of the huge shipments arriving in the port. Although the area was under control of the British military, the Americans had a small contingent of technicians based at Umm Qasr organizing shipments of grain made by the world food programme. At the time it was the only way to get anything into or out of Iraq in large quantities. The Basra area had been cut off from Baghdad due to the war and the people needed food badly. The main problem was keeping the peace while the food and other essentials were unloaded and transferred to waiting lorries.

Nobody took any notice of us as we looked up some old friends who were working in the port area. I had already called ahead to arrange our visit but there were a few surprised faces when we pulled into their camp in our two hire cars. I suppose it might have looked as if we were off on a fishing trip somewhere, only we were carrying pistols rather than fishing rods and there was spare ammunition in the boot rather than bait.

We were as pleased to see them as they were to see us and the usual slagging about receding hairlines, ageing physiques and dress sense was supplemented by banter about the differences in our respective roles. They joked about the soft overpaid life of a security team ahead of us while we laughed at their jealousy. Our client viewed this very British sort of teasing and ribbing with suspicion but we assured him that they really were happy to see us. Our serving friends did not look down on us for doing this sort of work. After all it was only a short term job and they might have done the same if they had left the service.

As we settled down for the evening, it was time to get information about what was happening in the area. We were not looking for specific operational information but we did want to know what to expect. Questions and answers about the locals, the environment, military camps and logistics problems criss-crossed between us well into the night. A few other faces from the past dropped by when they heard we were around and it was good to see them; we wanted as many of our old contacts to know that we were in the country. We never knew when we might want to call on them for a favour.

We stayed with our friends in Umm Qasr for a couple of days, checking out our routes and gathering intelligence. While we had most things we needed, we still needed semi-automatic rifles, or 'longs' as opposed to our concealed 'shorts'. Although pistols could get us out of a minor scrape, they were not much use in a country flooded with weapons. It did not take long to get a few contacts and a couple of Iraqi guys soon approached us with details of illegal arms dealers in the area. When the army was disbanded, villains and traders had secreted away arms dumps all over the country, hiding them away for a rainy day – not that it ever rained in Iraq. While food and clean water was hard to come by, there was a surplus of cheap guns, grenades and ammunition on the black market.

One of our contacts provided the name of a guy who was prepared to meet us at a discreet location and I arranged a meeting to see what he had on offer. I also took our guns specialist, or armourer, along to check the guns out for serviceability.

We met the guy in a secluded area where we could check out the guns in peace because our dealing was not exactly legal. After the usual pleasantries and posturing, he opened the boot of his car to reveal about fifty AK47s, the standard long arm of the Iraqi Army. The dealer talked away about how good his wares were, but it was obvious at first glance that some were in a sorry state. As I started haggling over the price, our armourer set to work dividing them into three piles which could be described as the good, the bad and the ugly. Those that worked, those that could be broken into spares and those destined for the scrap heap.

The AK47, with its distinctive banana shaped magazine, has been around for years, and for several good reasons. It is cheap to produce, simple to operate and easy to maintain. It has no gas parts, hardly ever jams and never breaks down. Our Special Forces arms training had often included the AK47, and its imitators, and I was happy to take the good ones and a few of the bad ones for spares. The price reflected the availability; $25 for a good one and $5 for a bad one; no questions asked. A stock of ammunition was included in the final price, along with the promise of more when we needed it. We were in business for only a few hundred dollars.

Our client's first port of call was in the centre of Baghdad, where the U.S. Military and the C.P.A. had established their headquarters on the west bank of the River Tigris. They had taken over the government buildings surrounding Saddam Hussein's Presidential Palace. The was area known as the Green Zone, the safe area, as opposed to the rest of the city which was known as the Red Zone, the dangerous area. We did not need to know anything about our client's reasons for visiting Baghdad, we just knew where he had to be and when. However, it was clear that he needed to meet the relevant executives in the C.P.A., to press the flesh, and learn about the scope of the contract before visiting the oilfields.

Those meetings involved a 1,000 kilometre round trip through southern Iraq, across what had been a war zone only weeks before. It did not take any time at all to decide the route; there was only one. The expressway, Route 1 or Route Tampa, was the U.S. military's Main Supply Route between Basra and Baghdad. It headed west through the Basra oilfields and then swung northwest past the cities of An Nasiriyah, Ad Diwaniyah and Al Hillah before heading to the capital. Although the first 150 kilometres was a straight forward asphalt motorway, Saddam had refused to tarmac the next 200 kilometres stretch to An Nasiriyah, limiting the amount of vehicle movements north. He had taken the decision after the Shi'ite uprising following the first Gulf War. Then it was back on tarmac for the long road to Baghdad.

So off we set, all loaded up for the big adventure. It would only take a day to get to Baghdad and we were well loaded with food, water, ammunition, spare tyres and as much fuel as we could carry. We had been told where the military camps were where we could try to get topped up. We also had plenty of cash tucked away in case we had to buy ourselves out of trouble along the way.

As we set off, it felt a little strange to be out on our own. We had all operated in Special Force units for many years and were used to operating as a small group in hostile situations. However, a lot of the forward planning and backup are sorted out for you in the military. If anything goes wrong you could call on your company headquarters and they would arrange to get you out of trouble. Not this time. We had to assess the threats, devise the drills to deal with them and make the contingency plans to escape from them.

As we drove north there was no doubt we were in a war ravaged country. War debris was scattered everywhere along Route Tampa; abandoned tanks, burnt out vehicles and unrecognizable lumps of metal. Wrecked buildings were a constant reminder that the Coalition Forces had used some heavy munitions to knock out Iraqi Army positions. It was a stark reminder of the power of modern weaponry, particularly as we only had our second hand AK47s and pistols for protection.

Although we were on edge the whole way, unsure what to expect, the Iraqis were pleased to see Westerners in those early days. The people, particularly in the Shi'ite south, were overjoyed by Saddam's disappearance and they looked on the Americans and British as their liberators from his cruel regime. Everyone expected prosperity under the new promised democracy and we saw real joy on people's faces as we drove by. It was only natural that they were looking forward to the day when their country would be built up again and money and trade would replace poverty and fear.

After five hours on the road, we cruised into the busy outskirts of Baghdad, becoming tangled in the mad rush of city traffic. Cars, vans, buses and lorries were everywhere, mingling with military vehicles loaded with grim looking soldiers armed to the teeth. So there we were, five white males sitting in two hired 4x4 vehicles with no number plates in the middle of it all. The situation was just crazy. But we just stuck to our route and tried not to draw attention to ourselves. We were on tenterhooks the whole time but most drivers were just intent on getting to their destination as fast as possible and they took little notice of us. A few registered their surprise and eyeballed us to get a reaction but we just watched our surroundings and each other.

I had been to Baghdad over ten years before on a covert reconnaissance mission before Operation Desert Storm and while the main buildings looked familiar, reminders of the recent invasion were everywhere. Burnt out office blocks and destroyed buildings reminded us that the Iraqi people had suffered over the past couple of months and they were struggling to get their lives back to normal.

It was around midday when we crossed the River Tigris and encountered the checkpoint on the edge of the new Green Zone. When the U.S. military had made their mad dash into the centre of Baghdad back in April, they had entered the heavily fortified zone surrounding Saddam's Presidential Palace. After brief, but heavy fighting, in which most of the occupants fled, the invasion force established itself in the area, taking over a range of palaces, government, military and residential buildings. The C.P.A. arrived soon afterwards and took over many buildings for offices while its staff moved into the nearby villas.

Over the months that followed an area of ten kilometres would be cordoned off by concrete blast walls and razor wire, turning the Green Zone into a city inside a city. However, when we arrived it was still a military controlled zone with new offices slotted between the garrisons. Our client had to meet representatives of the C.P.A., the Department of Defense and Iraqi officials and we had the job of ferrying him between meetings.

One of the main concerns in Iraq at that time was how to restore electricity to the country because the C.P.A. could not fulfil many of its promises without a regular supply. Iraq had a capacity of 10,000MW, one of the largest electricity generation capacities in the region, before the First Gulf War. However, international sanctions and obsolete technology reduced the capacity of the network to a third. Power stations became inefficient due to a shortage of spare parts and poor maintenance resulting in regular power cuts. Saddam responded by making his technicians reorganize the network to suit his political needs. They made sure that Baghdad and the towns in the Sunni Triangle, north and west of the city had first call on the limited supply. It meant his supporters always had electricity while the rest of the country was often plunged into darkness.

The network was badly damaged during the Second Gulf War because airstrikes and rocket attacks targeted the Iraq military infrastructure. Many military targets, including radar, telecommunications and signalling posts had been placed inside bunkers in built up areas, Saddam was using the residents as a human shield so the Allies hit generators and sub-substations, cutting the power to military installations. It also deprived the population of power. Intact generators and sub-substations were at the mercy of looters looking to sell valuable metals.

The C.P.A. placed the restoration of electricity services on the top of their agenda and the Commission of Electricity had been established to tackle the challenging problem. It was given complete operational authority and the promise of unlimited financial resources to get Iraq's electrical grid back on line. The Commission was a relatively autonomous institution and it coordinated the activities of eleven different companies responsible for assessing, repairing and replacing the network's infrastructure. It had the complex task of bringing together all the elements required to restore and maintain an adequate electricity supply; generation, distribution, construction, manufacturing and the all encompassing computing and information technology.

Work had already started on bringing power stations and sub-stations back on line but the supply was limited by what was still working. Running repairs had been carried out on the main installations and transmission lines by military engineers and Iraqi technicians but outside help was needed if the C.P.A. targets were going to be met. Our client worked for one of the U.S. companies invited to tender for the huge amount of work on offer and he was in Baghdad to discuss contract details with the relevant officials.

Although we were technically inside a military zone, we shadowed our client wherever he went. We had all worked with close protection teams during our military service but this time it was clear we were not welcome in many areas. It was an understandable reaction but we found it strange. When we had worked in a military capacity we had been welcomed everywhere and were often included in briefings. However, we were frequently reminded of our mercenary status when doors were closed to us over the next few days. We often felt like armed chauffeurs, driving our client to and fro from office block to military headquarters. We would just escort him into the building, show our passes and then be asked to wait outside until the meeting finished. There was a lot of classified information to discuss and no doubt a lot of money on the table; and it had nothing to do with us.

We had been issued with IDs which identified us as private security contractors and they kept us out of all sensitive places. We could only get through the front door of Ministry buildings and non-sensitive areas in Department of Defense buildings where we could obtain food or fuel.

We also had our British military IDs and in the future they would come in useful in British held areas. Even though we had left the service, we used them to obtain equipment or stores or even get intelligence information. They were always useful for getting food or a bed for the night. But while they worked around Basra, they did not cut any ice in the U.S. military held areas. As far as the average American soldier was concerned, we were just a group of mercenaries looking after one man. We were not soldiers anymore in their eyes, just five self-employed guys who had taken on a job to earn a lot of money in a short space of time. I guess if the roles had been reversed; I would have thought the same.

Meanwhile, our client was welcomed wherever he went. He worked for a well known international company which had a reputation for carrying out similar contracts in dangerous parts of the world. We, however, were viewed with suspicion. The Americans (whether working in a military or a civilian role) were curious as to why we were up in Baghdad and it often took a lot of talking to explain our role. The main question was why were British guys escorting a senior representative of an American company looking to work on behalf of the United States government.

The situation raised eyebrows in some quarters, especially as there were few American security companies working in Iraq at that stage. Virtually every Westerner in the city was in the U.S. military and driving around like they were in the military, in heavily armoured convoys. For us to be driving around covertly as a private armed security team in soft skinned vehicles was alien to them. PSDs would be seen everywhere in Baghdad over the next few years and they would become a way of life for us, but they were unheard of at this stage. The whole multi-million dollar private security industry had not been envisaged, but it soon would be and numerous contractors were starting to look for work on Iraq's infrastructure. Others were also looking to supply food and commodities, either to the military and the contractors or to the people of Iraq. If a company could secure one contract, establish a base and establish a good name, it was well placed to supply everyone arriving in the area. There was a lot of money to be made and it could be called the 'spoils of war'.

Looking back it is hard to see beyond the terrible events that seemed to occur with depressing regularity in and around Baghdad over the years to follow. It is hard to believe what the city was like back then. While there was a large military presence on the streets and many buildings bore the scars of war, the people had resumed their daily routines.

We often had time to kill while the client was safely holed up in a meeting and we took it in turns to explore outside the Green Zone. Dressed casually in cargo trousers and t-shirts with our pistols tucked out of sight, we mingled with the crowds, looking to see what we could pick up and get a feel for what was going on in the city. The shorts were only for personal protection against a mugging, there was no animosity shown against us, only curiosity.

We would have got into a lot of trouble with the authorities if we had walked around with rifles so we hid them in our cars. We did not have a licence to carry arms, not that a licensing process had been introduced yet; Baghdad was still technically a warzone. Although the need for arms was never raised when we were hired for the contract, it was clear that we would need them. No one asked how we would get hold of them and it was easier if no one saw them.

After a little sightseeing, our favourite place to hang out was the local market where the hustle and bustle of trading was a constant source of amusement. The locals welcomed us, waving and calling to us as we hung around, drinking tea. Everyone believed that the Coalition forces had come to save them and as Westerners we were seen as liberators, even though we had liberated nobody.

Although Saddam was still alive and on the run, no one talked about him when we were drinking in the teashops, they were more interested in their futures and were hoping for better things for Iraq. As far as we could see most people were too busy looking out for their families to be worried about causing trouble. The worst threats seemed to come from opportunist thieves and car-jackers, and as we were armed and switched on to threats, we were the last group of people a gang of robbers were going to tackle.

Eventually our client finished his meetings and we drove back to Kuwait, delivering our client back to his office. As we headed home we had time to reflect on what we had seen across Iraq. Although a lot of buildings were showing signs of war damage on the whole most things were functioning well. One thing that struck me was that Baghdad was not damaged as much as the press had portrayed; it appeared that they were focusing on the worst situations they could find and 'bigging them up' to enhance their stories. But for now we thought that our adventures in Iraq were over. The job had been a nice little earner but it was time to get back to my family and decide what to do next. I had always said that I would do occasional security jobs if they were offered, after all I had the right background and contacts; the money was also good.

Before the 2003 invasion of Iraq, the security industry was a very closed shop and there were only a few dozen people who made it their full time job. Most of them knew each other and from time to time they would call up old comrades to help them out on bigger contracts. I expected at some time to be asked to join one of these guys somewhere around the world and after a couple of months' work and I could return home. I suppose you could call it semi-retirement but I prefer to call it a sabbatical. Whichever way you want to look at it, it did not last long.

Chapter Four

We Are in Business

AFTER ONLY THREE WEEKS, I received a telephone call from the company our client worked for. They had been awarded a contract to work on restoring electricity in Iraq. To begin with the work would be around the Basra oilfields but there was potential for more work further north later on. While the company had the engineers they needed, they did not have the security personnel to escort them around the country. They also wanted us to provide advice on keeping work sites secure. In short we were being offered a security contract by one of the largest companies in the world, in what would soon be one of the most dangerous countries in the world.

It all sounded a little daunting to me and I started to explain how we were just a handful of guys who had only taken their man up to Baghdad for a bit of money. We were not an established company; we had no infrastructure, no financial backup or even the expertise to run the sort of operation they were looking for. The guy at the other end persisted, pointing out that this was not a military operation; this was a civilian operation working under rules laid down by the military.

Iraq was coming to terms with post war occupation and the huge problems it presented. While the U.S. military were controlling everything to the north, the British Army was busy in the south where we would be working. Our backgrounds would give us a unique insight into how things were done in the British sector and we could make use of our contacts in the area.

After hanging up the telephone, my head was in a bit of a spin as I came to terms with all the information. Twenty minutes ago I had been lazing about contemplating what to have for lunch. Now I was faced with asking the other four guys if they were interested in coming up with a business plan for a new security company.

They were all interested and after we had all had a bit of time to digest the idea, it was time to sit down and come up with a plan. The information was a little vague, so all we could do was come up with ball park figures for everything we could think of. We had all done a bit of moonlighting work, either intelligence gathering or close protection jobs, in the United Kingdom during our Special Forces days. But while we knew how to price small jobs up, this was completely different.

The figures soon started to tumble out for paying personnel, acquiring arms and ammunition, buying food and fuel and hiring vehicles and accommodation. That was the easy part. As we did not know what to expect in Iraq, we explained to the client that we needed a Forward Operating Base (F.O.B.) with a control centre, accommodation, vehicle parking and storage. We were assured that as we were working on the reconstruction of Iraq, the British military would provide us with a secure compound, complete with cabins and services, on their base.

We also had to arrange insurance. There was only one insurance company in London who covered this kind of work in hostile areas and it did not come cheap. As well as personal insurance for death and injuries, it also had professional indemnity, which covered mistakes made by the company.

We also had to consider how to deal with casualties and while we could find a company who would arrange for their evacuation from Kuwait, it would not operate in Iraq; it was still too dangerous. We would have to make local arrangements once we got to Iraq.

After a lot of deliberation we came up with a figure of around half a million pounds but we all knew it was a real 'back of a fag packet' calculation. The next question was where each of us would get the money from? But after a lengthy discussion, we all left the meeting believing we should give the business a go.

Over the days that followed the number of phone calls we all made to each other went through the roof. Each one of us pledged an equal share of money, giving us enough to buy an off-the-shelf security company. We did not have many details to give, so we took the decision to remain vague about our new venture. We decided against mentioning where we were working or what we intended to do to our accountant. A security consultancy can mean a hundred and one things, covering everything from patrolling building sites to guarding celebrities. Our type of security was going to be a little different, so different that even we were not sure what we were getting into.

The contract was very loosely worded; it only stated that we would be providing security for the personnel of an American company in Iraq and we deployed into Iraq on the strength of that. We were not sure what to expect but that is how you always work in the Special Forces. You are given an objective and you are expected to complete it starting with the limited amount of intelligence available. How you do achieve the objective is up to you.

Our client wanted to start by bringing ten people into Iraq to work on restoring power to the Basra oilfields. If the country was not producing oil, it was not making money and if it was not making money, it could not pay for its reconstruction. The fact that a lot of the reconstruction was needed to repair war damage did not seem to matter. You might think it would be more important to restore electricity to the populated areas first but we were not going to Basra to raise those sorts of questions. We had more pressing problems to attend to.

Now our client had told us how many staff he was deploying, we had to start recruiting, and fast. We needed forty men with Special Forces backgrounds who were looking for a career change. The five of us pooled our phone books and email addresses looking for people with the skills to hit the ground running. We did not have the time or money to train anyone.

At times like this you are grateful for the speed of emails and we were sending them out to everyone we could remember. They all started with "long time, no hear" and ended with "do you fancy a bit of freelance security work out in Iraq". As the replies started to come back, it was time for the five of us to head out to the Middle East and start work.

Once in Kuwait City, we were back where we had started at the hire car company, only this time as we set out for the border we had paperwork stating that we were legally entitled to enter Iraq as sub-contractors. Again the paperwork had been rushed through but it said we were working for an American contractor under the auspices of the United States Department of Defence and that impressed the border guards.

So once again we were in Iraq and heading for the British Army base at Shaibah Camp and our new Forward Operating Base. Shaibah Logistical Camp, or Log Camp was centred around an old airfield dating back to the days of British rule at the beginning of the 20th Century and it had grown into a huge military camp with security fences and vehicle checkpoints. It was situated in the middle of the desert, about ten miles south west of Basra and it was close to the oilfields and the main road connecting the city to the Kuwaiti border.

Heading north into Iraq, nothing had changed, only our reason for being there. It was all a bit of an adventure really as we had no idea what we were letting ourselves in for. As our two cars rolled up at the gates of Shaibah Camp, we drew a few funny looks from the guards on the gate. We were not convinced that the contract papers would work this time and as we had no other identification, we flashed our out-of-date army passes and gave a suitably vague story. The idea that five guys would be driving around in two hire cars was crazy enough so the squaddies assumed we must be Special Forces working undercover. They were nearly right.

Once inside the gate it took some time to negotiate our way around the maze of tents, huts and parking areas before we found our client's camp; a tiny fenced off compound smack in the middle. We were not impressed. All there was waiting for us was a single temporary cabin and our contact. He had been expecting us and proceeded to tell us about the cabins and supplies due to be delivered over the next few days.

So there we had it. After all the excitement of getting everything organized, here we were. We had no sleeping bags or blankets, because we had been led to believe that our accommodation would be ready. While the days were hot, the temperature plummeted after sunset at that time of year and all we had to wrap up warm in was our spare clothing. As we settled down for the night I just thought to myself, how crazy is this. Only a couple of days ago I was saying goodbye to my family and now here I was, huddled up in a freezing cabin in Iraq. I must have been mad.

The following day a couple of wagons loaded with the cabins which were going to be our new home arrived. While Kuwaiti workers set them up, all we could do was watch and explore. More cabins were due to arrive over the following week, twenty-five in fact; our accommodation, offices and stores. We were also expecting supplies, generators and water tanks.

The client also told us that the first technicians were due to arrive soon, leaving us only a limited amount of time to get the camp up and running before we had to start taking them to the oil fields.

Yet again tasks were listed, prioritized and divided out, ten to each man. They reported on progress at an evening briefing we called 'prayers', a name borrowed from our Special Forces days, where everyone was brought up to date on developments; and there were many. There were a million and one things to organize and new tasks were delegated during our morning meeting. One man was tasked to get as much current intelligence as he could out of British Army sources and then putting it into a useful format for us to use. He was also tasked with finding out what we could and could not do inside Shaibah Camp.

As soon as the cabins were in place, telecoms engineers were setting up phones, making internet connections and installing computers, putting us back on the communications map. It meant we could prepare to receive the first of our new guys, and we were all looking forward to meeting some old faces. Things were going to get busy because the client was looking to bring in ten clients and we had to have forty guys ready to escort them.

By the end of the week we had secured promises of twenty-five guys and a London travel agent was busy arranging flights. There were no flights direct into Iraq and everyone had to fly to Kuwait, presenting us with a logistical nightmare. We had to pick everyone up and bring them across the border to Shaibah.

Our answer was to set up an operations base in Kuwait city and one of our team went back over the border to find somewhere. After parting with a large amount of cash he rented six rooms, covering the entire floor of an apartment block. Five apartments were kitted out with bunk beds in every room ready to accommodate the lads. As time went on it would also serve as a rest area for lads on short vacations in Kuwait or as a stopover for those heading home for a longer holiday. The remaining apartment was our operations centre and while computers and communications equipment soon filled the desktops, maps covered every wall. Having said that, decent maps of Iraq were hard to come by and while the military had the best ones, they did not like giving them away. It left us with no option, we had to use bribery to acquire a set.

Everything was happening so fast that most things were done by the seat of our pants. We had little idea of what we could expect across Iraq but we had all served there at various times, so we could make educated guesses. We emailed a suggested kit list to our new employees and made it clear that it would be wise to assume that it would be impossible to acquire anything in Iraq. Most lads brought a few extra items and the company's field kit list evolved over time as we adopted items.

The script was that each guy was met at Kuwait airport and taken to the car rental office. They would hire a car in their name, using their own driving licence and our cash. After driving to the apartment they would be briefed on how to get to the border checkpoint and how to present their documents to verify their cover story. They would also be given an orientation briefing on what to expect inside Iraq.

The following day they would drive to the border, a kilometre wide strip which resembled a No Man's Land. Crossing that thin strip of land was more than crossing a border though; it was like stepping from one world to another. On the Kuwait side it felt safe. The last sign of normality was a petrol station where you could pay for fuel by credit card and buy a cold drink from a vending machine. A kilometre away it was a war zone, where the military or the mob ruled.

New guys were met by a security team in a car park on the Iraqi side of the border. They were issued with a weapon, magazines and body armour and then transferred to another vehicle so an experienced guy could drive the new car. Then it was time to make the 40 minute drive north up the expressway to Shaibah army camp. After they had found their bunk and dumped their kit, they were expected to attend an evening briefing before settling down for the night. No one forgot their first day in Iraq, they had just stepped into the world of security and it was a lot to take in.

Before long guys were flying into Kuwait and gathering at the apartment block nearly every day, filling the rooms with bodies and kit. I imagine the neighbours must have also wondered what was going on with all these men coming and going. If only they knew...

Once a new guy was bedded down at the camp we gave them a proper Operation-Group (O-Group) briefing in the mess room, explaining what was happening and what they could expect to encounter. Most of the guys knew what to expect from the First or Second Gulf War but it was wise to refresh their memories and make them aware of new threats. While everyone was eager for information, we did not always have it and sometimes we could only give them a flavour of what to expect.

Iraq was a dangerous environment and there were a host of things to be aware of just to stay in good health. What with the weather, nasty wildlife and contaminated water and food, it was a full time job keeping fit and well. We did not have the medical facilities to deal with illnesses, particularly any contracted through carelessness, because the medics we were recruiting were going to be busy looking after the teams.

While all ex-Special Forces men are trained medics, having undertaken hospital attachments and trauma training, the contract specified that each team had to have a trained army medic. That meant one in four recruits had to have dedicated medical training and they would have their work cut out when they were on the road.

You could not call 999 when you were out in the desert and the chances that a military patrol was passing were slim. Each team had to be capable of getting themselves out of trouble, even if it was something as simple as a stomach upset, a cut to the hand or a broken ankle. Injuries could also be as serious as a gunshot wound or multiple broken bones following a traffic accident.

The four man set up we adopted was based on the standard protection team but on occasions we modified it to suit specialized contracts. They travelled in two cars and if one car broke down, everyone could escape in one vehicle. Before a team set out, the cars were loaded up with everything needed on the road. While there was a spare tyre on the back door, two extras were strapped to the roof. Each guy had ten magazines for his AK47 but they could easily be used up in a two minute gun battle. 1,000 rounds were stored in an ammo box and packed in the boot alongside the trauma medic pack.

The Lead Vehicle, or Car 1, had the driver and team leader in the front seats with the client sat in the back. The team medic drove the Backup Vehicle, or Car 2, while the fourth man was the Tail End Charlie who watched the rear from the backseat. Most attacks came from the rear and the side and he was kept busy looking for suspicious vehicles approaching from behind or driving alongside. No one wanted to be Tail End Charlie, because travelling backwards makes you queasy and your body absorbs the shock every time the car hits a pothole; and there were a lot of potholes on Iraq's roads back then.

The two cars drove at least 100 metres apart in open terrain, making it impossible to hit both with gunfire at the same time. A lot of Iraq was flat and barren and it was possible to drop back as far as 500 metres from the lead vehicle as long as you maintained visual and radio contact at all times. There were military checkpoints on many roads and later on they would become targets for insurgents. It was important not to bunch up as you approached in case a suicide car bomber was waiting in the queue. While he might have been looking to blow up the checkpoint, he might change his mind if your two cars pulled up together. We would always stop 100 metres from a checkpoint and the second car would only move forward when the first had passed through and been given the all clear.

In the early days we installed Moto-Rola radio car kits and whip antenna in the hire cars. Each man also had a personal radio as well so he could speak to the rest of the team if he had to leave the car. While everyone was familiar with the standard army voice procedures we had to adapt them to suit travelling on Iraqi roads, adding new words to cover specific threats. To begin with each refinery was assigned a call sign while each road was given a code name. We also listened into the British military network so we knew what they were up to. The last thing we wanted to do was drive into the middle of one of their operations or be held up by one of their roadblocks. Before long, the British military allocated their own code names to the roads and we had to adopt them to avoid confusion.

The radio talk between the cars was always full of chatter about potential threats and they could range from people loitering on the kerbside or an overhead bridge, to cars driving suspiciously, to military convoys. Later on stationary cars were a worry because they might be loaded with explosives ready to detonate and our only defence was to veer away from the vehicle to minimise the damage from an explosion.

So within a short space of time we had a number of security teams escorting clients back and forth between a dozen refineries. While we had to be alert on the road, once inside the refinery gates the atmosphere relaxed. Well as relaxed as you can be walking around in 55 degrees with all your kit on for ten hours a day. Our clients were busy working with the Iraqi engineers, assessing the damage to the refineries and finding out what was needed to restore electricity. But while they had plenty to do, all we had to do was stay close by, keep our eyes and ears open and make sure no one did anything silly.

We were the only Westerners on the refineries and we stuck out like a sore thumb as we suffered in the simmering heat. The glare from the desert seared our eyes despite our sunglasses, the heat soaked us with sweat and no matter what sun cream we used our skin burnt. At times it was hell on earth and you often wondered how anyone could live and work in these unbearable temperatures. The only time we could cool off was when we jumped into the air conditioned cars during the breaks because we always kept the engines running, so they felt like ice boxes.

Sometimes the Iraqi police would turn up unannounced at the refineries as part of their routine duties but we would never let them enter or get near our clients. We were taking no chances and worked to the motto "best to be judged by twelve than carried by six". More than once we had heard of uniforms being stolen by criminal gangs who then used them for carrying out robberies. Our guys were told to trust no one and they had permission to fire warning shots to stop the police approaching. The real officers would put in a complaint and arrange a visit; the fake ones would go somewhere else. As far as we were concerned only the military had authority over us and everyone else was treated as hostile.

All our teams returned to the compound before it was dark because as they used to say in Vietnam, "the night belongs to Charlie". While it was quite safe to drive around during daylight, it was not worth the risk after dark; there were just too many bandits and robbers out there. Once back at Shaibah camp there was little to do, but we sometimes drove over to the NAAFI or the gym where we flashed our old army cards to get in. The squaddies knew what we were up to and we knew some from our army days. They never complained and let us help ourselves; after all it was not their money.

As the weeks went by a couple of other American security companies started working in the area and quite often we could be on the same refinery at the same time. There was no cohesion between companies at this stage and while there was a bit of macho posturing and verbal sparring between teams, we always helped each other out. We were always interested in how they did their work and what equipment they were carrying. Conversations back at camp often revolved around what we thought other teams were doing right or wrong and on more than one occasion we 'stole' a good idea; I am sure they did the same.

Those early days working around the Basra oilfields were quite easy and although they were risky by everyday standards, we rarely felt we were in danger. At this stage we were not being targeted by insurgents; it was quite the opposite. The majority of people were pleased to see us and welcomed us with open arms because as far as they were concerned, the war was over, Saddam had been deposed and the dreaded Ba'ath Party which had persecuted the Shi'ites for years had gone. We were there to restore their electricity and help get life back to normal.

While the client's engineers roughed it with us on Shaibah Camp, the managers preferred to live in the luxurious surroundings of Basra Palace. Every morning we had to drive from the military camp down to the palace to pick them up and then return them at night; a journey that added an hour at each end of the day. Their accommodation was in a massive compound with blast walls and high levels of security so they were safe enough, however, the drive across the city was a concern. Although Basra was fairly safe there was always the chance of an accident or a flat tyre and the inevitable crowds that would gather round. Four Westerners protecting a client with guns would bring attention anywhere and it was attention we did not want.

We would have preferred the clients to live in the camp but it was their call and all we could do was to work around it. It did not take long to plan because we had a fixed start point, a fixed finish point and there were very few sensible options in between. Although there were plenty of ways through Basra, most of them were potentially dangerous side streets that could easily be blocked, either by accident or design. That left us having to choose between one of the few main roads through the city.

At that time the Shiahs were on our side so the chances of anyone taking a pot shot at us were very low while IEDs had not been thought of at this stage. Our main concern was the high level of lawlessness, in particular the number of robberies and hi-jackings that were going on. There were also random riots across the city as people gathered on the streets to complain about power cuts and the shortage of food. Although we were armed, we just did not want to put our clients in any danger.

If anything, the main threat was in the crowded streets of Basra, particularly when food deliveries turned up late. Although the British military tried to keep order when the food was being dished out, fighting often broke out because there were too many people and too few sacks of grain. We just did our best to avoid the likely trouble spots and take detours. It was no worse than any other Third World country and we just had to stay alert.

We had to work out Standard Operational Procedures (SOPs) for everything in those early days, from driving drills and first aid to radio procedures and call signs. The work was new to us and while we could anticipate some things, there was always a new challenge around the corner. Most of the guys had a Special Forces background and we all had our own views on what worked and what was best to use. Practical experience and incidents often gave us the answer and we had to be very adaptable, introducing new drills whenever they were needed.

Like any other company we put together our risk assessments, only the threats we faced were a little more deadly than what you would find in your average office. Threats ranged from traffic accidents, to hi-jacking, to being shot at, to dangerous illnesses. We then had to assess the likelihood of an incident occurring and how deadly it would be.

To begin with our number one risk was a road traffic accident because the Highway Code does not apply in Iraq. It seemed as if there were no standard rules of the road and anything could happen; and it often did. Regularly we would see a smashed up or burnt out vehicle on the verge, the result of another driver's impatience or crazy manoeuvring.

We were allowed to practise driving drills on the airfield and we took what we had been taught about client protection from our Special Forces days and adapted it for the Basra environment. We came up with ways to defend ourselves if a car full of armed guys approached from the front, the rear or the side. We practised how to establish a defensive perimeter around the cars and how to transfer everyone into one car if there was a breakdown or accident. We trained how to manoeuvre out of trouble and escort convoys. Whatever situation we could think of, we had to sit down and devise a drill and then try it out to make sure it worked in practice. Then we could get the rest of the guys to practise it.

The first month of work saw our camp expand quickly as more people arrived. We had to split them into teams and allocate them to different clients, which was no mean feat in itself. Everybody came from military backgrounds and although they all had similar military ranks, we had to decide who worked together based on leadership and skills. To put it bluntly there were too many good men to begin with and it resulted in a lot of politics. Most decisions were based on personal choices and connections but from time to time there were discussions and arguments over who should be team leader. In most cases our initial choice worked well but we sometimes had to make changes when it was clear that a team was not working well together.

As the organization grew, we eventually had to recruit non Special Forces personnel and they usually came from the infantry, the Parachute Regiment and Royal Marines. We then split teams so that a Special Forces guy was leading three regular soldiers. Some of the Special Forces guys also moved up in the management structure when the organization expanded into other parts of the country.

The guy running the apartment in Kuwait was busy inducting new guys, organizing supplies and assessing intelligence but we all took our turn to run the flat for two reasons. Firstly, it gave everyone a chance to have a breather from working the long days on the refineries and secondly, it gave them an insight into the logistics side of the operation. When you are out in the field you do not realize how complicated the office side of the operation can be. It is easy to resent someone who appears to be sat on their backside in an air conditioned apartment while you are working out in the desert. But after a few hours of being bombarded with complicated questions, you long to be back in the field.

We soon realized that the logistics side of our operations was getting so complicated that we needed to appoint someone we knew from our Special Forces days who specialized in the work. He was tasked with greeting and briefing the new guys before taking them to the border. He also kept us supplied with a thousand and one things, all of which had to be sourced, delivered to Kuwait City and then carried by car to Shaibah. Later on the postal company D.H.L. would do all this for us, bringing whatever we ordered over the internet to our door.

We charged each man out at $500 per day, which worked out at $300 pay for the man while the rest went on food, weapons, ammunition, fuel and everything else. That worked out at $2,000 a day for every technician out in the field. Now $300 a day was a lot of money to a squaddie who had been on army pay for years so you can see why many decided to take the risks and hardships of working in Iraq to clear their debts and set them up for life.

We soon realized that we were spending money at an alarming rate and our initial wedge of money was not going to last until our first payment was due. Under the original deal we were due to be paid after three months and we simply did not have enough money to pay all the bills without getting a huge loan. None of us had dealt with large amounts of money before and we learnt a big lesson in sorting out our cash flow in those early days. Fortunately, our client agreed to change our payment structure so we could keep paying the wages and the bills.

So we had it all squared away moving what we needed between four key points; our main operation base in Kuwait City, our forward operating base in Shaibah camp, our storage area in Umm Qasr port and Basra palace. From there we had teams taking client staff out to the two main oilfields. The Al Zubayr oilfield lay east of the Basra to Safwan road while Rumaylah oilfield ran west of Shaibah, from the River Euphrates down to the Kuwait border.

In no time at all we had expanded to 40 personnel using 20 hire cars to escort ten clients around twelve oil refineries. The client was happy, the guys were all getting well paid and the risks were manageable. The hire company had not questioned what we were doing and if they had a clue why we wanted so many cars they did not ask. They were just happy to take our money. Everything was going well.

Chapter Five

Settling In

WHEN WE FIRST MOVED into the Basra area we looked at getting extra work in Umm Qasr, Iraq's only deep water port at the head of the Persian Gulf. Now we were not shipping experts or oil tycoons, but we knew it was going to be a busy place because virtually everything had to be shipped in through the port. The U.S. and British military were using it and so were the United Nations food programmes. It did not take a genius to work out that the deliveries were going to be targeted by all sorts of criminals, ranging from organized gangs down to opportunist thieves.

The British Army were busy looking after the port when we arrived, but they could not do it forever and while there were long term plans to train recruits for the port authority police, they wanted a security company to take over in the interim. Our client was working on putting power into the port, so we were in an ideal position to tender for the work. We were awarded the contract and soon had a small office based in the hanger unit used as the police headquarters.

Our security details were busy meeting the ships' crews when they docked and supervising the offloading of the cargo, making sure nothing was stolen. We also set up a training programme to teach men off the streets how to be security guards, turning them from zero to hero in only six weeks. The programme was intensive, maybe too intensive, but we did the best we could with them. As well as general security measures, we trained the recruits how to set up checkpoints, examine vehicles and search people. We also included weapons drills, unarmed combat and a few personnel protection techniques. To be honest we had our work cut out because most were hopeless but we did the best we could.

One afternoon I was working with our chief unarmed combat instructor. He would demonstrate the technique on me and then we helped the recruits to execute the move. Maybe I had been a bit too cheeky or we had paid him late, but he managed to dislocate my shoulder as he performed a takedown. Now there were no hospitals around and rather than head back over to Shaibah Camp to see if we could get any help, we decided to drive across the Kuwaiti border, and into Kuwait City. It wasn't much further and we knew I would get treated well.

However, the journey was a nightmare because the roads were as rough as hell. Although I do not remember much about the drive south, apparently every pothole brought moans of pain from the backseat of the car; followed by suitable comments from the front. I suppose it served me right for asking the instructor to make the training as real as possible.

The tribal leaders around the Basra area had been opponents of Saddam Hussein's Ba'ath party and they were anxious to install their own authority in the area once the British military had taken it over. The contrast between the living standards of the man on the street and the local leaders was astounding. While the majority of people of Basra lived in abject poverty, the mullahs had everything a man could want.

The military authorities organized meetings to build up mutual respect between the local leaders and the companies working in the area. As the representative of one of the security companies, I attended a weekly meeting with the mullahs, a military liaison officer and the heads of all the companies working in the area. We discussed progress and while the meetings were time consuming there were rarely any problems.

We would gather in one of the mullahs' houses where we were treated to their lavish hospitality. While we wanted to get a feel for how our work was being viewed and hopefully pick up snippets of information, they were trying to get the measure of you, fishing to see what you are about. They see you driving around their territory with your weapons and they want to know if you have the character and courage needed to back up the guns.

Fridays were the Holy Days and the local Shi'ah leaders liked to publically execute criminals before everyone went to the mosque to say prayers. A representative would come to our camp every week and invite me to attend as a sign of approval of their leadership. Now attending public executions was the last thing I wanted to get involved in but it was considered a big insult if you turned down the invitation without a good reason. Every week the guy would turn up at my office and each time I would make myself scarce or have an excuse ready about work commitments. Of course I could not keep up the excuses, so one week I felt obliged to attend.

I was taken to a huge open arena just outside Basra where thousands of people had gathered for the weekly spectacle. The air of anticipation in the area came to a climax as the mullahs and I climbed onto a large stage and took our seats ready for the proceedings to begin. A hush fell across the crowd as the police dragged the criminals out one by one while someone announced their details over the tannoy system. My hosts kept me fully informed, telling me in English what their crimes were and how they would be executed. Some had their hands chopped off for stealing or robbery, which was widespread at the time. Others were hung for more serious crimes and after the rope had been put around the condemned man's neck a mobile crane hoisted them into the air. While I was told that sometimes criminals were executed by firing squad, I did not witness one. But the ones which stuck in my mind were the beheadings. The criminals were forced to kneel down at the executioner's block and then held down by a couple of policemen while the executioner swung his axe.

This particular day the 'highlight' was the beheading of five prominent criminals one after another. As they were led out I was sitting with my hosts, drinking tea and trying to look interested. I nodded in approval as the mullahs told me about the criminals and their crimes while I was wishing I was somewhere else instead.

One by one the criminals were brought forward and beheaded in front of the expectant crowds. I knew the mullahs were all watching me carefully to see my reaction when the axe fell, looking for my approval of their method of justice. I did outwardly because it was their territory and as the saying goes, 'when in Rome, do as the Romans do'. They were interested to see if I flinched because it was a sign of weakness in their eyes. They were dealing with me on important issues at the time and they wanted to know that I was a strong willed man, one they felt comfortable doing business with.

The first three executions went to plan but the fourth guy caused a few problems by trying to wriggle free. He was finally held down but when the executioner swung the axe, it missed his neck, glanced off his shoulder and bounced off the block. There was an audible gasp from the crowd as the guy screamed and the police tightened their grip. As the executioner braced himself ready for a second blow, the head mullah stood up and shouted for the execution to stop. He explained that Allah had intervened; the wound was the criminal's punishment. Allah had spoken and the criminal was free to go.

The decision drove the crowds into a frenzy as the injured man was led away, blood pouring from his gaping wound. The mullah then turned to the executioner and made it clear that he was far from happy. After a short speech to calm the crowd, he told the executioner that he would be the next victim if he missed again. Shaking with fear the executioner took his stance while the prisoner was held down. You could almost taste the anticipation in the air as a hush fell across the crowd. This time the swing of the axe was perfect and the shouts and screams made it clear that everyone was satisfied.

As the crowds dispersed and headed to their mosques, the mullahs were full of appreciation for my visit. While they were thinking I had given approval of their methods of justice, I was thinking that I had witnessed one of the most bizarre experiences of my life. Either way my attendance had improved our relations and it was back to business.

Believe it or not I saw crueler spectacles than the Basra executions. The worst execution I witnessed was while serving in Kabul in Afghanistan when over 300 people gathered around to stone a woman to death. It took well over half an hour of excruciating pain before she succumbed to her injuries. The beheadings and hangings were nothing compared to that gruesome spectacle.

By the autumn of 2003 our lads in Umm Qasr port had their hands full keeping the Iraqi security guards on their toes. The huge market area alongside the port was jammed with trucks, market traders and civilians all haggling over deals. The truck drivers were anxious to get their vehicles loaded and on the road so they could start earning money. Arguments would often break out and they could turn into fights, some of them violent; there were even several murders as men fought to the death over a dodgy deal.

Most of the food and grain was distributed on a Sunday and one particular weekend in October we had a lot more on our minds than food distribution. While the Rugby World Cup had kept us occupied over the past couple of weeks, this game was the big one; it was England versus Australia in the final. We had begged the Americans to beam the match by satellite into our office but they had no interest in the game. Most had no idea what rugby was while a few confused it with American Football. After a bribe or two they relented and when the game kicked off, our little office was crammed with Brits, South Africans and a few curious Yanks.

It was a close game and we were riveted to the screen, cheering and cursing as the ball went from end to end. But our concentration was broken when a couple of Iraqi policemen popped their heads round the door and asked for our assistance. It was business as usual outside as the drivers and the traders argued and fought but this time the police had been unable to contain the problems. There was a full scale riot on the market place and they needed our help. "No way mate" was the reply, as we all pointed at the television. England was in with a chance, something that might not happen again for a long time, and there was no way we were going to miss it.

Despite their pleas we stuck to our guns, literally, and remained glued to the television until the final kick of the game. It was the kick that won the game and we erupted in cheers and congratulations. And that was it, check guns and ammunition and out of the hanger we went into the mayhem. Although it took a lot longer than normal to restore order the hassle was worth it to watch the game.

One of our jobs in the Basra area was undertaken in liaison with the British Army. There were water shortages in Basra and many people were relying on dirty water sources. Problems with the sewerage infrastructure in the city meant that there was a high chance of a cholera outbreak, the last thing the overworked military needed. Our client had been asked to supply power generators to a water plant so they could supply power to a large number of the wells across the city.

In no time at all we had planned the routes and a team was taking the engineer to the plant every day. We used codenames for all our locations and I had chosen the name Acid Bath for the water plant. So a call over the radio for "Bravo 9 at Acid Bath" meant something to our operations room but no one else.

The water plant was run down and had obviously been damaged during the air campaign against key infrastructure installations. While the compound had been covered in hardcore, the ruined buildings around the site were testament to the severity of the attacks. However, all our client had to do was set up power generators and repair the pumps to get the water flowing.

The work was straight forward and in no time at all we had organized an office and a storage area. Our clients worked on the generators, training the Iraqi technicians who had worked on the pumping station before the war, while Iraqi labourers were busy tidying the area. It was just another hot, dusty worksite.

We always parked our cars across the front of the gates with two of the team, to stop anyone driving in. The other two guys took it in turn to shadow the client wherever he went. Although the Iraqi workers were searched before they came onto the site, there were plenty of tools lying around which could be used as weapons.

After we had been on the water treatment plant for about six weeks, we found out how true the name Acid Bath was. Some of the pumps were leaking and the water formed a small stream which ran close to the main gate. Over time it had carved out a small wadi and although the amount of water was often only a trickle, at other times it filled the shallow ditch. From time to time the local children would come to the plant to splash in the water and watch what was going on inside the compound.

We always encouraged the lads to talk to the population, and try to make friends with them. You never knew what snippet of useful information you might learn following a friendly handshake and a smile. We also taught the lads about the local customs and the religious practices so they did not cause offence. For example our guys were told never to consume food or drink in front of Iraqis, they always went inside one of the offices or sat in the cars to have their lunch or quench their thirst. You definitely did not eat in front of an Iraqi during the day when Ramadan was on, their religious holiday when they fasted from dawn until dusk. Simple little mistakes could change the mood for the worse in no time at all.

Our approach was different to the one taken by Americans, who were used to plenty of everything. We believed that any bit of respect was appreciated and it was noted that we recognized their beliefs. The same applied to wasting food; we did not want to see guys discarding food or throwing scraps to dogs. We all had to remember that the Iraqi people were starving and short of clean water, yet we, the foreigners, had plenty in their country. It was a case of the old 'Hearts and Minds' routine.

The lads on the gate watched the kids playing in the stream and their happy shouts were a reminder that normal life still went on. Those kids lived in shacks and splashing in the stream was probably the best bit of fun they could hope for; but they were making the most of it.

The guys noticed that the kids were jumping on a square piece of metal, screaming at the loud noise it made, and they could see that it was an information sign related to the water plant. They asked if they could have a look and what they saw chilled them to the bone; the sign was painted with a skull and cross bones. It did not take a genius to work out that the sign had either fallen off the gate, or the kids had pulled it off. In no time at all I too was at the gate puzzling over the sign.

Our guess was that the warning sign had been put up by the American military. We had not been warned about any specific problems with the site but we needed to know before work continued. While it was clear that the site had been bombed during the war, the big question was, what had it been bombed with. While the client called their contacts, we called the military and between us we worked out what we were standing on top of.

There were suspicions that the Iraqi military had built underground bunkers on the site. One of Saddam Hussein's strategies was to hide important military posts under public buildings, like schools, electricity plants and our water pumping station. The idea was to force the Allies to bomb targets which produced negative publicity.

The U.S. Air Force had probably used one of their modern missiles to take out the suspected underground complex. During the First Gulf War smoke, dust and sand storms had interfered with the usual laser and infrared systems used to target missiles so the Joint Direct Attack Munitions guidance kits, or JDams, were developed to turn gravity bombs into smart bombs. An inertial guidance system and Global Positioning System receiver guided the bomb from a distance of 28 kilometres straight onto its target. It was believed that the system could direct the missile to within ten metres of its target. It made pinpoint attacks possible, reducing collateral damage and civilian casualties to a minimum.

However, it was not the accuracy of the missiles that concerned us, it was the type of missile used that really worried us. Bunkers were impossible to destroy unless the missile exploded deep underground, next to the structure. The ground absorbed the shock of the blast if the explosives detonated on impact and the military had developed a 'bunker buster' weapon to solve the problem. A depleted uranium tip, which was nearly two-and-a-half times denser than steel, made the missile travel faster so it would penetrate deep into concrete or rock before exploding.

What we were being told was shocking. The site had been covered over by hardcore to seal the radioactive material underground. If we had known we would have taken necessary precautions, starting with keeping our vehicles off the site. While I had only visited site once a week, the security team had been breathing contaminated dust for the past six weeks. No one had told the client and we had only found out by accident. That left a big question hanging over everyone; did they have radioactive metal deposits in their lungs?

We were assured that everyone was OK as long as they had not ingested it, however, no one would know for sure if their food or drink had been contaminated. As for breathing the dust in, we were told it was more dangerous to smoke – which was hardly reassuring. Ten years on, tests are still ongoing and the absolute results will not be known for decades. So much for pinpoint bombing – it had been achieved but at what cost to the people and the environment?

There had been a real lack of communications here. While the military knew about this, they had forgotten to pass on the information to our client when they awarded the contract. After the brown sticky stuff hit the fan a long list of do's and don'ts were issued. We were not allowed to drive inside the fenced off area because the vehicles would stir up the contaminated dust. While the hardcore layer had been put down to seal the area, our cars had churned it up. We were also told to put on our protective suits before we went on site. Err what protective suits, we replied? Radiation protective suits were the answer. Although we had a map marking unsafe areas, we assumed it referred to the bomb damaged buildings; there was no mention of radioactive material. No one seemed to care that the local kids were playing in the water. No one laughed when I joked that we code named the site Acid Bath.

A number of senior military commanders also showed up to take a look at what we had been doing on the site. It was a case of too many big-wigs too late. While they knew about the dangers on site, no one had told them we were there. Work stopped immediately while the British military cordoned off the area. Then there were a series of meetings to establish the new safety procedures as contamination experts from Kuwait came to test the radiation count of the area. But the worst part of it was telling all the guys on site. The engineers were also far from pleased with their head office.

The military took everyone who had worked on site to Kuwait for three days of tests for radiation contamination. They were all told that they had been exposed to low level doses but they could not tell them what the long term effects were going to be. All they could do was tell their doctors when they got home and report any unusual sickness symptoms over the next seven years. Even then it would be difficult to link them with the Acid Bath site. They had been left with a health legacy no one would wish on their worst enemy.

We talked to all the guys when they returned to Shaibah and put it to them that they were entitled to return home where they could have further tests and investigate instigating legal action. But squaddies, being squaddies, all said let us just get on with the job and they would deal with any health issues if and when they happened. Of course the Iraqi kids had no radiation tests and remained ignorant of the situation; there are probably still kids playing in the stream to this day.

Work recommenced with everyone wearing military style NBC suits and masks. The heat restricted your breathing and the sweat made it virtually impossible to function. Despite complaints about them, they just had to get on with the work; but not for long. A couple of weeks later work stopped forever on the site. It was never commissioned and the last I heard of Acid Bath, decontamination was about to start.

It was just one of those cock ups which occurred during the days when the military had its hands full and the new administration was still finding their feet in Iraq. There had been a conflict of interests at a high level, and the guys at the 'coal face' had been caught in the middle of them. The C.P.A. and the Coalition Forces wanted the work doing fast to reduce the chances of a cholera outbreak while our client was anxious to win the contracts. Asking awkward questions would jeopardize the chances of more work so it was easier to accept work and get on with it.

The engineers were sometimes being told to go into infrastructure sites with very little knowledge of what they were dealing with. They were the ones making the initial assessments and the decision to repair existing equipment or replace it was based on their findings. And wherever they went our lads had to go.

But the question that really bugged me about Acid Bath was this. Do you think we would have ever been told about the contamination if our guys had not taken the sign off the kids?

That was not the last I heard of Acid Bath. Work resumed on the plant after I moved north to Baghdad and while the area had been safe to begin with, the arrival of insurgents in 2004 turned it into a very dangerous place to visit. The plant was at the end of a long track leading from the main road and there was no other way in or out. It meant that it was easy for the bad guys to set an ambush and as you drove down the road you just had to keep your fingers crossed that they had not been busy the night before.

You really had to be switched on driving down that road, looking out for anything unusual. While you could often identify the likely places where an Improvised Explosive Device (IED) could be hidden, your only defence was to hit the accelerator and race past, limiting the chances of a direct hit. It was like playing Russian roulette and you just had to hope that luck was with you when the bad guys chose to set an ambush.

The pinch point on the road was a tight right turn on the last leg to the plant and you had to slow down or risk skidding off the road. There was also a low wall close to the edge of the road. One night somebody had fixed a pipe into the masonry, aimed it at the corner and then filled it with explosives. As our team drove the client up to the plant the following morning, the trigger man detonated the device as their car turned the corner. He was a fraction of a second too late and the blast hit the back of the car. Our guys looked back to see that the boot of the car had disappeared and the driver slammed his foot down, sending sparks flying as the car lurched forward. They did not stop until they reached the plant.

As the adrenaline subsided, they were able to take a step back and look at what the IED had done. It had not only shredded the tyres, it had taken off the back of the car, destroyed the boot and scrapped the back door. A fraction of a moment earlier and the driver would have taken the full impact of the blast. And that had been the trigger man's intention. While luck had been on the team's side that day, they had to keep driving to the plant, knowing that their every move was being watched.

A similar situation occurred not far away from Acid Bath when a security team was visiting one of the oil refineries. Again, there was only a single route connecting the refinery to the main road making it easy to set up an ambush. The team was hit as it slowed down to manoeuvre around the concrete blocks set up to form the checkpoint manned by Iraqi police. The insurgents had buried artillery shells next to the check point and then run the command wire into the scrub. The trigger man watched as our cars pulled up at the checkpoint and then flicked the trigger. Six of the Iraqi police were killed in the blast while the car was peppered with shrapnel.

Then the bad guys emerged from the scrub and riddled the cars with small arms fire. By the time they had made their escape, three of our guys were dead... I never learned the full details of the incident because I was working in Baghdad at that time but we were all shocked when the news came in and it highlighted just how dangerous the job was that we had undertaken.

Chapter Six

Spreading Our Wings

AFTER ONLY A COUPLE OF MONTHS, we were covering over a dozen oil refineries around Basra and our security teams had settled into regular weekly routines. Our client's staff were working hard with the Iraqi engineers to get the refineries producing oil as quickly as possible. Once it had been piped to waiting ships in Umm Qasr port, the revenue would generate income; income Iraq needed to get back on its feet.

The country was short of everything; food, clean water, electricity, everything, and reconstruction work was already starting in southern Iraq. While companies worked on the infrastructure, USAID was shipping grain into Umm Qasr and it was being transported via road across the country. The place was buzzing with activity and one thing was clear, the unsettled situation meant that nothing could move without security. While there were no insurgents around stirring up trouble at this early stage, there were plenty of robberies and hi-jackings and convoys had to be escorted everywhere.

While the military had been escorting the lorries, they had more important work to attend to and the amount of work being offered to private security contractors like ours was mushrooming. Most of the security companies were American but they were working further north around Baghdad. Basra was controlled by the British Army and it made sense that we would prosper there. They were happy for us to have a compound in Shaibah Log Camp; we knew how they worked, we had the contacts, and it did not take long to build up a good working relationship.

While we settled in around Basra, our client was trying to negotiate new contracts for more work across the rest of Iraq. The meetings were always held in the Green Zone in the heart of Baghdad and while the journey north was safe enough, the main complaint was the boredom during the 350 mile drive. Our client wanted a high standard of accommodation and there was nowhere suitable in the Green Zone so we stayed in one of the five-star hotels on the east bank of the River Tigris.

One hotel we used was the Hotel Palestine on Firdos Square, which had been built for a French hotelier back in the 1980s. Following the first Gulf War the French owner dissociated himself from the hotel and it was taken over by local owners. It still, however, remained a favourite haunt of journalists and news reporters.

After a day working in the Green Zone, we would head across the Tigris and drive through the crowded streets. The hotel was surrounded by a wall made of concrete segments and the only way in was through the Vehicle Check Point (VCP). While one guard checked your identification, another looked over your car for explosive devices. The whole process was done in tandem with Iraqi police doing the work while Iraqi and American soldiers watched. The strutting U.S. guards made it clear that they distrusted their Iraqi counterparts, making everyone uneasy. But once we were given the all clear we could drive through the chicane into another world.

While there was mayhem and poverty outside the concrete wall, there was luxury and tranquillity inside. After parking the car and unloading the kit, it was time to check in. While walking across to reception, the swimming pool beckoned across the hotel grounds. After the hustle and bustle of the city, the five star environment of the hotel was surreal. The staff did everything they could to make the customers happy and the background music in the reception area was supposed to get you in a relaxed mood.

However, we must have looked a rare sight as we walked up to reception sweating under our bullet-proof vests, with our grab bags over one shoulder and our long weapons over the other. While we were sweaty and covered in dust, the staff were dressed impeccably and their manners were perfect. They took no notice of our grimy appearance as they went through the checking in procedure and they gratefully accepted our advance cash payment in U.S. dollars.

Two guys stayed with the client in the foyer, while the other two went upstairs to check the location and status of the rooms. It did not take long because all the luxuries had been removed or stolen, including the televisions and mini-bars.

They also checked the view from the window to make sure it was not looking directly out on to the street. Finally, they looked over the stairwell, our escape route if the hotel was hit. We always asked for a couple of adjacent rooms next to the internal stairs, because the concrete walls would give us protection out if the electricity went off and the lifts stopped. We could either make good our escape to the car park or to the roof for helicopter extraction. It might all sound a little over the top but you never knew what could happen in Baghdad and a good routine is worth doing well, whatever the situation.

Once we were sure the rooms were OK, it was time to take the client to his room. It could get crowded in the lifts and comments like "can you mind your gun, its barrel is sticking in my side" or "watch my pistol as you squeeze past" were often heard. The sight of two armed security guys with a client squeezed in between must have looked comical when the lift doors opened.

The team leader was designated Close Protection (CP) officer and he had the pleasure of sharing the client's room. He could keep an eye on him while filling out reports and making calls back to the office. The rest of the team bedded down in the next room, taking it in turn to stand outside the door in two hour stints. If the hotel came under attack or the alarm went off, the CP officer would get the client on the ground and protect him while the rest of the team checked the escape route.

Although the east bank of the Tigris was relatively safe at this time, some looked on the five star hotels as a symbol of Western decadence. While the concrete barriers protected the ground floor from direct fire, the upper storeys were ideal targets for anyone wanting to take a pot shot. Angry young men would often stop their car in the street outside and take random shots at the upper storey windows with their AK47s. Mortar teams often fired rounds at the hotel, hoping to land one in the car park. A few brave souls would try their luck with a rocket propelled grenade and although they could cause superficial damage to the building, the chance of injuring anyone was negligible if you took precautions. The chances of doing anything more than breaking a few windows were minimal but the rattle of bullets did keep us awake.

The bad guys already knew about the power of the Western press and their attacks were often designed to get the maximum coverage in the news. After all an incident without airplay was a wasted effort. Threatening the press was a great way of getting publicity and as many journalists stayed in the hotel the bad guys knew every attack would make headline news. It did not take a genius to work out that the attacks were designed to get the sympathy of the press rather than alienate them.

Having said all that, the staff did what they could to make your stay a pleasant one and evening dinner was from seven until nine every night. While one guy stayed in the room with the kit, the rest of us went down to the dining room armed with our concealed pistols. Usually the dining room was full, with around 200 people seated at all thirty tables. Conversation would be buzzing and the diners ranged from clients and their bodyguards to journalists and oil executives. The press was often sniffing around asking questions, trying to find out who our client was and where we were working. We also saw a few guys we knew from our army days there on the same sort of business as we were. It was good to see a few friendly faces and even better to have a chat after dinner and swap information, particularly with the guys who were protecting the press.

The waiters never stopped, and they milled around serving food and drinks while clearing tables for new diners. It did bother us that we had no control over the food preparation but we did not have the influence or resources to control what was going on in the kitchens, so we tucked in like everyone else. The hotel had also laid on live music to keep us entertained and it created no end of amusement. I will never forget an Iraqi guy sporting an enormous Saddam moustache doing a Tony Christie impersonation. While he strummed his guitar he sang songs like Amarillo and other hits in English while trying to disguise his local accent. But as we sat there eating top class food, random gunshots outside reminded us that we had to go back out into the madness in the morning.

After dinner it was back to the rooms ready to settle down for the night. We kept the lights off because they served as an aiming point for anyone lurking down below with a weapon. The guys would take it in turn to sit on the balcony and watch the street for activity. If the lookout sounded the alarm, the CP Officer had to roll the sleeping client off the bed, tip the mattress on top of him and two guys would lie on top in their body armour. It minimized the chances of the client being injured by shrapnel or flying debris.

Although the client was always briefed in advance of what we would do in the case of an attack, it was always a big shock to be man-handled. It was a rude shock to be pushed to the ground and sat on; one moment dreaming of happy times and the next squashed on the floor struggling to breathe under a mattress while two guys sat on top of you. Most of our clients accepted the man-handling but a few objected, especially if they thought we had overestimated the threat. We always worked on the premise that it was better to be safe than sorry and it was worth being called a few bad names to keep everyone out of harm.

The hotel was always locked down when it came under attack and all exits were closed. If we thought we were in imminent danger we would move the client to a safe extraction point via the stairwell down to the car park or up to the hotel roof. Then we could sit tight and wait for the cavalry to arrive, in our case the United States cavalry.

One night the guard on the balcony raised the alarm after spotting a guy on the street shouldering an RPG and aiming it up at the hotel. As we rolled the client off the bed and piled on top of him, there was an explosion up above our window followed by the rattle of falling debris. It appeared that the guy had lifted the barrel up slightly as he squeezed the trigger aiming the rocket too high. Rather than slamming into a room, it demolished a section of the hotel roof and smashed a few windows.

When morning came, it was time to pack up, check out and load up the vehicles. Then back out through the checkpoint into the anarchy that was Baghdad. We usually collected any evidence indicating that we had been in a room, including papers, receipts and rubbish and we took it away and destroyed it. That was just habit from our Special Forces days. We never left a paper trail and we paid everyone in cash. It was just our training, and the three rules we stuck to were, 'deny, deny, deny'.

I said usually destroyed all the evidence because I kept one small memento from a stay at the Palestine Hotel. We were booked into room eleven on the ninth floor and the room receipt had the number 9/11 on it. That was the day that changed the world and my life more than most. I know

I should have destroyed the card, but I had to have it for the novelty factor.

As the number of infrastructure projects around Basra increased, so did the number of people knocking on our door. Our name and reputation was spreading and anyone looking for security in the Basra area was being pointed in our direction. Our main client was also getting more and more work. We could not lose but our main problem was getting enough personnel. As fast as we placed teams with companies, we were checking our contacts to see who was looking for work. We were so sure of getting more work we were inviting guys onboard, knowing full well that there would be work for them by the time they were ready to work.

We were all close to exhausting our address books and resorted to asking the guys to check their contact lists. We got a few new faces to join but it was becoming increasingly difficult to get British personnel; there were not enough ex-Special Forces lads around looking for a new career. American Special Forces guys were only interested in working for U.S. companies and we only employed one in Iraq. He was a larger than life character who served with us as a medic since the early days. He was famous for two things, firstly for being able to scrounge absolutely anything, particularly from U.S. military personnel. Secondly, every time a car came close to his team he put a call over the radio asking for permission to "put a cap in the driver's ass". I never worked out how he would fire his AK47 from his moving vehicle, but his constant calls either amused or annoyed the rest of his team.

We were put in contact with a couple of well connected South African Special Forces guys and we hired them. They put us in touch with quite a few names and we eventually had quite a few South Africans working for us. Although some were not technically minded, they were tough soldiers who would stand and fight. Most were used to getting stuck in and battering people and our American clients sometimes did not take to their blunt Afrikaans attitude. We tried not to put them on close protection roles, giving them tougher tasks to get their teeth into. We never understood what they were talking about most of the time because their Afrikaans radio chatter was full of tongue twisters. It also meant that the bad guys could not understand them either and we always let them work together. They also stuck together if they had an issue with the company and if one left, so did his mates.

We also contacted one of our old comrades who had emigrated Down Under a few years before. He had a couple of friends who were about to leave the Australian Special Forces and they were interested in earning a few dollars in Iraq. The Empire connection worked well and after a few emails we had others looking to join us until we eventually employed twenty-five Australian guys.

While it was good to get new faces, the main problem with employing guys from other countries was that reputations relied on word of mouth. We knew most of the British guys personally or were able to speak to someone who did. We had no contacts in foreign governments to check out their backgrounds. To put it bluntly recruitment standards had to get slacker because we were growing fast and we were up against competition from other security companies.

Most of the time we did not have a problem and if the odd rogue operator did make it onto our books we soon found them out. For example, on one occasion we obtained some new Glock and CZ99 pistols. After using second hand side arms for so long, the guys were all looking forward to having them. While issuing a Glock to one of the new Australian guys, I asked if he had used the pistol before, "yes, of course" was the reply and I thought no more of it. Not long afterwards I saw him fiddling with it, like he was working out how to use it. So I asked again if he was familiar with it and again the answer was "of course I am". I explained that one of the lads could train him on the Glock but he persisted so I dropped the subject. We did not have time to make an issue of it; we expected people to be switched on rather than hiding behind their egos.

Later that evening as everyone chilled out, the peace was shattered by the sound of two gun shots. No one knew what to expect next and there was general confusion and shouting as everyone grabbed their weapons and hit the deck. Then there was a shout from the next room "it's a bloody ND"; the military acronym for a 'Negligent Discharge'. It did not take long to find the culprit with his Glock. And then we followed the route the bullets had taken. They had gone through the internal cabin wall, passed over the client's bed, as he slept in it, and through another wall in the wash room. It finally hit the wall next to a guy while he was shaving and somehow deflected into the sink, sending him sprawling on the floor.

Talk about luck. Good luck for those who just missed getting shot by one of their own comrades, and bad luck for the guy who had fired the shot; he was sacked on the spot. Unfortunately, he had joined the company with three mates and they were expecting to work together as a team. They were determined to show solidarity with their friend and when we refused to keep him on, they resigned, leaving us a team down.

A couple of the South African guys also had negligent discharges and we had to let them go, and they too took their mates with them. But the craziest ND happened when a team came under small arms fire. One guy grabbed his long arm, caught the trigger and fired a round through the floor of the car. He was lucky it did not kill one of his mates...

Another problem with hiring so many people so quickly was that you never really knew who you were taking on until you had spent some time working with them. You hear all these stories of post combat trauma in the media, where ex-soldiers experience problems after they leave the forces.

Well we were recruiting these ex-soldiers and then deploying them into risky environments. I put the fact that we did not have any serious problems down to two factors; the standard of employee we recruited and our strict disciplinary code.

One example illustrates the concerns that weighed on our minds when we took on a new guy. In the early days in Baghdad we were still living out of boxes in our new villa and everyone was still a little disorientated. One night I was awoken by a noise, and as my eyes blinked open, I froze in my cot; one of the guys was wandering around in his boxer shorts while cradling an AK47 in his hands. I did not move in case he freaked out and silently watched as he shuffled across the room to the weapons cabinet and opened the door. My heart was pounding as he put the weapon away and then I leapt at him. There were curses as I pinned him to the floor, shouting for him to wake up. When the rest of the lads ran into the room to find out what the commotion was you can only imagine the amount of teasing we both got.

Joking aside, it would have only taken one lapse by an employee and our company name would have been splashed across the world's headlines. Just look what happened to the American security company, Blackwater, on 16 September 2007. A security team were escorting U.S. State Department diplomats through Nisour Square in western Baghdad. The guards said the convoy came under attack and they returned fire. The Iraqi investigation said the guards made an unprovoked attack. Whatever the truth was twenty Iraqi civilians were killed and another seventeen were injured. The following day Blackwater's licence to operate in Iraq was temporarily revoked. The incident further undermined Iraqi confidence in the C.P.A. and it made it harder for guys like us to get the people's Hearts and Minds. The court actions and investigations rumbled on for years. One mistake and our company would have faced the same problems.

Chapter Seven

Baghdad Cash

AFTER ONLY A COUPLE OF MONTHS in Basra, we got the news that we had been hoping for. Our client had finally been awarded work in the Baghdad area. We had Basra squared away and Baghdad was where it was taking off, both from an action point of view and a financial point of view. We were getting a liking for the business and it was time to increase our turnover and our profits.

There was plenty of competition amongst the security companies as to who would get to Baghdad first. I also believe that we wanted to see how far we could take the company. While the risks were going to be bigger, so were the rewards, and it was a case of 'Who Cares Who Wins', there was money to be made and we were not about to turn our backs on it.

So we were all on a high when the client gave us the nod about the work in Baghdad. I took on the task of expanding the company in the capital and had a month to prepare for it. A month sounds like a long time but there were 1,001 things to do before we could start. After tasking people to deal with our personnel and equipment needed for the new office, two security teams were tasked for a reconnaissance trip to Baghdad. It was time for a trip north to have a good look around and see if things had changed.

Well yes they had. For a start the U.S. military and their contractors had been busy turning the Green Zone into a fortress. The whole area was becoming surrounded by reinforced concrete walls and coils of razor wire and the only access was through a handful of heavily guarded checkpoints. Inside the walls were the offices and accommodation of the C.P.A., the military, contractors and security companies like ours.

Many of the main offices were based in the palaces and villas along the riverbank and Americans now lived and worked where Saddam Hussein and his Ba'ath party loyalists had once ruled. For many of the people of Baghdad it would soon feel like a home grown dictator had been replaced by a foreign one and it stirred resentment in many. Examples of Saddam's fantastic, and sometimes bizarre, taste in architecture could be found all around the Presidential Palace. The Tomb of the Unknown Soldier, the Believers Palace, the unfinished Ba'ath party headquarters and the Convention Centre, were just a few. There was also a large park where Saddam had once watched his soldiers march past.

The Green Zone was developing into a city inside a city. But while a safe environment was being created for the Americans and their Allies to work in, the streets outside were descending into chaos. No wonder the rest of Baghdad was becoming known as the Red Zone. However, it was going to be our home and workplace for the foreseeable future and we had plenty to do before we could open for business.

The first thing on our list was to find a base where we could live and work from. The American military put us in contact with an Iraqi property owner who was renting out villas on the north bank of the Tigris, a short distance west of the Presidential Palace. He was just one of many Iraqis who were making a living out of the new situation. The building had two blocks, one with three storeys opening onto a terrace on the roof of the two storey section. There were around twenty rooms which gave us plenty of space for the office, the operations room, a briefing room, a dining area and plenty of bedrooms for the clients and the lads. The roof terrace would be ideal for an open air gym.

The villa would have belonged to one of Saddam's loyal followers and the previous owner's obsession with security suited us down to the ground. A twelve foot high concrete wall, complete with security gate, surrounded the spacious grounds where we could park our cars. It was just the job for our Command Post, or CP. The Iraqi landlord also offered to organize local workers who could keep the villa clean for us and we snapped up the offer because the lads would soon turn the place into a pigsty. He also offered a cook and again we accepted because while we could always help ourselves in the U.S. military canteens or grab something from one of the takeaways springing up across the Green Zone, you could not beat coming back to a home cooked local dish.

Now we had somewhere to stay, jobs were delegated and the fact that it was possible to drive around the Green Zone on your own meant we could get on with them quickly. It was all starting to come together and things started snowballing. Once people knew that there was a new company in town, they were all eager to help us spend our cash, providing everything from arms and equipment to furniture and household goods.

One team was tasked with setting up the operations room and getting communications established so we could talk to everyone. With the help of the military we got a radio mast and satellite dish installed along with a high frequency radio link to our Shaibah office. The Americans also installed an internet server and told us which mobile phones would work in that area. What with satellite television and the internet, we had better facilities than I was used to at home. We could pick up the phone and speak to anywhere in the world, no problem. It made running the business a lot easier as both the client and our staff could ring any of our offices, either in Iraq or the United Kingdom at any time; we could also speak to suppliers anywhere in the world. Emails began to flood into the office around the clock and the time differences between the client's offices in America, ours in London, and the military offices in Baghdad meant that my electronic in-box was always full to the brim. Each piece of our jigsaw was fitting into place, making our work become easier.

Once we had our home and office established, it was time to explore the neighbourhood and meet the neighbours. A few American security companies, including Dynacorps, ArmorGroup, Aegis and Blackwater, were already established in the city, and it was worth putting faces to names and seeing what we could learn from them. Despite our experience working the Basra oilfields, we were treated like the new kids on the block and there was more than one raised eyebrow when they found out that we were British. Even more eyebrows were raised when they learned we had only been in business for a few months.

Although they all gave us useful information to get us started, we had to check it out for ourselves, to see if we could find out anything extra to give us the edge. That meant lots of work for all the guys and for the next two weeks everyone was busy driving around the Green Zone, checking out everything from hospitals and military headquarters to food stops and refuelling points.

We often used to blag our way into the U.S. military cookhouses and queue up in one of the massive food halls. No one asked who we were. Napoleon is credited with saying that an army marches on its stomach and when you checked out the fantastic range of food counters from around the world it looked like the Americans planned on marching round the world. You name it, you could eat it, from burgers to al a carte menus. It was all free and you could either eat in or takeaway. We used to think the food situation was obscene when we knew that starvation was rife across Iraq. It felt wrong to see the soldiers eating what they wanted and throwing a lot away when there were families with hungry children only a few city blocks away.

The state of flux in the Green Zone meant that it was possible to get your hands on most things if you were good at scrounging and blagging. Everything has its worth and the U.S. Army's policy to ban alcohol meant that a bottle of spirits or a few cans of beer could get us what we needed. I had brought our only American to Baghdad exactly for this reason; he talked the talk and could get anything off anyone. All you had to do was send him into one of the U.S. military camps with some goodies and he would return with all sorts of useful items; a real gem of a guy during those hectic early days in Baghdad.

We also had an armourer with us and he was fully employed checking out the local Iraqi arms dealers. There were all sorts of pistols, semi-automatic rifles and ammunition on offer but it was wise to check them out before you handed over your cash. Most of the equipment was ex-Iraqi army and the quality varied immensely. There was a fair amount of brand new arms and equipment stolen from the U.S. military stores. There were also a lot of rusted old weapons but lots could be broken down for parts and we were able to build up a stock of spares quite cheaply.

Our personal kit was unsuitable for Baghdad and it was time to change from desert kit to urban kit. Most of our time in the Basra oilfields had been spent driving around and we had always been able to park right next to where we were working. In Baghdad there was no need to drive long distances and we were spending more time escorting our clients in and around office blocks. We had to be able to carry everything on our bodies rather than in vehicles so we visited the local markets to get kitted out. The company did not have a standard kit and it was down to personal preference what everyone bought. Some liked the cop vests where your magazines were held in pouches across the torso. I preferred to keep all my goodies in my grab bag so that I could take it or leave it as I saw fit.

Whatever you wanted you did not have to go far in one of the large markets inside the Green Zone. The stalls overflowed with holsters, vests, utility belts and magazines and we were just spoilt for choice. Competition intensified when the American security supplier Blackhawk opened. They were able to get branded items from America, upsetting the Iraqi dealers with their imitation goods.

A lot of our initial work was going to be in Baghdad and while we could drive around the Green Zone without a problem, moving around the rest of the city needed a lot of planning. You could not just head off into the traffic and hope you would find your destination because you could not stop and ask a policeman or a friendly local for directions. The last thing you want to be doing is pulling up alongside the kerb to check the map or ask directions with a client in the back seat. You had to get it right first time or have an emergency plan to get back to the Green Zone.

We needed maps and large scale ones detailing all the streets and buildings. Believe it or not there was no such thing as the Baghdad A-Z and the only maps we could get our hands on were large scale and out of date. We did not want to risk sending a security team into a deadly short cut through a maze of back streets when there was a longer safe route on one of the many dual carriageways. So a bit of lateral thinking combined with some smooth talking and a bit of bribery made sure that a set of four large scale maps of the city found its way from the U.S. Army's map room onto the walls of our operations room. They showed every principal building, road, short cut and bottleneck; perfect for what we needed. Maps of the surrounding areas were soon being pinned up next to them. Now we could start studying what lay outside those concrete walls.

We only had a month to get to know Baghdad and we had our work cut out getting to know the city like the back of our hands. Every day each team would be allocated a district to check out and they drove around it all day before reporting back. There were a hundred and one things to look out for, ranging from checkpoints and chokepoints where the traffic could back up, to likely ambush points and places where IEDs might be used. The threat level rose considerably if you got stuck in traffic and whenever possible we wanted to avoid busy times. So our teams had to assess when traffic congestion was at its worst. Quite often a road would be busy in one direction in the morning rush hour and the opposite direction in the evening.

The team returned with a crib sheet of problems and mapped out the route with checkpoints; alternative routes were also prepared. Each route was allocated a colour and recognizable features such as intersections or landmarks were given a number. The team leader would report each point to the Ops room as he drove past it. It was an easy way to record progress without revealing your location to anyone listening into your radio.

It was the method we learnt on the streets of Belfast where a wrong turn could cost you your life as it did for two British corporals back in March 1988. They accidently ran into an IRA funeral cortege and the mourners, believing they were loyalist gunmen, dragged them from their car, beat them and executed them. We did not want to take any chances in Baghdad where some of the locals were equally unsympathetic to our presence. The month we spent planning out the city was time well spent.

Eventually our client gave us the nod that it was time to start flying personnel north from Kuwait City. Our first tasking was to collect them from Baghdad airport, one by one, and drive them to the villa before settling them into their accommodation. The U.S. military had built large checkpoints around the perimeter of the Green Zone using concrete barriers to force the traffic through chicanes. While soldiers watched from the heavily fortified concrete bunkers protected by sandbags, we showed our ID. The sentries would check that your car was on the list and if everything was in order you were allowed to leave.

Once you were out of the gate you were on your own and straight into the madness that was Baghdad traffic. The only way to describe it is like central London in rush hour, only madder, hotter and dustier. The River Tigris ran along the south and east sides of the Zone and the eastern Gate, known as Assassin's Gate, led out onto Al Jumhurlya Bridge and into the centre of the city; Arbataash Tamuz Bridge took you into the southern suburbs. But we followed the Qadissaya Expressway onto the road heading west to the airport, codenamed Route Irish. During these early days the trip was straight forward enough, but that would soon change as we shall see later.

Once the engineers were settled in, it was time to start making detailed plans. Their first job was to assess the state of the power network around the

Baghdad area. They had the locations of the substations they had to visit and we had to plan specific routes and allocate teams to them.

Working in Baghdad was going to be more complicated than working the Basra oilfields, so we decided to deploy personnel, moving experienced guys north and replacing them with new guys. This way they could get used to the basic risks in Basra before working in Baghdad. While some drove up, bringing hire cars with them, others flew up; quite a few blagged a place on one of the military flights shuttling to and from Baghdad.

It was not long before the villa was bustling with men and if we were not careful we would all start falling out with each other. A set of simple rules and regulations, similar to what everyone had been used to living under in an army barracks had to be drawn up and abided by. While we had the Iraqi cook and cleaner, we all had to respect each other's personal space and stick to rules regarding everyday tasks such as eating, storing weapons and sleeping.

Once we were settled into the villa and teams were going out regularly to work sites, we could establish a regular daily routine. The routine was a pretty tight one because it was tied to three time zones around the world. While we worked to Iraq time, our London office was four hours behind, and the client's office in the United States was another six. They say that New York is the city that never sleeps, well it sometimes felt the same in our office. While advanced telecommunications and emails were great for keeping in touch, they just kept coming in and we had to reply quickly.

After a good night's sleep, gunfire, mortars and helicopters excepting, we held a morning team briefing with all the team members after breakfast. Each team leader was told who he was escorting, where he was going and at what time; he was also told who was in his team. Each leader then sat down in his personal space and worked out his route, discussing any questions with the operations manager before collecting his team members together. Leaders never discussed destinations with each other and they only told the guys when they were ready to go. It was our way of eliminating security leaks, because as much as we liked our Iraqi house staff, we never really knew what they thought of us...

Then the team leaders held their O-Group meeting in a quiet corner, where the conversation could not be overheard. He explained the scenario for the day, including the weather forecast, the road conditions and anticipated problems, so the guys could grab what they needed. Then it was time to tell the men what position they were; a driver or the dreaded Tail-End Charlie. Finally, it was time to load the cars, check the weapons and collect the client. And the day's work had not started yet.

Vehicles leaving the Green Zone had to get advance clearance unless they wanted to wait in a horrendous queue. The idea was to reduce traffic congestion at the security checkpoints, but you always felt that it could have been done better. You had to notify the U.S. Military in advance about your security convoys; including details on the number of cars, the required exit gate and the hoped for time out of the gate, along with a host of other details. You never went early because of the dreaded rush hour and later on the risk of being hit by an IED set during the night was higher. Hopefully, you were given a good exit time and you could get a flying start to your day.

We used satellite phones to monitor team movements around Baghdad to begin with and relied on the code names devised by the reconnaissance teams, because we never knew who might be listening in. So for example the call would be 'Team Bravo at Red Four' and our operations guy would move a coloured pin on the map. Simple but effective and it was all we had in the beginning. If anyone got into trouble it was easy enough to work out who could get to the scene first.

Later on we went high-tech when AEGIS took over the coordination of all the security companies. They installed a satellite tracking system, fixed a huge screen in the operation room and put GPS receivers on all the vehicles. The screen automatically updated vehicle movements but while you might think it did the operation manager's work for him, the number of teams moving around had increased. Every team leader checked their tracker signal before they left the villa and while it gave the guys the assurance that they were being watched, we still made them radio their position in every hour to check everything was working. All day the lights flickered across the screen as the teams went about their work, a constant reminder of all the work going on around the city.

The teams working in the city were always back at the villa by six in the evening because it was never a good idea to get stuck in Baghdad's manic evening rush hour. Once everyone was back in safely, it was time for evening 'prayers'. Apart from finding out how everyone had got on, it was also a chance to share intelligence passed onto us by the military or other security companies. Generally we knew in principle what the following day's workload was, and we discussed events which affected them, for example, new no-go areas or lockdowns.

The client would then spend the next few hours coordinating his work load with his guys in the villa, those on site, and his head office in America, where it was still only late morning. He could brief his technicians on the other side of the world over the internet while we talked to the work sites.

Apart from getting clients out to sites or to meetings, we also had a lot of our own work to coordinate. Guys were going on holiday and had to be collected from the sites, illnesses had to be dealt with and new guys had to be given experience. It always helped if the teams got on with each other as well, so it helped if you knew who liked or hated who when you placed them. On the logistics side, we had to sort out the transport, getting parts out to mend cars, getting them back to the villa to be serviced, getting the computer guy around to deal with problems; you name it, if something could go wrong, it would go wrong and usually when you needed it most. There were no Yellow Pages or call out numbers to rely on, you had to get on with it all yourself.

If the client had equipment en route from Kuwait, we had to safely transport it from base to base. The amount of deliveries eventually grew to the point when we were permanently running convoys between Basra to Baghdad. The client also had a lot of equipment delivered by the postal courier, D.H.L., to our villa in Baghdad. They had their own wagons coming north from Kuwait and they would join US military convoys for the long haul north.

Everything had to be planned in advance and whenever possible we would try and sneak our stuff in with the client deliveries. Usually it was just routine stuff but every now and again something silly would crop up. For example one of the worksites was moaning it had run out of breakfast cereal. Now some of our guys ate more than three of those famous wheat biscuits every morning, and they were far from happy when we forgot to send some up in their food delivery. Well the reminders kept coming in until they were stressing me out, so I took action. The next time a security team went up with a couple of clients, the cars were loaded up with a month's supply. After weaving through the streets of Baghdad to one of the power plants, the security team climbed out of their cars, escorted the clients to the office and then proceeded to unload the cereal boxes. As anticipated, there were cheers all round. Sometimes it was the little things that counted. I never found out what the Iraqi workers made of this bizarre sight.

By ten o'clock at night the client's tasks for the morning would land on our desk and the fun part began as we matched it up with as many of our own requirements as possible. Then it was time to sit down with the operations manager and begin allocating teams to tasks. There was always a lot of chopping and changing on the work schedule to even out the work load. Moving teams around involved all sorts of problems and you could not just swop overnight because neither team had local knowledge of the other's routes.

While you might think it was easier to keep guys on tasks they knew, each one had a different risk level and you had to do your best to reduce tension between teams. No one liked the risky jobs, and if they did then they needed a rest before they became adrenaline junkies. At the opposite end of the scale, anyone who spent too long on an easy task would get picked on. Little niggles became major problems if we did not keep them in check and it was never a good idea to have a lot of angry armed men falling out with each other.

Altogether it was a bloody nightmare and of course we, the guys sitting on our backsides in the villa, making all the changes, were always to blame. I tried to get out to sites as often as possible, but the mobile phone never stopped ringing and I always came back to a mountain of electronic paperwork. So it was Catch 22; office or sites, sites or office. The main factor in my defence was that I had started as a team leader on that very first run across Iraq and then as project manager in Basra before I became a boss at the Baghdad office. It meant that I could always tell the new starters that I had done what they were doing.

All the guys spent a week in the operations room during their time in Iraq to give them an insight into what a complicated job it was. It reminded them that they were part of a bigger team and it gave them an appreciation of the difficulties of running all the sites at once; it also gave them a break from driving the streets. It was a great way of reducing tension between the villa and the sites by removing the illusion that the grass is always greener on the other side.

Chapter Eight

Getting Down to Business

WHEREVER WE WENT IN IRAQ there was one factor that worked in my favour. I was British; or rather I was not American. It also helped that I could speak enough Arabic to start a conversation and usually find out what we wanted or get what we needed. Whether I was in Basra, Baghdad or anywhere else I did find that the Iraqis quite liked the Brits. However, there was a general intolerance for the Americans. Right across the country the general consensus of our guys was that no one had any time for the Americans. The Iraqis put up with them, got what they could out of them but never had a good word for them.

In the early days after the invasion, when we were one of the few companies operating in Baghdad, I saw American security teams act with no consideration for the Iraqis and no thought for the consequences of their actions; either the immediate backlash or the lasting impressions. Our company philosophy stemmed from our Special Forces background, and it was a philosophy that had been learnt the hard way working undercover in Northern Ireland during the Troubles, watching the activities of the Republican and Nationalist paramilitaries.

The golden rule was not to draw attention to your vehicle because there was always someone looking to kill you; if not this time, the next. Only there were several crucial differences between working the streets of Belfast and Derry and those around Baghdad and Basra; and it was not just the heat. The insurgents in Iraq and their supporters were quite content to walk or drive right up to you and blow themselves to pieces to kill a target for the price of a second hand car in Northern Ireland.

While the universal use of the mobile phone in the 21st Century was a godsend to many people, they caused us no end of worries as youngsters notified their paymasters that we were heading their way. Communications back in the days of the Troubles were far more rudimentary when the paramilitaries primarily relied on runners to pass on messages.

We were also painfully aware that no matter how good our suntan was, or how cheap our sunglasses were, we always looked like Westerners. During our first trips up to Baghdad, we had worn shemaghs, the local desert scarves, wrapped around the face as protection from the sun and dust. While they concealed our identity and allowed us to blend in, they soon became a liability as the number of military checkpoints across the country multiplied rapidly. Even close up we looked like locals to friend and foe alike. It was soon clear that the risk of being shot to pieces if we pushed our luck at a checkpoint was far higher than being blown to bits by a suicide bomber.

One of our golden rules was that drivers stuck to the rules of the road unless the team was under threat. It was far safer to keep a low profile rather than draw attention to ourselves. While courteous driving did not attract attention, it took nerves of steel to weave through the traffic. But that was how we liked to conduct business; calm and alert.

The American security teams often worked in a completely different way. Their driving style sometimes reminded me of a cross between one of their cop television shows and a Mad Max film. They drove huge 4x4 cars, often beefed up with armour plating and mounted weapons on the roof. The open back trucks with a 50 calibre machine gun mounted on the back were a favourite. The security teams carved their way through the traffic with headlights on and the horn blaring. You could either hear them or see them from quite a distance as they raced across the city, often on the wrong side of the road. And if we knew they were coming, so did anyone hoping to take a pot shot.

As they raced past pedestrians would stop and look – and we thought if they were looking at the American teams, then they weren't looking at us. As the 4x4s pushed through the traffic, the occupants brandished their weapons out of open windows, pointing them at anyone who dared get too close or look at them. They also used to point their weapons at us until they realized that we were in the same line of business and then it was all smiles and friendly gestures as they roared away at speed.

We often saw teams pull up with a screech of tyres and then clamber out to form a defensive perimeter, carrying their weapons tucked into their shoulders, finger on the trigger. Angry shouts and gestures made it clear it was unhealthy to take a step closer. They all wore cop vests jammed with ammunition and side arms strapped to the thigh. Most sported a goatee beard, shaved head and sunglasses; some would have Stars and Stripes bandanas around the head. Their whole attitude was "the Americans are here; we shoot first and ask questions later – so back off and get out of my gun sights." It was real Rambo stuff; sometimes all that was missing was Sylvester Stallone and a camera crew.

Despite all the bravado, the way they conducted themselves told me one thing; their actions were driven by paranoia because they were scared of the Iraqis. The American security teams viewed them all as possible insurgents and did everything in their power to keep them at arm's length. Their display of power was regarded as disrespectful by the Iraqis; another knock to the campaign for winning the Iraqis' Hearts and Minds – that is if there really was one.

Our teams were taught to blend in as much as possible, stopping their cars as normal as possible when they arrived at their destination so as not to attract attention. The team would exit the car with their guns down, and take up their positions watching intently for anything or anyone out of the ordinary. It only took a fraction of a second to shoulder a weapon and squeeze the trigger to stop an insurgent in his tracks. Well it did if you practised regularly.

Each time our client was awarded a new contract, we had to check out what it entailed. We were always given plenty of notice and by the time the client was ready to place staff on site, the place was as safe as we could make it. All our scouting was carried out by our two Forward Reconnaissance Teams, call signs FRT 1 and FRT 2, and they both spent most of their time looking at new jobs.

The FRTs had a whole list of issues to investigate before work could start on a site, starting with getting to the site. Now the safest route might not always be the obvious route but you never knew until you checked it out. The FRTs would drive along all the options, looking at the timings, ambush locations and choke points. They travelled up and down them at different times of the day to check the traffic flows and the rush hour.

The FRTs also assessed the site, looking at a wide range of issues and threats. They always worked alone, often a day's drive from the nearest friendly team, and they had to be careful not to get involved in any fire fights. Their arrival would usually be noted by an informer working at the site and within hours of arriving something unpleasant might happen. That was when the team was at their most vulnerable; they never knew what to expect. The FRTs often spent several days out on the road, living rough in their vehicles which were jammed full of food, equipment and ammunition. But it was just the sort of covert work we were used to carrying out during our military days; travelling unseen, lying low and reporting back.

Part of the threat assessment involved checking what happened at night around the site. This involved lying low, watching and listening through the long night hours, recording any activity. While they were not in a position to stop any unsavoury activity, such as thieving or sabotage, they were able to make recommendations on how to stop it.

By the end of the visits our Baghdad office would get a fully illustrated report of what the situation was and the security measures to be put in place before the client arrived. Then the planning could start, organizing the personnel, accommodation, defensive equipment and weaponry. The project manager was also involved in the planning so he could understand what he would be doing.

Our best guys were chosen to work on the FRTs and we were always monitoring newcomers to see if any were suitable. Most of the guys aspired to join one of the teams, maybe because of the additional sense of adventure and freedom that the work involved.

As the day for the client to start work approached, it was time to let the FRT pass on their knowledge to the site staff. Team leaders would be driven to site, listening to the FRT's instructions along the way. There was a lot to take in and everyone had to be totally switched on during the handover phase. Once on site the FRT would hold site briefings and escorted the team leaders around the site, explaining security issues and what needed to be done. They would also introduce them to the local contacts working on the site. By the time the team leaders were back at the Baghdad villa they were totally clued up on their new contract and ready to take the client's staff, confident they knew what to expect.

Emergencies happened all the time in Iraq and you never knew what was around the corner. Apart from getting shot at by gunmen or getting blown up by an IED, cars could break down, get stuck or crash. There was no end of trouble our teams could get into. Our contingency plan for emergencies was the Quick Reaction Force, or QRF. We always had two fuelled up cars loaded with ammunition and equipment parked in the villa compound ready to go. Any guys off duty or who had returned early from a job would be on standby for the QRF; in other words anyone hanging around the villa. They would grab their gear as soon as the operations room received an emergency call and drive out of the Green Zone. Most of the guys made a point of listening out to see how their mates still out on jobs were getting on and no one relaxed properly until the last team was home.

Most times the QRF was scrambled when someone had broken down. Remember how anxious you get when your car lets you down on the motorway and it seems like an eternity until the breakdown lorry arrives. Well add to that the possibility that any one of those cars passing might be full of guys who would love to take a pot shot at you; all they had to do was call home to get their weapons. It is enough to send your stress levels through the roof.

The sight of the QRF cars rolling up the hard shoulder was a welcome sight, especially if you had broken down on your way home and it was getting dark. You would always breathe a big sigh of relief as the QRF team set up an all round defence while the mechanic set to work fixing the problem.

When security teams work with VIPs they always deploy an extra level of protection known as protective surveillance. While the overt team carried out close protection (CP) on the client, an over watch team worked covertly, shadowing their every move. They went ahead of the team, checking the route, and then waited at the destination. It meant that the CP team could concentrate on keeping the client safe, knowing that someone was watching their backs.

As much as it would have added an extra level of security, we rarely used over watch teams because the client usually refused to pay for them. Sometimes we ignored the cost and sent out a guy on a motorbike to check the route out. They also made sure that the destination was not mobbed with people or traffic.

Occasionally we deployed a bit of heavy backup, just in case things went wrong. We had converted a battered old camper van into a mobile support unit by mounting a 50 calibre machine gun in the back. The van driver would be able to shadow the team, ready to move closer if there was a problem. The man inside the back could then open the rear door and give the bad guys a nasty surprise. Cheeky but necessary.

In the early days the operations room tracked our teams by radio messages and a map board. The operations manager watched to see if anyone stopped unexpectedly but usually a team would put in a call, "Contact - Wait - Out"; it meant they were under fire, but so far so good. Everyone else would stop to listen and wait for instructions, hoping that their mates were OK. Usually they would report that the contact was over and they were continuing on their way but sometimes they would request help from the Quick Reaction Force.

Occasionally a team had to abandon their vehicles and put their Escape and Evasion plan into practice. In other words make a run for it on foot, taking only what they could carry easily with them. That was their arms, ammunition and a grab bag filled with goodies to help them survive 24 hours in the harsh Iraqi environment. We reckoned our procedures and backup could locate anyone in that time and if not, then chances were they were a dead man. We had no backup from the military so we had to have our own SOPs in place if things went wrong. It would be our own guys going out to find their lost friends and we did not have helicopters to search the landscape.

The grab bag provided for five things; food, water, warmth, navigation and a weapon. Each bag had a survival pouch, with items such as fire lighting equipment, candles, a fishing line and a good survival knife. You also carried dried fruit and water. Everyone carried a map of the area they were working in and a compass; some people carried a spare mobile phone and sim card in case their regular one stopped working. Maybe you could stuff a jumper, a hat, gloves and a space blanket inside because the nights could sometimes be as cold as the days were hot. You always carried a couple of spare clips of ammunition and a Makarov pistol with a couple of magazines, in case you had a problem with your usual weapon.

It was essential to keep the operations room informed of your location, what had happened and what you were going to do before you abandoned your vehicle. That information just might save your life, or at the very least make sure that you were safe as soon as possible. While every team had a satellite phone, the batteries only had a limited life and mobile phone coverage across Iraq was patchy.

If the radio went dead and the operations room could not raise an answer, the assumption was that the team were in difficulties and the QRF was scrambled. The operations room would also inform the nearest military base in case they had a patrol or convoy in the area. They would help if they could, but often they could not. If you worked on the premise that it was every team for themselves, then you would not be far wrong.

Every route had pre-planned Emergency Rendezvous (ERVs), a list of regular points marked along the route where a team could head for and wait to be picked up. The QRF would first locate the abandoned vehicles and then head for the nearest ERV. Once the QFR team reached the ERV, they started backtracking towards the team's last point of contact. They would soon be found and brought home safe and sound. While planning the ERVs took a lot of time, it was well worth the effort when the time came.

Each work site also had an ERV in case it came under attack and the team had to make a run for it; something that rarely happened. The only time I had to use an ERV was at Al Quds, an important power station in the Rashidiyah area, northwest of Baghdad. When we started working there it was protected by rusty old wire fencing patched with corrugated iron. There were more holes in it than a string vest and the perimeter was a nightmare to monitor, particularly at night. While our clients worked away on the turbines, an Iraqi contractor had been appointed to build a concrete perimeter wall and our guys were looking forward to the day when it was finished. The wall was close to completion when I decided to make an overnight stop to spend some time with the team.

The Iraqi construction workers failed to turn up the following morning and when the Ministry official called the contractors, he was told they were not returning to work. Armed men had visited the supervisor and his foremen during the night and made it clear that their lives would be in danger if they finished the wall. No matter what the Ministry man offered or threatened, they were not going to return.

The wall still had a gap of 70 metres, leaving the turbine compound and our camp wide open to attack. Anyone could work out that the insurgents were determined to damage the power station before the compound wall was finished. All we could do was prepare for the inevitable attack later that night.

The military were not interested in sending troops to support us on the off chance that something might happen but we could not abandon the power station. After mounting a guard I sat down with the project manager to plan our defence; it did not take long. There were 100 Iraqi guards employed to patrol the perimeter but we did not know if they had been paid or threatened to turn their guns on us or desert us. Even if they did stand and fight, it was unlikely they would put up much of a fight. They were only armed with AK47s and a few clips of ammunition and had been given very little training. So we decided to post them along the perimeter and hope that at least one of them would fire a few warning shots if they saw anything.

There were ten of us and all we could do was prepare to make a last ditch stand. The office and dormitory were two half buried steel containers and we planned to put our three clients inside one while we manned sandbag positions on top of them. All day long we sweated in the heat, filling sandbags and building sangars and as the sun went down it was time to set up weapons and distribute ammunition. With so few guys involved we kept our plan simple. The sangars had interlocking fields of fire and were close enough so we could rely on visual signals to run the defence. Hand signals were much easier to understand than radio calls, particularly in a fire fight in the middle of the night.

The project manager had assessed where the insurgents were likely to attack and our outer line of defence covered the approaches to our compound. It was likely we would be unable to hold this extended line for long so various ways of withdrawing to the inner line of defence were devised. We called this collapsing a position, in which men moved back one at a time while the rest gave covering fire. It was the only way to stop the enemy realizing you were withdrawing.

Each position was given a number and every man knew where to go when the alarm was sounded and who was to his left and right. It meant that we could find anyone and check for casualties. While it sounds too simple to be true, it works.

As we were putting the final touches to our work, four U.S. Marine Corps snipers checked into our compound and they were a welcome addition to our tiny force. These snipers often worked in pairs out on their own, setting up observation points along the main roads to watch for unusual activity with their night scopes. One of their tasks was to watch where IEDs were being set up to see if they could catch the perpetrators. As luck would have it they had chosen tonight of all nights to stop by at the power station for a few hours' rest. We doubted they were going to get it...

As we settled down for the night in the dormitory, the lookouts took up positions on the roof. Not long after midnight gun fire was heard outside the perimeter wall. More shots and screaming followed as the Iraqi guards exchanged fire with whoever was approaching. Great stuff, they had given us the warning we needed. Shouts from the lookouts followed, warning us that it was time to man to the sangars.

I crouched on the roof of the bunker behind the PKM machine gun with my number two ready with the ammunition belt and opened fire, aiming towards the gap in the concrete wall. The PKM is the machine gun version of the AK47 and it is mounted on a sturdy bipod for fire support. Although these weapons date from the 1960s, they are lightweight, reliable and, above all, it was easy to get our hands on ammunition belts. The rest of the lads were in the sangars below in a semi-circle in front of us, firing their AK47s and M21s. While we were squinting into the darkness the Marines were putting their night vision equipment to good use and taking aimed shots.

From my elevated position it was difficult to make anything out in the darkness apart from gun flashes and darting silhouettes. As expected the Iraqi guards were looking for the nearest exit, leaving us to face around fifty armed guys. While we could probably hold our own, we were well aware that we did not have enough ammunition for a sustained fire fight. We had no idea if there were more bad guys around and we did not feel like guessing who would run out of ammo first. After a brief chat with the project manager we agreed that there was a good chance that this was only the first wave of insurgents; others could be moving in for the kill.

The bottom line was we did not want to get trapped and after alerting our Baghdad operations room and the Quick Reaction Force, the order to withdraw was passed around the sangars. One by one the guys pulled back to the inner defence, while the project manager told the engineers it was time to leave; we were going to put our Escape and Evasion plan into operation.

We left with the clients first, heading across the basketball pitch away from the shooting. After ducking through a hole in the fence we slid down a steep slope into a dry river bed, where we were out of sight and out of the firing line. The next bit involved scrambling along the wadi and although we had checked to make sure it was passable, it was tough going in the dark. One of the clients was about twenty stone and while there was no chance of us breaking into a jog, I remembered thinking "It is surprising what big guys can do when they are under pressure".

As we headed off down the wadi, we hoped the rest of the guys could escape from the compound without being seen. The promise we made to each other was always that no one would be left behind and the team leaders made sure that all their guys were accounted for. We just had to hope the insurgents did not find our escape route for some time or we were in trouble. We faced a five kilometre walk to the Emergency Rendezvous, where a road crossed a riverbed, giving us a place to hide.

The four snipers were following and they had also been busy talking to their operations room. Only they had access to far better firepower than we could ever dream of. As we scrambled along the wadi we could hear the sound of two helicopters in the night sky. I felt a big grin stretch across my face as they swooped low over the power station. The cavalry had arrived.

The AH-64 Apache is a twin-engine attack helicopter, designed as a flying killing machine armed to the teeth with a wide range of weapons to take out a multitude of targets. The nose-mounted sensor suite has a sophisticated target acquisition system and night vision equipment which would light up the power station compound. While we could hardly see who we were shooting at, the helicopter's crew of two had a grandstand view from their tandem cockpit. The pilot only had to look at the gun flashes below through his Helmet Mounted Display and the 30 mm M230 Chain Gun underneath the helicopter followed the aim of his eye. He could then open fire at will, unleashing 625 bullets a minute from the electrically operated chain gun.

As we looked back from the lip of the wadi we could see the streams of tracers spewing from the chain gun towards the gap in the security wall. The Apaches just hammered the bad guys; they did not stand a chance. The mayhem allowed the rest of our guys and the Marines to escape and we were soon making our way to the rendezvous point.

After an hour of scrambling along the darkened river bed the road bridge loomed in the horizon where our Quick Reaction Force was waiting. We were safe. Our Escape and Evasion plan had worked like a dream and by the early hours the clients were tucked up safely in the Green Zone. I never did curse again when the noise of an Apache helicopter woke me up in the middle of the night; after all the crew could have been the one who saved our skins that night.

Chapter Nine

The Iraqi Highway Code

WE CONDUCTED THREAT assessments of our work, the same as you would conduct risk assessments in your office, only we had more to think about than trip hazards and lifting heavy items. We had to identify hazards, and there were many, and then suggest ways to reduce the chance of them occurring and limit the risk if they did. We then organized training to work out ways to escape from bad situations. In gangster and cop films the driver slams to a halt and everyone clambers out, taking cover behind the doors to return fire. Forget about that, it never happens in a real fire fight. The doors give little protection while the car makes a great aiming point. In many cases the first couple of shots are fired to distract you from the main ambush. We did not have time for heroics; our job was to get the client to safety as quickly as possible. Having said that things did not always go to plan... And when they did not we relied on our Quick Battle Orders, or QBOs. These were short instructions decided in advance and everyone knew what to do when they heard them; no questions asked. After all there was no time to issue complicated orders when the rounds started coming in.

To begin with our number one threat was the road traffic accident. Driving on Iraq's roads, particularly in built up areas was erratic, to say the least. If a car was involved in an accident then the team members transferred into the remaining car and made good their escape before the incident escalated. The main priority was the safety of the client; and the team. We could retrieve the car, or pay to have it removed later.

We used the same driving techniques for changing cars we had used in the Special Forces. The two members of the team in the stationary car would get out and shoulder their weapons, ready to suppress or drive off approaching insurgents. The moving car would manoeuvre alongside the stricken car and the client would be manhandled between the cars; he was sometimes pushed to the ground behind the steel wheel hub if there was heavy fire.

Different scenarios were devised depending on which car broke down and which direction the fire was coming from. Drills were then practised on Festivities Square, the huge parade ground in Zawra Park, built to mark the end of the Iran-Iraq War. The area was famous for the twin 'Hands of Victory', a triumphal arch in the form of two forearms based on plaster casts of Saddam's arms. The hands held swords and each sword is 43 metres long, with the blades meeting 40 metres above the ground. It was an impressive memorial and one that features in many photographs.

Saddam Hussein had ridden a white horse beneath the swords on the inauguration day before firing rounds into the air on the grandstand as the Imperial Guard marched past. Since the U.S. military had taken over, the parade ground had been designated as a training area where we could practise our manoeuvres. It was only a couple of minutes from our villa, across the Qadisiya Expressway, and we pushed the guys to spend their free time out there practising.

Even after all that training, things could go wrong. I worked back-to-back with one of my best mates in the Baghdad office. We went back years in the Special Forces and instinctively knew how each other worked. After a long stretch of working it was his turn for a holiday and he jumped in with a convoy that was heading south to Shaibah Camp. He met a client there who was going on leave and after a stopover they left early the following morning for the border. It was only a short drive in a safe area of the country and there was no need for security. All went well until they crossed the stretch of No Man's Land at Safwan, on the border with Kuwait and they were involved in a car crash.

I could not believe it when I got the phone call telling me that they were both dead. I never found out what really happened but the car hit one of the concrete barriers, killing them instantly. After all those years on Special Forces duties and then working in Baghdad, and that happens. He was a popular man in the armed forces and several hundred turned out for the funeral; no one could believe what had happened. His death hit me hard because we had worked so close together for a long time; it was a real choker. The roads across Iraq were at best in a poor condition, at worst appalling and occasionally our teams had to leave the road to get around an obstacle. What with the state of the roads and the heat, it was a wonder our cars did not break down more than they did. They did sterling work and not only were they reliable, they would go virtually anywhere.

But from time to time they gave up. The drill was to pull over in a safe place, set up an all round defence and then try to fix the problem. Quite often cars just overheated and they needed time to cool down, not that you could always stop where you wanted. Sometimes it was something more serious like a broken prop shaft or damaged steering while the armoured cars we used later were almost impossible to drive if the power steering stopped working. If the guys could not make a roadside repair, they could try and tow the stricken vehicle back to the villa but their slow speed and inability to manoeuvre would make them vulnerable.

Sometimes the weight of a loaded armoured car was too much for the strongest tow rope and the car had to be left behind. Then while two guys kept a watch, the other two switched all key items, like weapons and ammunition, into the serviceable car. Cars were only abandoned as the last resort because there was no point returning with a tow truck; thieves would either steal it or strip it down before the day was out. I always told the guys to do absolutely everything to nurse both cars home; it was just too much money to lose.

Another way of escaping when you find yourself in difficulty was to hi-jack a car, however, it was a hi-jacking with a difference. Under our rules of engagement we were entitled to stop a local at gunpoint in his car, drag them out of the car and drive off; we introduced a cash incentive so there were no complaints later, after all technically we had bought the car.

The difficult part was getting a driver to stop, particularly when you consider we were wearing our 'Rambo gear' and carrying weapons. When you did get a driver to pull over, you waved him out of the car and then gave him a handful of cash in exchange for his keys. Cash could get you most things in Iraq, as long as it was in dollars, and everyone carried $1,000 cash on them for emergencies.

You then drove off in your new purchase, hoping you had 'bought' one with some tough tyres and some petrol in the tank. Most Iraqi cars were battered old things which seemed to keep mobile through ingenuity rather than good maintenance, and while they were only worth a few hundred dollars, they could be a life saver.

Our guys rarely had to hi-jack a car but occasionally a team would roll into the villa compound in a battered old banger, accompanied by cheers and jokes referring to Arthur Daley the famous second hand car dealer. You could only imagine the phone call the driver made to his wife as he explained why he was going to be late home for dinner; "Hi honey, I have some good news and some bad news..."

While driving in the city we quickly learned that attacks were very rarely random and at times it felt like everyone was watching you. Any insurgent worthy of his trade in death would know who was heading his way and when they were likely to turn up. Keeping a lookout for dickers could drive you paranoid as you went about your daily business. Anyone looking in your direction for too long came under suspicion, particularly if they had a mobile phone jammed to their ear or if they appeared to be signalling. Of course they might just have been calling the wife or waving to a friend across the road, but we did not know that. They might just be setting us up for an attack.

One little trick that used to get on our nerves was making kids hang around traffic lights with an old cloth and a bucket of dirty water. They would try and wash your windows as you waited for the green light but as they wiped with their cloth some would try and look inside the car. Our only defence was to be a bit ruthless and threaten them with a weapon to make them back off. It was not nice to do it but we were not going to take the risk.

However, the prize for the best dicker had to be awarded to a woman who lived in a rough shack she had built in the middle of a roundabout in south east Baghdad. She would sit there all day with her kids, begging for food or a few coppers from the drivers stuck in the traffic jams. Whenever I drove past, I used to feel sorry for the poor woman. That was until I found out she had been working as a dicker, watching and reporting the to and fro of vehicles into and out of the Green Zone. Talk about being cheeky; the bad guys had an observation post bang on our route and they had us feeling bad about her...

Another of our biggest threats while driving in an urban area was getting lost, or rather being forced off your route by an unexpected event like a lockdown, an incident or a good old traffic jam. Once you had to change direction you needed all your wits about you, a good sense of direction and a bit of luck to get to where you wanted. The following example illustrates what could happen if it went wrong.

On 31 March 2004 the world was shocked to see how low insurgents would go when a Blackwater security team was ambushed in Fallujah. Four guys were escorting food delivery trucks to a military base when they took a wrong turning because the insurgents had repositioned the road sign. Before they knew it, they were in a narrow street and facing a dead end. The ambush had been set and they were shot dead in the trap. But it is what came next which shocked the world.

The bodies were mutilated and set ablaze as the mob cheered, then tied to the backs of vehicles and dragged through the streets as gruesome trophies. At least two of the mutilated bodies were hung from a bridge over the River Euphrates. As we watched the Brigades of Martyr Ahmed Yassim claiming responsibility on television, we were reminded how evil the bad guys could be. While it sent a shiver down all our spines, no one talked about the incident.

One team I went out with faced a similar situation as we headed back to the villa after a long day at one of the sites and our route went past one of Baghdad's many mosques. We knew there had been an incident during the afternoon and anticipated that people were heading to the building to demonstrate. We contemplated whether to risk the main road past the mosque or an alternative route through the side streets to avoid the inevitable crowd. We decided to stick to our route but minutes later we wondered if we had made the right decision.

We faced the traffic jam from hell because there were hundreds of people gathered in the square outside the mosque creating a huge traffic jam and we had to get through it. We were soon spotted and the brave ones in the crowd pushed up against our cars, making hostile gestures. We had nothing to do with the reason they were at the mosque; we were in the wrong place at the wrong time. And they were going to focus their anger on us.

We needed to drive to escape the crowds but the easiest way to get vehicles to move was to get out of our cars and threaten them with our weapons. But the way it was looking, we would be dragged out and our weapons ripped from our hands the moment we unlocked the doors. If we were lucky we would be beaten and taken hostage; if we were unlucky, we would be killed on the spot.

So we just had to brazen it out, and our drivers nudged the cars forward, inch by inch through the crowds. Dozens of people pressed their angry faces against the car windows while others slammed their hands or rocks against the bodywork; all we could do was remonstrate and show our weapons. It was scary stuff but no one in the crowd had a weapon and we were soon at the opposite end of the square and back into free moving traffic. The whole thing had taken less than five minutes, but it had felt like a lifetime. A real white knuckle experience and one we did not want to try too often.

Some might say why we did not get out of the cars and shoot into the crowd to disperse them, after all they are intent on killing you. However, it is far from easy to fire on unarmed civilians, no matter how much you are threatened. It was easy to show your weapon as a show of force, aiming at the crowd, but to pull the trigger is another matter; would your conscience let you? Returning fire on armed insurgents is straight forward but it is a totally different situation when you are facing an unarmed mob.

Some might ask why the guys in Fallujah did not open fire and try to escape? Believe me it is a very difficult decision to make and while you can plan for it, it can take you unawares when it happens. Although I had always been trained to use reasonable force to resolve a situation, I can understand why people cannot bring themselves to squeeze the trigger even when their lives were in danger.

While driving through Baghdad had its own dangers, travelling on the open road had its moments too. As the months passed and operations spread across Iraq, the number of military convoys moving around the country increased. Some of the convoys were over two miles long, with over thirty vehicles moving in a long line. They were forced to use main roads and had to move so slow, they were an insurgent's dream. The long line of lorries and transport vehicles were interspersed with tanks and Humvees, and you could spot them from miles away.

IEDs could easily stop a convoy in its tracks and spotters mounted in the leading vehicles had their eyes glued to the ground, looking for suspicious signs. Specialized vehicles equipped with scrapers drove alongside the road, detonating IEDs planted in the verge. Armoured Personnel Carriers armed with flails followed, slicing any wires dug into the verges. While the two vehicles disarmed IEDs, they forced the convoys to move at a snail's pace. The insurgents sometimes used rocket propelled grenades (RPGs) against the huge, lumbering targets and if they hit one, the rest ground to a halt, making them sitting ducks.

The convoys were protected by a lot of trigger happy guys armed with powerful weapons. Many were twitchy and inclined to shoot first and ask the survivors (if there were any) questions later. We did not want to be around the convoys for a moment longer than necessary because if the bad guys did not get you, the good guys might.

The column's 'Tail End Charlie' always had a large sign with the words "Stay 100 metres away or we will use deadly force" in Arabic and English fastened to the back. That did not help us and we never wanted to be stuck behind one of these convoys, in case a suicide bomber was in the queue of cars tailing the convoy. After all we were a softer target and they might have decided to target us.

Our usual tactic to get past a convoy was to slow down as we approached and then get the attention of the guy watching the traffic over the sights of his gun. Flashing lights, our white faces, the style of the car and even the Union Jack flag on the sunshield were hopefully enough to convince him that we were friendly. He then radioed the convoy commander for permission to let us pass, who in turn warned the rest of the convoy that two cars were about to drive past at speed. Once we were waved through, there was no stopping us. Our driver checked for oncoming traffic and then floored it past the convoy as fast as he could. And then it was back to miles of boring tarmac.

You never knew when you would meet one of these convoys on the road and it pushed our adrenaline levels through the roof every time we saw one on the horizon. We had seen numerous reports of Americans firing warning shots at security teams as they pushed their luck trying to squeeze past a convoy and you will soon see why they became our number one risk.

One evening we were in a rush to get back to the villa after a long day on the road and the sight of a military convoy ahead made our hearts sink. An M1 Abraham's tank, a huge chunk of metal weighing over 60 tonnes which dwarfed our cars, was at the back of the convoy. Our attempts to get the attention of the gunner poking his head out of the turret were not working, so we just kept edging a little closer. When we did eventually catch the gunner's eye, we did not get the signal to drive past, instead he shouted down into the innards of the tank.

We realized he thought we posed a threat to the convoy when the tank turret swung slowly round until the barrel of the 120mm gun was pointing directly at us. Our eyes widened like saucers and our guts tightened as the barrel waggled up and down, in the same manner as a mother would wave her finger to her naughty child. Only we knew we were heading for more than a smacked backside if we did not back off, we were heading for the mortuary. The message was "do not push your luck boys, we do not know who you are and if you do not back off we will turn your car into a pile of twisted metal." We dropped back and waited until we eventually got the all clear to drive past.

While approaching another convoy near Samarra, about a hundred miles north of Baghdad, we were given the all clear from the Tail End Charlie to drive past. However, he made it clear that we had to pass on the nearside of the convoy, along the dirt hard shoulder. As we drove at speed past the line of vehicles, kicking up a cloud of choking dust behind our car, I spotted that the turret man of one of the Humvees had nodded off. Hours in the baking sun, staring into the desert had become too much for him. His shoulders were slumped forward and his head was resting on his 50 calibre machine gun, with his helmet over his eyes, while he dreamt of a woman waiting back home.

My driver and I just looked at each other, half in envy at his slumbering state and half in resignation at the laxness in discipline. But it turned out he was not asleep, just dozing, and the noise of our engine roused him from his slumbers. He then proved that he was not as lax as we thought as he came to terms with the problem confronting his bleary eyes. He did not expect to see a civilian car driving fast down the hard shoulder and made the snap decision that we were suicide bombers about to drive into his convoy. He swung his machine gun in our direction, squeezed the trigger and let off several rounds in our general direction. The noise from the gun panicked us as three rounds bounced off the tarmac and went through the roof of the car; the rest missed completely.

As we braced ourselves for more bullets, our nemesis disappeared rapidly from view as one of his mates grabbed his knees and pulled him down. We could only imagine the conversation inside the Humvee and our contribution was to scream obscenities and make appropriate gestures as we drove past. They waved sheepishly back and mouthed "Sorry". Sorry indeed but that small lapse of concentration nearly killed us.

Looking back I had to feel compassion for the young guys on the convoys. While the soldiers taking the fight to the insurgents were fully trained Regulars, the young men guarding the convoys were usually National Guardsmen; the equivalent to British Territorial Army soldiers. Many had joined up for the weekly training, annual camps and financial boost to their hard earned pay cheque. National Guardsmen were usually only deployed if there was a national emergency, like the floods in Louisiana following Hurricane Katrina; they did not expect to have to go to war in a foreign country.

However, the United States military had a problem. Twelve months after the 2003 invasion it was becoming difficult to maintain the number of Regular soldiers across Iraq as they came to the end of their twelve month tour of duty. Many support services looked to the National Guard to keep the combat troops supplied and their equipment maintained. Some of the guys on the convoys would have just recently finished college while many others would have been called up from their regular jobs. After only a brief refresher training they found themselves a long way from home in a strange country, working on military bases and escorting convoys.

The National Guardsmen had a different attitude to the Regular Army soldiers, like they were annoyed with having to put their lives on hold for twelve months. Many had a career back home and a girlfriend or wife waiting for them. They had not joined the Army to see the world and they just wanted to get back home to pick up where they left off as soon as Uncle Sam let them.

Once as I waited for our client to have a meeting on Camp Spicer, I chatted with a National Guardsman on gate duty. He was protected by a concrete bunker, blast walls and sandbags and armed with every type of weapon you could think of, all laid out neatly, along with a lot of ammunition. He also had the face for the job with the obligatory sunglasses perched above a fixed grimace which went round and round as he chewed gum.

He was happy to explain the hazards of working the front gate of the camp and he was equally pleased to explain what all his weapons were for. "This weapon is the best for stopping taxis in their tracks, they can rip the engine block to pieces, not to mention the driver" he explained. "4x4s were more powerful and a larger weapon was needed to stop them in their tracks" he went on. He had been led to believe that every car which drove up to the gate was a potential suicide bomber and the only good suicide bomber was a dead one. As he pointed out, the driver was going to die anyway, so he was doing the guy a favour.

The guard's attitude justified our reason to make the U.S. military our number one threat. Quite simply they had an overwhelming amount of firepower and tended to shoot first and ask questions later; well that is if the target survived to answer. A few innocent people might get killed but that was considered acceptable collateral damage in the bigger picture of keeping the peace. The gate guard did not understand about winning the people's Hearts and Minds and did not care to learn how to do it either.

To begin with we could virtually drive anywhere around Baghdad and across the country without being questioned. However, that all changed as the U.S. military and the C.P.A. got a grip on the situation and began installing checkpoints everywhere; some permanent and some temporary. While the military and the police were entitled to check the movement of traffic, it could cause us a big headache for several reasons. Firstly, a military checkpoint could stop a team to search the cars for contraband. Secondly, an Iraqi police checkpoint could be false and manned by bad guys intent on killing or capturing Westerners. Thirdly, the checkpoints and the queues of cars around them were ideal targets for the insurgents.

While we tried to force our way through Iraqi held checkpoints, there was no way we would do the same at a U.S. military one because the guards would put a few bullets or something bigger into your engine. The soldiers always looked twitchy as you drove up but they usually relaxed their guard a little when they realized you were a security team. However, they always stuck to their rules as if their lives depended on them and there was no way you wanted to get into an argument because they could really screw your day up...

If the guards thought anything was out of order or if you upset one of them, you were in for a long wait. They would make you park to one side, empty all your gear out of the car and then start looking for contraband. The whole process could take a long time if you had a jobs worth and some checkpoints were notorious for being a real pain. The rules seemed to change every day and at times I felt that they just did it for the fun of it. It was just one more thing for our team leaders to factor in when they were planning their routes.

Repeated problems at checkpoints could mess up your schedule and the client would become irritated if he was forced to cancel or miss a meeting. We could do nothing until the company AEGIS was employed to coordinate all the security companies' activities and act as our representative to the military. All we could do was voice our concerns at the weekly security meetings and AEGIS would pass on the message.

Some of the permanent checkpoints became very sophisticated. For example the airport checkpoint eventually had a card reader. You pulled up, handed over your ID cards and the guard swiped them in the machine. We never knew what came up on the screen but the guard's reaction told you if it was good or bad. We assumed that it was similar to passport control and it showed your mug shot and your misdemeanours.

However, the system was in its infancy and the machine often failed to verify the card. We have all had the computer saying no to our credit card at a supermarket checkout and faced the embarrassment of asking the cashier to give it another go, while everyone smirks in the queue. Now imagine the same situation when the cashier is an armed soldier and the queue is a line of cars full of irate Iraqis and other security teams. Now they would not just turn you away, oh no. The team had to park in a quarantine area and wait to be searched thoroughly.

The card reader also told the operator what clearance our personnel had and again the rules often changed. Some days a team were allowed to carry their weapons and other days they were not. It meant they had to lock them into vehicles, compromising our client's safety. The clearances were set by the shift commander according to the daily intelligence and our team leaders never knew what to expect when they pulled up. Ever changing rules just made it harder and harder to operate efficiently.

Many times as I stood watching a young soldier searching our cars I used to think, there was none of this in the good old days. Back then our ID was our business card with the company logo and a passport size photograph sealed in a laminated pouch. A bit of sweet talking and maybe a bit of bribery helped us more than once. We also stuck small Union Jacks to the back of our sun visors and flipped them down as we approached a checkpoint. That often resulted in a smile and a cheeky comment from the guard on the checkpoint.

As the C.P.A. and military got to grips with the situation, the standard of identification became very advanced. Everyone had to have a sophisticated identity card which not only had eye iris ID like the modern passports; they had a 3-D photograph of your head. I am not sure about the technical details but you basically sat in a chair while cameras compiled your facial profile. The idea was that CCTV footage could identify you from any angle. Chips were also installed in every car and by 2006 virtually all American vehicle checkpoints had a portable chip and pin device. When you pulled up the guard would swipe all your cards and your details would come up, similar to airport passport control.

Our teams took a completely different view when we faced a roadblock manned by the Iraqi police. The following examples show why. In February 2006 insurgents dressed in stolen police uniforms set up a roadblock near Baqubah, north of Baghdad. They stopped several cars heading north to a protest at Samarra and executed 47 people, leaving their bodies in a nearby ditch. In November 2006 dozens of men, again many dressed in Iraqi police uniforms stopped a convoy of over thirty lorries near Basra. They kidnapped the five American security guards and held them hostage. A finger from each of the five men was delivered to the U.S. military after eighteen months of waiting; their mutilated remains were not found until much later.

These are just two examples of what you were dealing with when you approached a checkpoint. You never knew who the scruffy guys in blue shirts who were waving you over for an identity check were. Had they joined the police to earn an honest wage or had they bought the shirts on a market, hoping to collect a ransom. You never knew whether they were the real thing or not as you drove slowly towards one of their checkpoints.

Temporary checkpoints could be as basic and bizarre as a policeman sitting in a plastic sun chair under a parasol. If it was not for the uniform and the pistol, he could have been sitting by a hotel swimming pool. Instead he had to sit by the side of a road, hoping that drivers did not mind stopping to show their identity cards – he also had the worry that the next vehicle was driven by a suicide bomber. So there was suspicion and fear on both sides.

Our SOP made it clear that our teams must not stop and must not open their doors or windows. You slowed down, and drove through, looking them straight in the eye while you flashed your IDs. The real ones would get angry as they tried to make you pull up and they might report you to their superior officers (not that we had any registration plates). But we would rather get a telling off from the Americans than risk our lives.

One deadly situation I faced at a checkpoint illustrates how sophisticated and dangerous the insurgents were getting. Towards the end of 2004 American intelligence had picked up news that a group of around seventy guerrilla fighters had come from Chechnya to help fight the Coalition Forces and guys like ours. These guys had been fighting the Russians for years and had now decided to support the wave of Islamic fundamentalism sweeping across Iraq. They were mercenaries, hardened terrorists who were paid to teach the home grown ones how to step up their game.

One of their tricks was to mimic a typical security team. They dressed in the same clothes, obtained the same weapons and stole similar 4x4 vehicles complete with tinted windows and aerials. They even drove around in pairs, copying our driving techniques. From the reports I read, it was impossible to spot the fake teams until they opened fire on you and it grated everyone's nerves to know that these guys were out there looking to kill.

Another security company had been given a large one off job which they could not staff themselves. They asked if we could help and we supplied a couple of teams to help ferry a group of clients to an important meeting. The convoy set off with six vehicles and our two cars were bringing up the rear. All went well until we halted in front of a U.S. military checkpoint in the outskirts of Baghdad. Due to reports of suicide car bombers making the rounds, the guards were taking no chances and they were making all the vehicles stop 100 metres away from roadblocks. So we had to wait as the cars and vans were called forward one by one by the grim faced guards. There was scrub and trees either side of the road where anyone could hide with an AK47 or an RPG and our cars were spaced fifty metres apart to guard against this eventuality. Although we were all on the lookout for trouble, we all felt uneasy as the minutes ticked by.

We had a digital camera on the dashboard, recording the soldiers going through their routine. Every car had one and the lads used them to record difficult situations and we always switched them on when we stopped at a roadblock. The film could be used as evidence if there was a problem but it could easily be deleted, and ready for the next one if all went well. It was a crude but effective method of covering our backsides...

Suddenly the radio clicked into life; "cars moving towards us at speed from the right". Glancing across, we could all see about half a dozen Land Cruisers and Pajeros spewing dust into the air as they raced along a dirt road running parallel with the main road. This was looking bad. We were stuck and had nowhere to hide. We could not back up because the road was blocked with traffic and the checkpoint would shoot at us if we made a sudden move forward. Talk about being trapped.

As the cars came to a crunching halt alongside the head of our convoy, we scrambled out of our cars, taking cover. The bad guys also climbed out of their cars, around thirty of them, and we watched helplessly as they opened fire on the first three cars, making an incredible noise.

Within moments two guys in the lead car were dead while the third hid behind the bonnet. It looked as if the client had been hit in the second car and one of the security guards had dragged him behind the rear wheel and was checking his injuries. The other guard managed to get out and was in the scrub returning fire with his bipod mounted machine gun. The situation in the third vehicle was similar with one guy on the ground mortally injured while his mate crouched down, administering first aid.

What a mess and although it all seemed to take a long time, it was all happening so quickly that we could not do much to help. Rounds seemed to be coming in from all angles. One of the guys in my car threw out a smoke grenade and as the grey wisps of chemical smoke filled the air, we returned fire in the hope of drawing the bad guys' attention. To begin with our fire did not have any effect and the bad guys were certainly not scared by it, but as our fire became more concentrated, some turned to engage us instead.

Then as quickly as the gun battle started, it ended. As a handful of the insurgents gave covering fire, the rest clambered back in their cars. We would not follow because we were outgunned and too busy attending our casualties. They just spun their cars round and drove off into the distance, leaving us to pick up the pieces.

Watching it later on the camera film was surreal, like some badly choreographed war movie; only this was for real and we had been the actors who had survived. It was mesmerizing to see how badly it all went in a short space of time. You can train all you want but at times like that you really felt like you were in the lap of the gods.

The military's increasing tendency to throw out random checkpoints without warning was a worrying feature and one that we had to plan against. It was obvious that as soon as we came to a halt in traffic we were sitting ducks. All we could do was change our SOP to counter the threat. In future our security teams had to roll slowly towards the checkpoint rather than standing off at a distance. If we suddenly went from a standing start towards the checkpoint we would be a threat to the soldiers at the checkpoint. At least if we were moving forward slowly we might be close enough to them to benefit from any covering fire they might want to give us.

Finally it has to be said that apart from the dickers, the checkpoints, the convoys, the suicide bombers and IEDs, driving in Baghdad was just plain mad. The Highway Code did not apply and it did not help that many traffic signals did not work. All in all the traffic was busier and madder than downtown London during rush hour. And once you passed the city limits, the risks on the open road were just as dangerous.

Chapter Ten

Keep on Running

A CAR IS GREAT UNTIL IT BREAKS DOWN or it runs out of fuel, then it is just a useless lump of metal and more of a liability than anything. But when you are driving back home you always know that there will be a petrol station in the next town or maybe on the next roundabout. On the motorway the road signs let you know how far you have to travel before you can fill up. Even if you run out of fuel you can call up the recovery truck and they will get you home. There was none of this when you were in Iraq.

Although Iraq's wealth is its oilfields, you would not have known it because it was difficult as hell to get hold of any. Our cars guzzled a massive amount of juice on the long journeys and the air conditioning increased the consumption. No one wanted to climb into a stifling car and most teams kept their engines running all day, keeping the car as a little haven from the heat.

Team leaders had to assess how much fuel they needed, and it was sometimes a difficult decision to make on the longer runs. You could supplement your tank full by loading jerry cans in the back but if you carried too much it could turn your car into a potential bomb. A random bullet could engulf your passenger compartment in a fireball.

Functioning petrol stations were few and far between, and there was always a huge queue snaking around the block. The last thing you wanted to be doing was waiting in a queue because in no time you would have been dicked and it was easy to block you in, leaving you a sitting target. Our SOP banned our teams from using road petrol stations unless it was an absolute necessity. As far as I know I think I was the only one to do so, and only once during the early days down in Basra; if any of the lads stopped at one, they never admitted it.

While there were few authorized petrol stations, there were plenty of unauthorized petrol stops. Everywhere you would see men or kids squatting at the side of the road with all manner of containers filled with fuel. All you had to do was pull up, fill up one of the jerry cans in the back and hand over a few U.S. dollars; no one wanted Iraqi dinars because the value was falling fast. And the price was dirt cheap, typically as low as 10p a gallon, or the equivalent.

Whenever possible our cars were filled up at one of the Petrol, Oil and Lubricant stops, (POL) in the military camps. They were usually an open space with a few dozen temporary pumps at regular intervals linked to fuel tankers. One of the soldiers would note what company you were from and the amount you were taking. It was as simple as that, a complete contrast to what the locals had to do to get a couple of gallons. Having said that I don't know where the bills went because we always gave a false company name. Just think seventy cars, each using a tank of fuel a day; that was a fantastic amount of fuel and no one questioned it.

Keeping the cars going was a nightmare. To begin with in Baghdad we often blagged our way into local U.S. military workshops and bribed the mechanics to work on them but their patience started to wear thin as our fleet expanded. We also used an Iraqi run garage and while they did a good job, the cost of servicing, repairs and modifications started to soar. The chances of getting a car fixed when you needed it was also a bit of a lottery; not something we wanted to chance too often.

We eventually had 40 cars based in Baghdad and as many working out on the sites, so we rented a piece of land next to the villa to park them all on. Maintenance problems were getting out of hand so we also decided to set up our own repair shop where we could prioritize work and keep on top of problems; after all if a car was not moving, it was not earning. We built a small hanger for the workshop, hired a good military mechanic we knew and took on board a couple of ex-Army engineers. And away they went...

Before too long, the cars were rolling in and the number of breakdowns and problems dropped. The team of mechanics not only kept on top of our own work, they started to do work for other clients. A lot of security teams were upgrading their vehicles to suit their contracts and they were looking for a variety of DIY modifications. So the mechanics employed two Iraqis who were soon welding anything from armoured plates to weapon mounts onto vehicles. We even had U.S. military Special Forces bringing their vehicles into the workshop because our team could do the work quicker than their own mechanics.

Our little idea mushroomed and it ended up making over a quarter of our revenue in Baghdad; it just showed there were business opportunities everywhere in the Green Zone. However, it took us a while to work out that the garage operation was soon spiralling out of control. While it was always busy, it was sometimes too busy because the mechanics were doing work for cash on the side.

Our cars were getting battered on the training ground as well as the road. We had set training drills for the typical situations we would face but the team leaders devised their own manoeuvres based on real experiences. While the training was evolving, some of the new drills were more suitable for a James Bond film than downtown Baghdad. While it was commendable that the guys were taking their training seriously, the amount of damage the cars were sustaining was not. Vehicles were returning from the training ground with crumpled bodywork or ripped off doors far too often for our liking. Maybe they were trying to make their training as realistic as possible or maybe they were spicing it up to relieve the boredom. Either way the problem became so bad that we threatened to deduct the cost of damage out of their wages.

Of course I had to eat my own words one day. I was driving the second car in a two car convoy racing round the training area. The lead car disappeared over the brow of a hill when the driver slammed the brakes on, coming to a halt out of my sight line. I also hit the brakes but did not stop in time and ran straight into the back of him. You don't need much imagination to imagine the ribbing I got when I nursed my damaged car into our garage.

Another of our biggest threats was a punctured tyre. While regular maintenance and extra jerry cans of fuel kept the cars going, you could never plan for a flat tyre. The distances we travelled, the terrain we had to cross and the mad manoeuvres we carried out battered the tyres. Potholed roads and dirt tracks constantly hammered the tyres and now and again the familiar unresponsive steering and rumble from beneath the car warned the driver that he had a puncture.

A flat tyre turns a fast moving car into a useless lump of metal and you could have a puncture anytime, anywhere with no respect for the amount of danger you were in. We used to be on the guys' backs all the time about practising tyre changing and every other day they went out on the training ground to practice. It would get on the lads' nerves, sweating and heaving in the heat, but a quick tyre change could save their life and we insisted that it had to be done in less than ten minutes. That was the time we estimated that locals would need to tell their friendly neighbourhood insurgent. Any longer and we believed you could have a serious problem.

Although the guys preferred practising all the flashy car drills they had learnt in bodyguard school, the fast turn rounds and the fancy J-turns were mainly for show. Nobody liked having to do the boring stuff over and over again but when the time came, the nuts and bolts stuff saved you; a good tyre changing drill could be a life saver.

A puncture would be reported over the radio while the driver selected a place to stop. The second car pulled up alongside so two of the team could work on the tyre while the other two kept a lookout. Of course that was the ideal situation, sometimes you just had to stop where you could and get on with it. I personally only experienced a few flat tyres, most of them in Kurdistan where the roads are virtually non-existent and the ruts and potholes hammer your tyres and suspension. The only saving grace was that the puncture usually happened in the middle of nowhere and you could change the tyre without fear of interruption.

However, one puncture during a run north up to Bayji power station did turn nasty. We heard the familiar rumbling from underneath the car as we drove through the Samarra area, about 75 miles north of Baghdad; smack in the middle of the Sunni Triangle where no one was friendly. The driver confirmed that the car had become difficult to handle but we kept going a short distance, eventually coming to a halt on top of a bridge. While we had excellent all round visibility anyone could see us from miles around and what a lovely target we made.

The second car pulled up alongside and while two of the team started work in the searing heat, my mate and I walked a short distance away from the cars to get a better view. It did not take long to take in the scenery because there was desolate scrubland as far as you could see, typical of northern Iraq. You would have thought no one lived there, but there was a small group of houses, well what passed as houses in this part of the world.

As we sweated in the heat, the only noticeable movement in the desolate wasteland was a small child playing in a dry streambed. He stopped his play as soon as he spotted us and ran towards the houses, as fast as his little legs would carry him; bless him. We could hear his screams, alerting his neighbours that we were there and he would no doubt have his hand out, hoping for a few coins for being so vigilant.

Brilliant I thought, now we are going to have to get a move on. News that there were four Westerners having a spot of bother with their cars on the highway was welcome information indeed. Most Iraqis had an AK47 in their house for personal protection and now was an ideal time to try them out. All we could do was watch and wait as dozens of men gathered around the houses, and their shouts and gestures made it clear that they were going to come and investigate. We did not for a moment think they were going to give us a hand with the tyre; this was going to turn nasty...

As the two of us checked our weapons, I shouted back "Come on lads, I don't want to hurry you but we need to get moving." They did not need any encouragement and their curses got louder as the mob came nearer. Firing a couple of warning shots into the air can go either way in a situation like this, the crowd might back off or someone might decide to return fire. It all depended on how brave they were feeling. By now though there was no time to be philosophical about the situation, and as a couple of rounds cracked off the mob froze.

The good news was that no one had returned fire; the bad news was that they were still walking towards us. This was going to go down to the wire. As the tyre guys toiled with the final stages of changing the wheel, the language got worse. "Hurry up, they are nearly on top of us", we shouted as we shouldered our weapons and aimed them at the mob. They did not stop and we were facing having to shoot civilians, possibly unarmed ones, to save our own skins.

Breathing deeply, fingers on the triggers, the pair of us braced ourselves for the inevitable screams and shouts that would follow our shots. We could not wait any longer when suddenly we heard what we had been waiting for; "All done, let's get the hell out of here." Jerking our weapons into the air, we let off a stream of rounds into the air to scare the mob and give us a few extra seconds. Then we sprinted for the cars, diving in as our drivers floored the accelerator. Looking back we could see the mob cursing us; we felt otherwise. After a big sigh of relief, a few nervous laughs and jokey one-liners broke the tension. That had been damn close but now it was time to put the foot down and let the air conditioning do its work. It was time to get to Bayji.

While we had been able to set up our own car repair shop, finding good tyres was far from easy in Baghdad. We were always on the lookout for reliable tyre suppliers while we scrounged and bribed them out of the military workshops in the early days, the mechanics' patience wore thinner every time we turned up. The trouble was you could not make do and mend or convert something like you could under the bonnet; each style of car had to have its own size of tyre.

On one occasion we had just used up our last spare tyres for our Pajeros, and could not source any new ones inside the Green Zone. After a few phone calls, one of our Iraqi contacts came up with the name of a tyre dealer. Another call by our contact and we had a deal; we could collect as many as we could carry straight away. Great we thought, but as always in Baghdad, there was a catch. The dealer was northwest of the Green Zone, in a part of the city you did not visit unless you had to; and we had to.

After clearing out three cars, six of us jumped in and off we went with our Iraqi contact directing us. We found the garage no problem; it was a typical car dealership on a main road. While four of the guys stayed outside with the cars, two of us went into the office accompanied by our contact who would act as our interpreter. Nothing unusual there you might think but the guy behind the counter stood bolt upright and stared at us as we walked through the door. You rarely saw Westerners in this part of town and then only driving past at speed in armoured 4x4s. Maybe it was the fact that we were armed that unsettled him. Who knows? But after a few minutes of tense negotiations, our interpreter explained that we were there for tyres and not to rob the place.

The car dealer was happy to do business with us but he had one request before he started sorting our tyres out. Could we please park our cars inside the showroom? The reason was simple; although he wanted to do business with us, he did not want anyone to know. Any dicker could drive past, note our cars and let the bad guys know the dealership was dealing with a Western security company. He explained how he never knew who was spying on him and he did not want to draw attention to his garage.

Sure we said, and the drivers drove the three cars into the workshop and turned off the engines. As they clambered out of the cars, the steel roller doors closed and slammed shut, locking us in. Then we had one of those 'Doh' moments as we looked at each other. Had we just driven into a trap or were we safely hidden from the passing traffic? Was the garage owner on the phone to the local bad guys, hoping to claim a cash reward for capturing us, or was he checking his stock levels on the computer? All we could do was stay calm and vigilant...

After reading the daily list of emails on events around Baghdad we knew that you had to expect the unexpected in the city. Anything could happen and we just hoped that we were not going to be on tomorrow's headline news. No matter how well you drew up your SOPs new situations cropped up all the time and if we had carried out risk assessments before every job, we would have never gone to work. Anyway Baghdad was such a complex place and there was always the chance that something could go wrong. All you could do was rely on your training, your evaluation of the situation and your gut instinct; in other words make an on the spot risk assessment and work it out on the move.

Our assessment was that the chance of the owner being corrupt was lower than someone dicking us to the bad guys – or so we hoped. It was going to take some time to get all the tyres off the shelves and load them into the cars, so we took the cashier's advice and waited in the garage's upstairs café. It sounded like a good idea because we could keep an eye on the road outside and watch the cars being loaded at the same time.

So there we sat, drinking tea and watching the road below for signs of unusual activity: and we did not have to wait long... We soon noticed the traffic stopping and wondered what was going on up the street; and more important did it have anything to do with us?

We soon saw three large flat bed trucks driving at a snail's pace and they were the ones causing the traffic jam. Each one had over 100 men on board and they were all dressed in loose black clothing with red and green bandanas around their heads. Black flags and the sound of beating drums completed the bizarre parade; but it got worse. As the convoy moved closer we could see the men whipping their shoulders with cat of nine tails one after another until they were red raw. It was a pilgrimage remembering the suffering Iman Hussein endured at the battle of Karbala in the 7th Century and they were heading to Karbala, south of Baghdad.

Shi'ite Moslems celebrated the Iman's sacrifice by travelling slowly across the country, particularly from Basra, where there are many Shi'ites. Thousands joined en route until the convoy became a huge gathering of people who walked for days on end in the intense heat. The pilgrimage was the people's suffrage and while it was highly commendable, we just did not want them marching past the garage while we were there.

Brilliant timing we thought, as we looked at each other across the teacups. This is just going from bad to worse. But all we could do was shrink back away from the window and hope that no one had seen us and if they had, that they did not betray us. After what seemed an eternity, the tail of the procession disappeared into the distance and the traffic in the street returned to normal. Our tyres were loaded and it was time to pay the bill. And then we reversed out of the garage and it was heads up and we drove back to the Green Zone with another tale to tell.

But we had not heard the last of the Kabala processions that day. As they stopped at mosques across the city for prayers, Sunni insurgents detonated four bombs, killing dozens of people and injuring many more. They caused mayhem across the city and what should have been a day of celebration became a day of mourning. In accordance with Muslim law, the bodies had to be buried within 24 hours of death and the streets were going to be packed as the funeral corteges made their way to the mosques.

We had not been back in the office long when a television company called and asked us to provide a security team so their camera crew could film the funerals. Now the official line was that we could not carry arms while escorting the press because they had a non-military role. However, there was no way we were going to put a team onto the streets without weapons; they would carry concealed pistols and stow their long weapons inside the vehicle.

Reports estimated over 50,000 people were going to attend and we were going to have to force our way through the throng to get the film crew close to the action. While the camera crew had permission to film around the mosque, it was still a potentially hostile area to enter. Our armoured cars would have attracted a lot of unwanted attention so we chose to travel covertly in our old camper van with blacked out windows we had acquired for such occasions. No one would take any notice of the battered old vehicle and there was enough space to get the security team, the film crew and their equipment inside.

The journey started well but the crowds filled the streets around the mosque, forcing the camera team to cover the last leg on foot. While the security team stuck with the journalists the camper van followed on a parallel street ready to pick us up if we needed to make a quick getaway.

As we pushed through the crowds the camera started rolling, filming the coffins as they were carried through the crush of bodies towards the mosque. The emotion and hysteria was incredible and it was difficult to know where to watch as the crowds pressed closer. Our little group was soon in the sea of people pushing forward to get closer to the coffins and the camera crew stuck out like a sore thumb. Everyone had a reaction when they saw the camera and while some expressed their feelings other people objected to the filming.

Either way our presence was aggravating a lot of people.

While you always see the reporter talking on your television screen, you never see the security team trying to keep them out of trouble. There was a conflict of interests because the film crew repeatedly pushed the boundaries of safety as they tried to get better footage. They wanted to grab the headlines and we wanted everyone to get home safely. After all we were only armed with concealed pistols, and while our getaway vehicle was only a hundred metres away, the chances of reaching it if the atmosphere turned nasty were small.

Journalists were seen as viable hostages around that time and rather than searching for the big story, they became the big story. We argued many times as the reporter and his camera team pushed their way deeper and deeper in the crowds. It was a real battle of wills and not one I wanted to do again. We were relieved when they said they had the footage they needed and we could start pushing our way out of the crowds and back to the camper van. We were all glad to get out of the crowd and back to the villa that evening so we could wash off the sweat and grime after another crazy day.

We often worked with the same press company, escorting camera crews around the city. They would want to get close to the aftermath of a car bomb or a shooting and get pictures, film footage and interviews to sell the newspapers. This involved going to the very heart of the action, where there would be angry crowds in a standoff with the military cordoning off the area; the Iraqi emergency services would also be milling around, trying to be helpful and rarely succeeding.

Working with the press guys had the benefit of keeping us up to date with what was really happening on the streets, and it meant that we did not have to rely on the television news for information. The crews often roamed the streets, making random interviews and paying for juicy bits of information in the hope of getting a lead on a story; the all elusive exclusive they craved. They often turned up better intelligence than the American military and while some of the information could not go on the news, it was useful to us.

One of the phenomena of the insurgents' dirty work in Baghdad, was their grasp of the press's desire for good film footage and how it was easily turned into propaganda. They wanted to make sure their handiwork was on the news that day. While the press wanted an accurate record of an incident, there was nothing better for raising support than footage of a big explosion and pictures of casualties and wreckage on the world wide web. Sometimes the camera would even be in place before the bomb went off.

One thing we did learn was that people were paid well for a successful attack. Insurgent groups would offer considerable financial rewards to a family if a relative blew themselves up; and the more Westerners they killed the higher the reward. However, the detonation had to be filmed as evidence and no footage meant no money.

Once we heard this tit-bit of information we became paranoid about anyone filming with cameras. It unnerved you because you never knew if they were hoping to film your final moments. We took the view that no one was interested in filming Baghdad's architecture; they were either studying our security techniques or waiting to film a suicide bomb. If anyone came too close with a video camera while we were stationary, one of the guys would get out of the car and take it off them at gun point, taking the batteries out to stop them filming. It was just another layer of paranoia to add to those we already had.

Chapter Eleven

Whose Side Are We On?

WHEN WE FIRST ARRIVED in Baghdad the military only supplied very general intelligence with random bits of information. Facts which influenced how we worked were few and far between because our teams were more in tune with what we wanted to know. But as the months passed, and the C.P.A. and the military became more organized it was clear that security companies were going to be in Iraq for a long time. Although the military were getting the upper hand over the insurgents they could not protect every infrastructure site across the country. With the amount of construction work going on, the security industry was really taking off. You have to remember that everything the military got involved in was news worthy; whether it was the cost of keeping them there, the rising number of troops stationed in the country or the rising cost of casualties. They were all figures that the governments and the press referred to as a mark of success or failure of the reconstruction of Iraq. President Barack Obama would later refer to them as the country's blood and treasure.

However, the rising cost of deploying private security companies, the increase in security and the rising number of security personnel who were killed or injured carrying out their work was rarely in the news. It was as if we did not count; after all, many called us well paid mercenaries.

The death of a security guard did not make the headlines and it was not reported in the House of Commons. There was no military style repatriation and the public did not turn out to line the streets like they did in Wootton Bassett. Yet these guys had all racked up years in the military, serving all around the world, and many of them had been the elite of the country's Special Forces in their day. It was convenient for governments to distance themselves from the work we were doing and to forget that we were also doing our bit to achieve their goals. The only time that our work appeared in the headlines was when it was bad news and the C.P.A. was determined to make sure that it did not happen.

In June 2004 we were issued with C.P.A.'s memorandum number 17, the 'Registration Requirements for Private Security Companies'. The document laid down the minimum financial and operating standards that we had to adhere to. If we complied with them we would be awarded a business licence and an operating licence; if we did not we were in breach of Iraqi law, subject to prosecution and out of business. There were 150 pages of rules and regulations which we had to adhere to. While they covered all types of incidents, the main items were covered on the Rules of Engagement card. It told us to cooperate with the Coalition Forces and the Iraqi Security Forces. It also warned us not to aim guns in their direction; which I thought was a fair point even though U.S. military patrols were always pointing theirs at us...

We were only allowed to use deadly force, in other words shoot at someone, under three circumstances; in self defence, to defend your client, or to save a civilian's life. Now that is all well and good until you are under threat and you make a snap decision. The incident would immediately come under the scrutiny of military investigators and you had to hope that they saw things the same as you did.

Whenever possible we had to use what was called 'graduated force' and there were four stages. You had to shout at the people threatening you, telling them to halt. If they ignored your shouts then you could shove them out of the way or restrain them. If that did not solve the problem you could show your weapon, aiming it in their direction. And finally if they still persisted you could shoot 'to remove the threat only where necessary'. If you had to open fire then they had to be aimed shots and you had to 'fire with due regard for the safety of innocent bystanders'. So the order of play was 'Shout... Shove... Show... Shoot!'; just one of many catchy statements we heard bandied about the Green Zone.

That sounds nice and neat on paper but in the madness of the streets of Baghdad you did not have the time or inclination to be nice and neat. You just could not risk it. You only have to consider the earlier example where we were stuck in the traffic jam outside the mosque. Our cars were blocked in and the crowd were banging on the windows. You could shout all you like and it would not work; you could not shove either.

All you could do was make an on the spot risk assessment and act on it, knowing that you might be judged later if the outcome was messy. While the Iraqi police could not arrest you because you were immune from prosecution while working, you still had to abide by the C.P.A. standards.

You had to interview the team following every incident and then submit a contact report for examination. Your evidence would be compared with that given by any other witnesses. You faced a military tribunal if your conduct was in question. This all changed in 2006 when Iraqi law began replacing military law and a few security companies left because they did not like the new regime. We did not like working under it either because we felt we were judged guilty until proven innocent because we were a security contractor, or rather in their eyes, a Western mercenary.

The C.P.A. regulations also stated we had to prove that our employees were of a minimum age, physically and mentally fit and willing to respect the law and the human rights of Iraqi citizens. They also had to pass a security check, removing anyone with a criminal or terrorist background.

They also checked the villa and our weapons and our training programmes to make sure they were up to scratch. One issue they focused on was the issue and storage of arms. During the early days everyone was responsible for their own weapon, the same as when you were in the army. You carried it at all times, maintained it and you stored it in your locker at night. Under the new regime, everyone was issued with a Weapons Card and weapons had to be checked and registered before they could be used. It was a bit of a change from the early days when we were handing over cash to dodgy arms dealers for second hand weapons...

We also had to install a lockable armoury and delegate someone as armourer who would check weapons in and out. The whole idea was to stop security guards wandering around with weapons when they were not working. Although I agreed with the ruling, I did not register my specially designed pistol. It was the sort of pistol used by secret service agents who worked with the United States President and other VIPs. Although the C.P.A. constantly reminded us that the Green Zone was safe, I was not taking any chances and hid it in my bum bag when I went running.

We were eventually given the stamp of approval to continue working. We had to expect further visits for audit purposes, to make sure we were continuing to follow the rules. Eventually AEGIS International, a well known and respected British security company, was awarded the contract to provide Reconstruction Security Support Services. It would provide command, control, communication, intelligence and a framework to coordinate security work across Iraq. They would introduce and oversee regulations, address health and safety issues, arbitrate during disputes and, above all, make sure professional standards were adhered to.

I do not know why a British company was chosen because the majority of security companies in Iraq were American but I suppose it did limit the chances of favouritism and rivalries. I do know that when the news was announced, the Americans went crazy because they had all expected an American coordinator to win it.

One of AEGIS's tasks was to coordinate work, making sure security companies cooperated with others rather than hindered others. We had to submit a report, summarizing our work for the following week, so they could coordinate security work across the city with military operations and other external events. We also had to email our work schedule on a daily basis, including the routes, the teams and the purpose of our business. Your routes would be compared with others to limit the number of teams in an area and they would also be checked against military operations to make sure your work would not interfere with them. It made you feel like you were a small piece in a large jigsaw and whether you liked it or not, you had to abide by the new rules. It was like Big Brother watching over your every move and it did somewhat limit our flexibility.

AEGIS acted as the mediator if there was a problem and you could report bad practice for investigation and issues for arbitration. Fortunately for us, the company was run by a lot of ex-British Special Forces guys, so when we were invited to the weekly brain storming meetings, it was a bit of a reunion for me. We had also worked with them on a couple of small contracts and we had established a bit of rapport with the guys who were checking on us; which made our lives a bit easier...

Our teams spent a lot of time moving between the Green Zone and worksites and many of the problems occurred while they were on the road. We often had to shunt a car out of the way if we thought it was getting too close, driving aggressively to get out of a tight corner. Drivers would often tailgate one of our cars and our defence was to slam on the brakes, so they ran into the tow bar at the back. We could see the driver standing by the side of the road, shaking his fist at us, while his radiator steamed. We would think, well at least it is just a fist this time. If a car persisted in coming too close alongside, we would show our weapons, occasionally opening the window and putting rounds into the engine block to scare them off.

You had to do whatever worked to get about your business some days. Road rage in a mad city like Baghdad was widespread and it seemed at times the only way people got around was by honking of horns and shaking their fists at other drivers. Over and over again we would come up against a car or van that would not get out of the way. Usually it was possible to get the message across by showing our weapons and telling the driver to get out of the way. But many times they took no notice or wanted to argue and we did not have time to argue, we had to get our client to his destination safely. We had no option in cases like that but to get out of the cars and show our weapons; only then would they get the message.

Having said all that we did encourage our teams to only use aggressive driving when it was absolutely necessary, for example if they felt threatened or their route was blocked. We had seen how aggressively some of the American security teams drove around, ramming cars, waving weapons in people's faces and being verbally abusive. We felt there was no need for it; it only antagonized the people and after all it was their country.

Although AEGIS was always asking for information about your activities, they also gave things in return and the best one was a global tracking system for all our vehicles. It meant we did not have to rely on radio reports and manually plotting on maps. The system was high tech for its day and the huge tracking screen covered one wall of our operations room. Cars were tracked through the global satellite system, and displayed their position on the screen. I have no idea how it worked but it made our job a lot easier. At a glance we could see all the teams working in the city, their positions marked by little lights. However, the real advantage of the global tracking was that AEGIS could also see where the U.S. military patrols were and could direct one to give assistance if a security team was attacked; well in theory they could.

AEGIS also forwarded intelligence reports to our office every morning and we had all day to sift out the relevant intelligence ready to brief the lads at evening 'Prayers'. It took time, knowledge and experience to be able to cherry pick the useful bits of information out of the reams of material.

Personally, I thought it was a good thing to have a governing body for several reasons. When we started in Iraq we just acquired a licence from the British and the American military to work and we were then left to our own devices. As explained earlier, it took a lot of hard work, a fair bit of blagging and a bit of bare faced cheek to get by in those early days. We had to work out everything ourselves and learned many lessons the hard way.

AEGIS standardized the way security work was carried out, laid down the rules and made companies aware of their responsibilities. They also weeded out the rogue contractors who were giving the industry a bad name and making it harder for the rest of us to carry out our work.

The downside with everything becoming settled in the Green Zone and standards being introduced was that military base style regulations were introduced. That involved piles of paperwork, lots of box ticking and strict health and safety regulations. Any violation or breach of the regulations was investigated in detail, taking up valuable time. The fact that it was mayhem outside the concrete walls did not matter.

The number of jobs-worths also rapidly increased and at times it felt that they were more interested in maintaining the speed limit than allowing us to get on with our work. After the madness of driving out in the city streets it was sometimes hard to relax and drive at the low speed limits set by the authorities. I remember at one point the military police in Shaibah twice copped one of our cars speeding with their speed guns and then issued a warning that we would be asked to leave if we continued to flout the rules.

The amount of intelligence sent into our office just snowballed and we had to sift through a stack of correspondence every day; and they never brought good news. The list of problems was endless; people throwing bricks, gun men taking pot shots, IEDs exploding, suicide bombers; in short general mayhem. For example our report for October 2003 showed that there had been 113 life threatening incidents in the month, an average of over four a day. There had been 86 attacks against military patrols and 23 against the Iraqi police, the Iraqi Civil Defence Corps or government buildings. There had also been four against International Organizations.

They included 29 IEDs detonated, 18 attacks with RPG, 16 small arms attacks, 15 mortar attacks, four rocket attacks and two car bomb attacks. To top it all off, four SAM ground-to-air rockets had been fired at military flights; two of them at Baghdad airport.

Eventually so much information was flooding in that it became harder to work out what was and what was not relevant. But it was no good just forwarding information without checking it carefully, in case we missed something. It was also dangerous to give the guys too much information because they would switch off and miss the relevant stuff. We eventually employed an ex-Intelligence Corps guy to look through it all and he identified useful snippets of information, drew useful conclusions and wrote them up.

Attacks against security companies did not feature in the official figures but we created our own intelligence ring. We would analyze attacks against our teams and circulate the information to the rest of the companies and some days we received around 20 reports in return. We had to study them to see if there were any new developments and we quickly learned that the insurgents did not lack ingenuity when it came to dealing in death. They were willing to try anything once and then would study what worked and what went wrong, looking to improve. While we sometimes anticipated the natural development of their ambush techniques, every now and again they did something that shocked us. The bottom line was that the bad guys were not as stupid as the authorities and the military wanted you to think. You had to respect them or pay the penalty...

So every evening at six o'clock our Prayers gave a summary of the day's events. As hard as we tried to keep the lads interested, it often turned into a monotonous list of bad news. An endless nightmare, like the film 'Groundhog Day'; only each day seemed harder that the one before. A case of same crap, different day; oh and here are a few new things you need to look out for.

One source of information we had was a newsletter known as the 'Word on the Street' or the 'Baghdad Mosquito'. At regular intervals the C.P.A. and military sat down with knowledgeable Iraqis from different ethnic and religious backgrounds to talk about the latest rumours circulating in Baghdad and the mood of the people. Iraq was a country where rumour and fact intertwined and facts were dispelled as rumours as often as rumours were accepted as facts. Saddam Hussein even had a department of the intelligence service dedicated to spreading rumours so he could control the people.

Although a lot of information gathered by the Word on the Street staff was false, it was important to learn what the Iraqi people were thinking. One common theme was fear and anyone who was seen to be speaking in public support of the Coalition Forces could expect to be targeted. For that reason alone the information was called into question. Were they telling you what you wanted to hear or what they thought you wanted to hear. One thing was certain though; Baghdad was a crazy place and it was getting more dangerous by the day...

When we started work in Baghdad we were left to our own devices and we could send teams out when we pleased and to where we wanted without too much interference. But as the weeks passed, the C.P.A. increased its control over the city and we had to adapt to working inside a changing military framework which grew stricter by the day. At times our work was severely disrupted by operations and we were constantly reminded that the military had the final say about what happened on the streets. The first we heard of an operation was when the restrictions were announced. Roadblocks appeared overnight, city blocks were cordoned off and curfews were implemented at a moment's notice as troops moved in to search an area.

If there was military activity in an area there was bound to be temporary checkpoints and heavy traffic. Not only that, insurgents might move into the area looking to target one of the military patrols and the last thing we wanted to do was to be an alternative target. The changing military situation kept us on our toes and it was important to study the intelligence every evening to know how operations would affect our teams.

Lockdowns also occurred on a regular basis. The military would just tell us that no one was allowed out of the Green Zone and work had to stop; no questions asked and no answers given. Lockdowns associated with Ramadan and other religious festivals could be anticipated but they were often implemented without warning. We rarely found out why there was a lockdown and although you heard rumours, you never knew what to believe. One favourite story was that an unspecified intelligence source had reported that a suicide bomb team was driving around town looking to take out a security team.

The longest lockdown lasted for a week following a series of coordinated attacks on mosques across the city. It made it difficult to keep the men busy and all we could do was focus on training and drills. Lockdowns were trying times and tempers flared due to the frustration of being cooped up. From the company's point of view, it did not help that we were not earning money, only spending it.

I was entitled to a lot of sensitive information concerning what was going on in and around the city in my position. However, there were many areas in the Green Zone, particularly near the Presidential Palace, where I was not allowed to visit. Blast walls and checkpoints manned by soldiers who seemed intent on carrying out the instructions on the signs which made it clear that 'deadly force would be used'.

Some of these buildings were occupied by the likes of Paul Bremer, the head of the Coalition Provisional Authority, and his officials. It did not take a genius to work out that other areas were occupied by the Special Forces and the C.I.A. While the U.S. Regular Army dealt with us when it came to deciding where and when we could operate, my own Special Forces background made me aware that clandestine operations, otherwise known as Black Ops were going on. In the past, Special Forces have been involved in all sorts of covert work during insurgency conflicts, from the kidnapping or assassination of key leaders down to the wire tapping of headquarters and the booby trapping of arms dumps. Was it going on in Baghdad? Well our training told me that something was going on but it also told me that it was unwise to ask. It did not stop me speculating about what might be happening whenever I saw something unusual.

We believe we came into contact with a Black Ops team while we worked on Al Quds power station, northwest of Baghdad. There was a big military push going on in Fallujah at the time and there were concerns that activities were being organized in Rashidiyah, the district surrounding the power plant. If you think laterally, the power station was an ideal base for covert operations because it had site security and a secure perimeter but no soldiers to draw attention to it.

We were providing security on the plant alongside another American subcontractor which was, in our opinion, a shadowy organization. We could never prove it but our guys were convinced it was a front for American covert operations. The employees were more interested in what the insurgents and the local mullahs were doing rather than getting on with the work on the power station. Their vehicles looked the same as the ones we used to the untrained eye but a closer look revealed that they were far more powerful than anything we could afford; the high range frequency antennas on the roof were far better than anything we needed.

Many times the company's teams would tag along behind one of our security convoys as it drove out of the compound only to turn off after a short while without a word over the radio. The next time you saw them was when they returned to camp later on and not a word was spoken about where they had been. It was none of our business either and whatever our thoughts were, we knew better than to ask questions.

During my Special Forces days we were always kept up to date on the latest intelligence during operations; we had to be. This had continued in the Basra area where our background helped us to work closely with the British Army. But in Baghdad it was a different story; the U.S. military only told us what we needed to know to carry out our work. Although U.S. patrols and convoys would often stop and help out if one of our teams was in trouble, it was down to the unit commander to make the call; after all they had their own missions to complete.

Even the British Special Forces operating in the Baghdad area kept us completely in the dark because they were working in a U.S. military area of operations. Although we had served with one or two of the commanders in the past, we knew better than to ask questions. This wall of silence left us 'out of the information loop' and it did leave us feeling exposed at times.

We knew from our military experience that local intelligence was always the best and while we tried to get informers to work for us, they were too suspicious of Westerners. A lot of Christians and Jews lived in southern Baghdad's suburbs, just across the Tigris from the Green Zone. We thought if anyone could be persuaded to help us, it would be Christian Iraqis but we were wrong. While they welcomed the fall of Saddam, fundamentalists were soon threatening them and while many Christians headed north to Kurdistan others left the country. Those left behind lived in fear and did not want to be linked to Westerners.

As work was hard to come by, we employed a couple of young men and women and they kept us fed and clean, carrying out domestic duties, shopping and fetching. A few moved immediately into the villa but the rest preferred to live at home. Every morning they turned up for work with snippets of information they had been given from friends or heard while out and about. But they were being watched and before long people were knocking on their doors, trying to persuade them to spy on us. These midnight callers were constantly asking for information on our movements and our vehicles and the questioning became more threatening until it was too dangerous to carry on. They either stopped working for us or moved in with us. We were only allowed to give them a few dollars a day or whatever was the going rate. They would have been treated badly if word got out that we were paying them more; such were how things were seen in Baghdad. All we could do to help was provide free lodgings, food and any other bits and pieces we could spare.

But information sometimes came from the strangest sources. Iraqis were employed on many of our sites to carry out menial tasks we did not have time to do ourselves. As helpful as they were, we had to be mindful that they were only on a small wage and they could be easily bribed to get information on our work. The easiest way to limit what they could see was to keep certain areas out of bounds.

The cleaners soon worked out that the Americans had provided us with satellite television, with sport, music, films; in fact just about anything you could think of and more on the 500 channels. They also worked out that you could get the porn channels on the television and some days it seemed that every time I turned my back they gathered around the television fiddling with the remote control. I was forever getting them out with the cries of "Please Mr., please Mr., can we watch the television". Believe it or not, my room was always spotless and we were always provided tit-bits of information in exchange for a few minutes of pornography. And they were not the only ones who felt the need to watch a bit of cheeky television.

We needed internet connections to keep up to date with emails from the client, the military, the work sites and even from loved ones. Nowadays everyone has the internet and it was the same in Iraq. An office could not function without an internet connection, and it had to be running around the clock. But there was no high speed Wi-Fi back then, it was all cable internet and while the military eventually installed the best system of its day, to begin with we had to cope with Iraq's finest and it was frustratingly slow at the best of times.

We eventually employed a guy to keep our internet connections going across Iraq. But while he was kept busy installing new connections and upgrading existing ones, he spent most of his time fixing computers. The problem was that many of the lads were downloading porn movies, music and computer games. Naughty but no big deal you might think; they were all over eighteen after all. The problem was that downloading huge files took ages over the internet connection and overloaded the computer memories. I am no expert; but in layman's terms, it buggered them up. A lot of these websites also added undesirable software or viruses to the computers. Most of them could be easily fixed by our computer expert but you have to remember that we were linked into the military computer networks. Some guys argued that that they were downloading their goodies onto their own laptops but what they did not realize was that they were using the U.S. military servers and it was screwing up their internet and putting their hardware in danger. And that could cause a real problem, especially if there was a military operation going on.

While the whole porn thing started as a bit of a joke, it ended up as a real big problem and became a big issue with many security companies. We had regular meetings over internet issues and it became clear that it was not just our guys; it appeared that lonely British and American soldiers were anxious for a bit of internet action as well. After a few incidents we had to ban certain types of websites and we made it a sackable offence to download certain material. The military were able to trace virus attacks to particular computers and times, so keeping a log of who was online became just another of those things we had to keep track of.

But just when you thought you had everything squared away, another problem would crop up. The problem was head hunters enticing our guys to go and work for them. The company was starting to get a good name around the Green Zone and one-off jobs started coming to our door. Everybody needed a security team before they could move around the city but not everybody had a security team on call. Some companies only needed to send their staff to a meeting outside the Green Zone once in a while; others had to bring staff into Baghdad to sign contracts or attend a meeting. Sometimes we had to escort a visiting executive around worksites for a day or two. We were becoming a one stop shop for guided tours of the city, including the most exciting part of the visit; the drive along Route Irish, to and from the airport.

The new client forwarded details of their personnel, the locations to visit and a schedule. We then assessed the dangers, worked out the requirements and submitted a price. We were grateful for these one off contracts and they did open doors to other things but they did have their drawbacks. The main one being that we did not have the time to check out a one off job, usually because they came into the office at the last minute. We also had to make sure that they did not interfere with our main client's work. But while we were always on the lookout to expand our business, so were some of our guys...

Despite the salaries we were paying, there was always someone out there who could put more money on the table. Terms and conditions, living conditions and perks could always be improved on as well, if only in the short term. The tribal heads and religious leaders (known locally as the sheiks, mullahs and imans) had become powerful men following the fall of Saddam's regime. They often had the police in their pockets and they controlled the local population; they could also dictate who worked on the projects on their patch.

As always, power and money go hand in hand with envy and greed. These local leaders would often become targets for hit men hired by their rivals or by families looking for revenge after suffering at their hands. They knew their lives were at risk and they wanted security and security guys like ours were considered the best; and they had the money for the best.

Our lads were often head hunted on behalf of a local leader and offered healthy payouts. They would be asked to provide close protection and provide training for their own people, and rewards were offered if they enticed their mates to join them. Men were being offered $1,000 a day and it did not take much to convince some guys, after all they were in Iraq to earn money fast.

The problem we faced was that it was far more attractive to work for a well connected sheik, living the high life in his large villa, than work on a power station in the middle of the desert. There were so many deals on the table and at times it was difficult to keep men. Several times we were faced with an entire team handing in their notice and as their contracts could not bind them to working for us, we had to let them go.

Our biggest problem occurred when three four man teams working on the Bayji power station left at the same time. There were a large number of local workers on the Bayji site and the sheik's men decided who could and who could not work there. They also turned nasty and forced workers to try to sabotage the plant if they did not get the deal they wanted. There were two sheiks in the area and they were always posturing against each other in true Iraqi style. Our way of smoothing over local politics was to meet them both and if you think of a scene from Lawrence of Arabia, then you are not far wrong. We visited their tents in the desert where lots of gesturing, bowing, feasting and small talk preceded the discussions. They were impressed I could speak Arabic and in both cases they agreed to a compromise. One would provide labourers for one month and then the other would do so. Job sorted.

Of course they both kept a close eye on how our guys supervised the improvements to the power station's security arrangements. One of the sheik's was impressed enough to offer them double their money and added some off the record style perks. Now ask yourself, would you rather be sweating it out behind a rusty barbed wire fence, wondering when the next mortar round is going to hit or would you rather stand around watching a sheik while he entertains?

Before they left we had to make it clear that they were on their own and did not have the backup of the company or the U.S. military. Personally I thought it was a bad move because you never knew who you were working for or what the sheik really thought of you. Bayji was a hotbed of trouble at that time and you had a lot of enemies when you looked after one of the head honchos. While the whole mercenary aspect had great financial rewards, you only had to put one foot wrong and the sheik could turn on you; then who were you going to call?

These freelance operators had a shock when AEGIS regulated security work across Iraq, introducing rules covering weaponry, transport, safety and a host of other issues. One by one the freelancers were paid a visit and given the option to join one of the certificated companies or stop working. Some asked if they could come back working for us while some went their own way.

Chapter Twelve

Blackout City

SO WE WERE IN BAGHDAD and our villa was established. Our client had given us a list of work sites in and around the city and we had assessed what we needed to do to keep the risks to a minimum. In those early days getting to and from Baghdad was relatively straightforward but as time passed the bad guys upped their game and gave visitors an experience they would not forget...

We sometimes booked guys onto one of the small, ancient planes used for internal flights across Iraq. While there were few problems at Basra airfield, on one occasion a mortar team decided to try its luck while my plane was on the runway. My knuckles were whiter than usual as the plane's nose pulled up and we took off with mortar shells landing around the runway.

As soon as the plane levelled off the South African air hostesses would serve coffee as the passengers settled down. Usually the flight passed quickly and there was time for a short nap as you tried to block out thoughts of returning to work. But on one occasion I was startled to see an engineer lifting up part of the floor to tackle a problem. I did not sleep at all on that flight... Then in no time at all, the pilot, again usually a South African, was on the intercom telling the crew to prepare for landing. The plane then banked while still at a high altitude and circled, waiting for clearance to land.

Flying into and out of Baghdad International Airport (or BIAP) was always an experience. Although the Americans had the airport and Camp Victory sealed off, there were still random attacks by surface-to-air missiles. The insurgents were always looking for a good news story and bringing down a plane or helicopter was always high on their agenda. When the all clear was given by the control tower, the pilot would press his control stick forward, sending the plane into a terrifying spiral, limiting the chances of a rocket hitting the plane. They always seemed to time the levelling out to perfection and then you were on the tarmac.

It was not long before you were through security and being met by a couple of the guys, teasing you about how you had got fatter while you were away. There was hardly time to catch up with the news before you were in the car and heading to the Green Zone.

We often had to make the run out to Baghdad International Airport to pick up clients, new guys and those returning from holiday. At 12 kilometres long, Route Irish was only a short run along a three lane motorway, but it soon became the one most hated by the guys. It was the only way in and out of Baghdad unless you were important enough to ride in a helicopter. The rest of us had to take the ride along what became the most dangerous stretch of road in Iraq. All the bad guys had to do was drive up and down the rough concrete road or wait on one of the over bridges. Every day we received reports of attacks along the road and they ranged from drive by shootings, to suicide car bombs, to roadside IEDs.

In the early days the attacks along Route Irish were rudimentary and you could avoid most incidents by being observant. We believed that the insurgents were like muggers who had time to pick and choose their targets, while people like us had to keep making the journey. We also believed that they were looking for the easy target and our motto was "why kill a tiger when there are plenty of sheep about".

As a team left the Green Zone, the call would go out Alpha One Zero through Red One, the call sign where the slip roads joined the main road. And then it was 'heads up' ready for the drive of your life. On the first half of the journey there were four over bridges in quick succession connecting housing estates either side of the motorway. There were usually guys hanging around on top, either with a mobile phone to their ear or waving a piece of rag. These were the 'dickers' who were looking to 'dick us' by signalling to their mate which lane we were driving in. He would pop up from his hiding place and open fire with his AK47, hoping to hit our car. We could see the bullets hitting the tarmac in front as we drove under the bridge and our best response was to swerve left or right and hit the gas. Everyone in the car tensed up as we roared away, hoping that the gunman was slow to react; if not we heard a thud or two as bullets hit the bodywork.

These crude attacks became more sophisticated as the insurgents stepped up their game. It was like a game of cat and mouse and we had to be vigilant, checking the intelligence reports to see what new tricks they had devised. Some were frustrated opportunists releasing their anger while others were testing your driving skills and drills, looking to see our reaction. They wanted to find out what worked so they could plan more sophisticated attacks.

Sometimes a dicker would call his waiting friends and they would come roaring down a slip road in a stolen car. Then we would see the barrel of an AK47 poke out of the window and open fire. Our only defence was to put distance between us because you never knew who else would join in.

The bridge top dickers often worked with a couple of drivers who spent their time cruising Route Irish. They used every trick in the book to interfere with our driving, pulling in front to slow us or alongside to stop us changing lanes. At times it felt like you were in one of those crazy computer car games, only in this game you could not press the start button to play again if you got killed. It was game over for good.

The second half of the journey ran between the Presidential Palace to the north and the Presidential Grounds to the south. There was open ground either side of the road where insurgents could work away at night setting IEDs. One popular method was to load a stolen car with old artillery shells and then rig it with a detonating device. The loaded car would then be abandoned on the verge while the bad guys waited for a passing security team or a military convoy. Then BOOM!

Smaller versions were made by stuffing rubbish sacks with shells and dumping them on the verge. These bombs were usually rigged to a command wire running through the undergrowth to a hiding place. It takes a fraction of a second from pressing the trigger to the bomb going off and in that fraction fast moving cars can be over twenty metres past the blast. To begin with many bombs detonated behind a speeding security team but the insurgents soon learned the art of setting a 'lead target'; positioning a marker at the best point to press the switch. They had already noted how fast we drove along the road and anything from an oil drum to a plastic cone would be used; the trigger was pressed the moment the target went past the marker and a fraction of a second later, BOOM!

As the months went by the insurgents introduced secondary devices to try and catch us out. They would set off a small device, maybe in a rubbish bag tossed onto the central reservation, in the knowledge that drivers would react by slowing down and steering around the scatter of debris. As a traffic jam formed the secondary device would detonate and an abandoned car on the hard shoulder would erupt in a shower of metal and dust.

Route Irish was attacked every day, sometimes more than once, and the team's eyes were everywhere looking to make sure that it was not their turn. You had to look for likely ambush points, suspicious vehicles or dickers on the bridges overhead, calling out the threats over the radio. Holes blasted in the tarmac and wrecked vehicles on the roadside were a grim reminder of what could happen if it wasn't your lucky day.

The radio commentary was constant as the cars weaved between lanes to avoid threats. A team leader notices two men standing by the side of the road and he has no idea if they have explosives strapped to their bodies or AK47s tucked under their bulky clothing. He doesn't want to find out the hard way and the radio crackles into life when he presses the send button, "Watch Out! Watch Out! Two X-Rays right in 200 metres... swerve left to increase the gap..." A quick check on the traffic and both cars suddenly change lanes almost in tandem. And so it went on...

The only time you would stop is if a car broke down or was hit too bad to carry on. There was no time to check out the damage, you just switched everyone to the running car and got the hell out of there. You did not hang around because there was always someone about who would take great delight in finishing you off.

On the morning of 5 June 2004 a two car convoy was making a routine run along Route Irish towards Baghdad airport. While the leading car was soft skinned, the second car was armoured and the guy who dicked them noted the difference. As the two cars hurtled along, two vehicles drove alongside at high speed and focused on the leading car. Leaning from their windows, they opened fire, using tracer bullets to damage the engine and set the fuel tank on fire. The driver of the armoured car manoeuvred into a blocking position during the high speed chase; it suffered a flat tyre and caught fire in the crossfire.

Both of the cars came to a halt further down the road but the insurgents had not finished with them. They stopped 100 metres away and clambered out to get a better aim. Another one or maybe two cars, the survivors did not know, also pulled up and joined the gun battle, turning the burning cars into death traps. With four of their number already dead, and their cars disabled, the three remaining men made a run for it across the carriageway; all three suffered injuries making their getaway. As they ran into the oncoming traffic, still under fire, they managed to stop a car and forced the terrified driver to let them drive it back to the Green Zone. In the space of a couple of minutes a normal run along Route Irish had turned into a disaster. Four lay dead on the roadside while the other three were on their way to the hospital, thanking their lucky stars that they were still alive.

One convoy I was leading encountered a different type of hazard as we travelled to the airport. We were a short distance behind a security team working for another company when the road in front of them suddenly erupted like something out of an earthquake movie. Our eyes widened and our mouths opened as a cloud of broken tarmac and dust rose in the air. The insurgents had spent several nights packing artillery shells in a culvert under the road before laying a detonation wire to their hiding place.

My driver was not the only one to slam the brakes on, bringing us to a screeching halt about 300 metres from the rupture across the road. As the noise of the squealing tyres and falling tarmac subsided, it was replaced by the sound of gun fire. While most of the traffic had come to a standstill, six cars raced past us heading for the team stuck in front of the damaged road.

We were on a different radio net and unable to warn them, so all we could do was watch the gun battle unfold in front of our eyes. The cars halted close to the stricken team and four or five armed men clambered out of each one. As they riddled the cars with bullets, I decided we had to do something and shouted over the radio to my guys "get out and engage".

Three security guys were already dead and the other two were doing their best to return fire, in what was a very uneven contest. We opened fire at long range and a few bad guys turned around to return fire while others ducked for cover. While we could not hope to beat the insurgents we were giving them something to think about. After trading shots for what seemed an eternity, we heard the welcoming wail of sirens in the distance; the Iraqi police were on their way.

There was no way we wanted to get mixed up in the inevitable police round up; it was time to get back in our cars and get the hell out of there, our client would have to wait a little longer at the airport. The insurgents had the same idea and as the Iraqi police cars pulled up we were all making our getaway.

The entrance to the airport was very heavily fortified and the queue of cars stretching back from Checkpoint 1 was always a worrying sight. Once you were in that queue you were stuck and there was very little you could do except hope that you were through the choke point as quickly as possible and behind the blast walls of the holding area.

A shuttle bus would take two of the team to the passenger terminal and they would have to get through airport security and then wait for the client to arrive. Once back in the car they were issued with body armour and a helmet, as stipulated in their contract. If we were picking up one of our own guys, we would also issue them with a weapon with instructions to use it if we came under fire. Welcome to Baghdad mate and then guess what? Yes, you are right; we had to do it all again to get back to the villa. It was one hell of a welcome to your new place of work.

Route Irish was a classic case of not dominating the ground. Despite all the tanks, armoured fighting vehicles and helicopters operating in the Baghdad area, the U.S. military could not control the short stretch of road from the Green Zone to the Airport. It told us one thing; they did not have the resources.

In the end construction contractors were employed to make Route Irish safer, a process which took many months to complete. They started by building concrete walls along the hard shoulders, making it impossible to plant IEDs. They finished by removing the bridges, removing the dickers' observation platforms. It removed the only way across the motorway and the locals had to take their lives in their hands when they crossed the road. A case of taking a sledgehammer to crack a walnut; something we often saw in Iraq.

The bigger issue was that the Americans never dominated Baghdad during the night. While their patrols were out on the streets in the day, manning checkpoints, carrying our sweeps and making searches, they withdrew to their barracks at night. The only guys who stayed out at night were a few Black Ops guys on specific missions and sniper teams tasked to watch certain routes. So the whole routine was that the bad guys spent all night doing their dirty deeds and the military spent all day playing catch up. It was another case of "the night belonged to the insurgents"; all the bad guys had to do was to wait until darkness fell and they had virtually a free rein to move across the city.

So where did we fit into the huge undertaking to restore Iraq in the aftermath of the Second Gulf War? The country was facing many problems, some of its own making under Saddam Hussein's rule, some due to military action and some due to the poverty you found in that part of the world.

Iraq's electricity network suffered from a number of problems before 2003. Many power stations and substations had been installed by foreign contractors many years before Saddam Hussein came to power in 1979 and the oppressive nature of his regime stopped companies sending technical personnel to maintain them. U.S. warplanes targeted the grid during the first Gulf War in 1991, cutting electricity supplies to military and civilian installations alike. Although the country was able to restore the power system to 4,400 megawatts following the war, it was not enough. The United Nations then implemented trade sanctions which left power stations and substations short of spare parts and maintenance suffered.

There was also another problem. Hussein made sure that the capital was favoured by the power network. The people of Baghdad were the ones who had the electrical appliances and they were also the ones in a position to demonstrate. By giving the capital city full power and giving other cities less than half what they needed, he was appeasing the people who were most influential. It meant that 20% of the 24 million people in Iraq were consuming 40% of the country's electricity.

By the time the Coalition Forces invaded in the spring of 2003, Iraq's power system was struggling to keep the supply at 4,400 megawatts, resulting in blackouts across the country. The pre-invasion air strikes again took a heavy toll on Iraqi infrastructure. Many power related targets were destroyed because they stopped important military functions, including communications and radar systems. The attacks tipped the country's power system over the edge, leaving many people without electricity.

Once Iraq had been conquered, the problem of restoring the country's power system became the C.P.A.'s and restoring electricity was high on its list of priorities. The Army Corps of Engineers assessed the power network under the Restore Iraq Electricity project and they found it in a sorry state. The Iraqi electricity minister, Karim Hassan, also admitted it was going to be difficult to repair the country's ailing grid, putting extra pressure on the C.P.A.

In July 2003 the C.P.A.'s head, Paul Bremer, promised to increase power supplies back to pre-war levels within sixty days. The plan was to invest about $230 million on emergency repairs to raise production to 3,500 megawatts by the end of the summer and 4,400 megawatts by midwinter; the goal was to reach 6,000 megawatts by June 2004.

At the same time the senior U.S. coalition advisor to the electricity commission, Peter Gibson, argued that electricity had to be distributed evenly across the country. It meant that while many rural areas would be better off, urban areas would be worse off. The power-sharing programme cut city supplies to 50%, with the power being switched on and off every three hours.   Eventually the rural areas were getting as much as ten hours electricity a day while cities only received half of that; Baghdad's massive metropolis was the worst hit with less than four hours on some days. It was not good for us...

The problem was that the country's basic needs had to come first. The C.P.A. had to guarantee power supplies for strategic sites including hospitals, water plants and oil installations. For example if there was no power for the clean and foul water pumping stations, the people had to get their water from the sewage filled rivers. This in turn led to a rise in illnesses, putting extra pressures on the hospitals; it also increased the chances of a cholera outbreak.

The shortfall left families without electricity and resentment rose in line with the temperature due to the lack of air conditioning, electric fans and refrigeration. Many families bought diesel generators to keep the appliances and lights on. When the power went off, they would switch to generator power. While richer families could afford to buy their own electricity source, most families had to rely on suppliers who set up generators in their area. These makeshift arrangements led to dangerous wires strung across every street while greedy suppliers charged extortionate prices resulting in a large part of a family's weekly budget being spent on fuel or electricity.

Even while the assessments were being made, protests over lengthy power cuts were underway, particularly in the cities. A poll by the International Republican Institute (a U.S. funded non-profit organization) asked people what the government's priorities should be. The need to deal with the insurgents came eighth, a desire to see the Coalition Forces leave came seventh, while tackling crime came fourth but the need for 24 hour electricity was number one. Only the scale of the problem was huge and it would take months, if not years, and millions of dollars to solve but the C.P.A. had to start somewhere. While contractors were employed to repair and upgrade electricity installations, they in turn had to employ security contractors to protect their employees and the power stations. And that is where we came in.

In the summer of 2003 the Army's repair crews were reporting a new phenomenon; sabotage. To begin with thieves stole power cables, melted them down to extract the copper and then sent it in barges down the Shatt-al Arab Canal to sell. But sabotageing the power network soon turned into a national past time as reported incidents rose to over 300 a week. Large areas of the power grid were being shut down by looting and sabotage and Baghdad's power system was particularly vulnerable. The pylons and substations around the city were impossible to guard and easy to damage making them a saboteur's dream and the foreign insurgents soon knew that a disrupted power supply increased public anger against the Coalition Forces. So they began working hand in hand with the criminals. And that is when we started to earn our money.

There is a history of random violence following a war of liberation these days. In some countries, like El Salvador, there was a bloody civil war. In other countries the people turned on the liberators. Occasionally, insurgents would take advantage of the vacuum of power left by the invasion. Iraq was a unique mixture of all three with its own problems added but it meant that we were up against a mix of bad guys with different motivations and they were all armed with a variety of weapons. On a good day it could be a local guy having a pot shot with an old AK47 and on a bad day it could be a group experienced insurgents armed to the teeth.

Iraq was a multicultural country with three main religious groups, the Sunnis, the Shias and the Kurds, and each one dominated a part of the country. While the majority of the Shias lived in the southeast around Basra, the majority of the Kurds lived in the north. The Sunnis dominated the central area and the area west of Baghdad became known as the Sunni Triangle after Saddam Hussein was deposed. They also dominated the country while he was in power.

There was potential for trouble when the three groups mixed, as often happened in the cities. While Hussein's strict regime did not accept religious intolerance (unless it was state sponsored), it reared its ugly head once he had gone. It was intensified by the lack of basic needs in the aftermath of the invasion, in particular, food, clean water and electricity. A lack of work and money added to the tensions in mixed communities.

The United Nations Development Programme estimated that over half of Iraqis were unemployed in the aftermath of the war. Bored men with too little money and too much time on their hands often protested against the lack of jobs, deteriorating living conditions and the lack of basic services. They often saw, either in the news or at first hand, that Westerners had plenty of everything while their families had nothing. American insensitivity to their social and religious customs only added fuel to the fire.

Frustration often boiled over and demonstrations could turn into riots. Some inevitably wanted to strike back at the military or the likes of us, even though we were working to improve conditions around the country. Of course we also came up against criminals from time to time in what was becoming an increasingly lawless country.

As stated earlier, one of the C.P.A.'s first decisions in May 2003 had been to disband the Iraqi army, putting around 400,000 soldiers out of work at the stroke of the pen. At the same time the C.P.A. sacked everyone connected with the Ba'ath Party and it meant that the over stretched Allied military had to take over basic security issues normally carried out by the police. If they did not, or could not, problems arose.

Many Party members had access to funding and some sought their revenge by paying people to kill soldiers. $5,000 was enough to set up an Iraqi family for life and some young men sought paradise in the afterlife by accepting the blood money. They would either carry a bomb into a crowded area or drive a car loaded with explosives into a checkpoint in the hope of killing as many Westerners with them as they could.

While there was plenty of home grown resentment, the presence of United States and British troops on Iraqi soil was a huge motivator for Islamist terrorists. The situation made Iraq an ideal place for Jihadi operations against the Western infidels. They crossed the porous borders and patiently watched the breakdown of law and order while accumulating weapons and ammunitions. When they were ready, they struck and the results often made it on to the international news. Only a heavy military presence on the streets would deter them and there were never enough soldiers to go round.

While President Bush's administration exaggerated the al-Qaeda threat in Iraq, the organization was happy to accept the blame. Many times the press gave al-Qaeda free propaganda and in October 2003 Osama Bin Laden referred to the situation in Iraq as his chief motivator. While there was very little evidence to support organized al-Qaeda activities, suspects occasionally admitted working for it; but where they? The overall intelligence picture was sketchy but over time everyone thought that Bin Laden's supporters were smuggling money, weapons and insurgents into the country.

There were also the freelance terrorists slipping across Iraq's open borders. There has always been fighting in different parts of the Middle East and there was no shortage of experienced warriors looking for a fight or hoping to train others to fight. They came from far and wide, but the majority came from Saudi Arabia, Jordan, Syria and Yemen. While many were motivated by ideology, others were motivated by money; ironically the same reason they were fighting was the reason we were there.

So where did the bad guys get all their arms and ammunition from? Well again it was another problem caused by the rapid fall of Saddam's regime and the inability of the Allies to deal with the aftermath. During the invasion of Iraq the Coalition Forces moved quickly across the country, driving the Iraqi Army back in disarray. Although it disintegrated rapidly and soldiers shed their uniforms so they could go home, they left behind a legacy which would haunt the country for years. It was believed that there were around 2,000 abandoned stockpiles of small arms, light weapons and ammunition scattered across the country and anyone could take what they wanted. Saddam Hussein had made sure that every town with a population of 30,000 or more had a large arms dump and after the Iraqi soldiers had fled there was no one to secure them.

It was believed that Iraq was littered with upwards of 650,000 tons of ammunition and it would take years to destroy. In September 2003 General John Abizaid told the United States Congress that"there is more ammunition in Iraq than any place I've ever been in my life ... I wish I could tell you that we had it under control but we don't".

Armed criminals were busy collecting what was saleable and anyone with money could buy a weapon and ammunition on the street. The glut of arms available drove prices down to a minimum, so that virtually anyone could get their hands on a gun; we reckoned that a Kalashnikov cost around $72, an AK47 would be $110 and a grenade was only around $1. It was just mad... Even we had taken advantage of the cheap prices to arm ourselves from one of the many arms dealers. In Basra alone, a city of 1.3 million inhabitants, it was reckoned that most families had a gun. Frightening stuff.

One example illustrates how electricity problems in Baghdad made our teams the focus for people's frustrations. It also shows how attitudes to our work turned from indifference to anger to armed confrontation; even though we were part of the solution. One of our contracts involved visiting an electricity generator in the heart of Sadr City on the northeast side of Baghdad. The area was a grid of low cost housing, around twelve square miles on the north side of the Army Canal, built in the 1950s to solve housing shortages. Thousands of people flocked to the area from their slums and shacks in the surrounding countryside and the name Revolution City was coined because the area was a base for the Iraqi Communist Party.

In 1963 the Ba'athist-led coup overthrew Prime Minister Abdul Karim Qassim and the area was renamed Saddam City after the country's new leader. Resistance to the new regime intensified, Shi'ites moved into the houses and the government neglected the area, leading to deprived conditions. Conditions deteriorated over the next 40 years and it became the poorest district in the city. Unemployment, poverty and crime increased in the warren of poor quality, low rise buildings. Rumour had it that Saddam Hussein allowed many criminals to go free just before Operation Iraqi Freedom and it was believed many had disappeared into the maze of buildings, where they formed gangs and preyed on the population. It was just another of the many problems facing the C.P.A.

The area was also known as Al Thawra but many residents referred to it as Sadr City in memory of the Shi'ite leader Mohammad Sadeq al-Sadr. Whatever it was called, it soon became known as a hotbed of insurgency. The U.S. military established Camp Marlboro in an abandoned factory on the east side and over 1,000 soldiers backed up by tanks were based there.

A small Civil Affairs team started working with the local leaders, aiming to rebuild the crumbling infrastructure which had been left to rot following the invasion. In June 2003 the U.S. military hired contractors to make the torched shell of a municipal building habitable. Three weeks later a district advisory council was meeting inside the building.

The locally based Mahdi Army, a hardcore of armed insurgents led by Muqtada al-Sadr, a young Shi'ia cleric who was calling for the creation of an Islamist state, took advantage of the situation. The Mahdists found it easy to recruit from the masses of young unemployed Shi'ias in the area and as the number of attacks on patrols increased, the military had to respond. In October twenty Abraham tanks and Bradley fighting vehicles rolled through the streets. While the Americans and the Mahdi Army squared up against each other, the people of Sadr City cowered in their homes.

The Civil Affairs teams had their work cut out liaising with the locals and their attempts to build up a rapport with the people were dashed in November when the District Council chairman was killed during a confrontation with an American soldier. Tensions flared as everyone blamed the occupying forces for their problems. Angry youngsters flocked to the Mahdi Army and on 17 December 2003 an American convoy was ambushed. After IEDs showered the vehicles with shrapnel, gunmen fired down on the troops from the rooftops, inflicting many casualties. Mahdi snatch teams nearly took soldiers hostage in the chaos.

The ambush showed the American military how strong resistance had become and they responded by establishing two more military camps over the winter. Camp War Eagle was set up at the north-east corner of Sadr City while Firebase Melody was built on the university campus next to the Army Canal.

Confrontations continued throughout 2004 and the worst battle occurred on 4 April when eight soldiers were killed and another fifty-seven were injured. Conditions continued to deteriorate because contractors were banned from entering what was effectively a war zone. As a result tens of thousands of people were left without electricity, water or sewage.

Sadr City was a real area for concern and while rubbish piled up on the streets and sewerage ran down many streets, clean water was hard to get hold of. Many buildings were overrun with rats and the chances of an epidemic were rising rapidly. At the end of 2004 a cease-fire was announced on humanitarian grounds.

The intermittent electricity supply had always been a key part of the problem because without it water and sewerage pumps could not function efficiently. Prolonged blackouts were also making life uncomfortable, especially during the hot summer months. That is where we came in because one of our client's engineers had to visit Sadr City's main substation on a regular basis; and we had to make sure he was kept safe in the Lion's Den.

After weaving through the centre of Baghdad, we joined Thawara Street and drove towards the combined American and Iraqi checkpoint over the Army Canal. The river is just a narrow canal but Saddam had relied on the three bridges to stop the people of Sadr City heading for the city centre if there was unrest. The Americans blocked the bridges for exactly the same reason, stopping criminals and insurgents escaping into the warren of streets north of the canal.

We would drive slowly up to the chicane of concrete units leading onto the bridge while the guards watched from behind the concrete blast walls surrounding their guard huts. Machine guns and recoilless rifles were on hand if anyone tried to rush the road block and the Americans sometimes stationed an Abrahams tank or a Bradley fighting vehicle next to the guard post as an extra deterrent.

There was another chicane at the far end of the bridge and then it was into the massive slum that was Sadr City. The advantage of the gridded streets was that it was easy to find your way out if you ran into a problem. To escape a potential ambush site all you had to do was turn left, left and left to get back on your original road and you could either find another route to the substation or head back to the canal.

Normally we drove straight on through Sida Square and on to Jumilla Square, deep in Indian country. We would take the left after Jumilla Square and there was the substation humming away in a caged compound.

We never had any problems during our early visits and the locals did not take much notice of us parking up and taking up a defensive position. One of the team would stand by the compound gate, one would get a good view from the roof of the cage and the other two would stand by the cars, keeping nosey people away.

There we waited while the engineer went inside the compound to check the generator's gauges and make sure everything was running smoothly. It usually only took him about twenty minutes and we could drive from the safety of the Green Zone to Sadr City and back in around an hour and half; from our haven to hell and back in no time at all.

There was a café right next to the generator and we sometimes stopped to have a drink of coffee and a chat with the guys because they were all friendly and eager to exchange news and rumours about events around the city. They were also curious why five Westerners were visiting their area.

The friendly attitude soon turned against us as the weeks passed. They had been used to having power 24 hours a day under Saddam's regime but since the C.P.A. had taken over they were getting less than half that, and sometimes hardly any at all. So it was easy to understand why they were getting angry.

The daily blackouts left the people with no lighting, no air conditioning, no refrigeration and it impacted on every aspect of their difficult lives. It did not take long for the word to spread that our visits were to do with the electricity supply and locals were convinced we were turning it on and off. The engineer was doing quite the opposite but we were obvious targets for the locals' hatred and the bad guys were not going to dissuade them.

Young kids often played near the generator and as soon as we pulled up they ran to their elders to announce our arrival in exchange for a few coppers. As the engineer started checking the generator, word soon spread that the Westerners were messing with the electricity supply again. The team then had to play a waiting game, watching the crowds gather at a distance. It did not take long before there were hundreds of men shouting and hurling abuse, while the youngsters threw stones. The only hope was that no one fired a shot.

On some occasions the team had to force the engineer to abort his work as the crowds grew bolder and moved closer. There is only so much four armed guys can do to keep an angry mob at bay. As the crowd edged down the street, the team had to decide when to stop the engineer and get the hell out of there. Leaving was always a dodgy moment because the crowd would surge forward the moment they sensed the team were leaving. And then it was the mad drive back to the Army Canal checkpoint.

There were lots of places across the city where contractors were working to restore normality but the people's patience was stretched to breaking point. Their frustration boiled over into demonstrations which the insurgents were only too eager to encourage. Meanwhile, contractors like the one we were working for had to carry on while guys like us had to keep them safe.

Chapter Thirteen

Power to the People

WHILE SADR CITY IS AN EXAMPLE of how we worked at the delivery end of the electricity network, we also worked at the generation end of it too. Iraq's ageing infrastructure system provided many soft targets and the insurgents were quick to gather around them. The fact was that hitting the power grid had an immediate impact on Baghdad and the people always blamed the Americans when the electricity went off. So hitting one was a double whammy and the bad guys were quick to pick up on this. It was very difficult to protect something like a power station because you could not move it to a safer location. You just had to carry out what is called 'target hardening', installing blast walls and checkpoints.

There are several power stations supplying electricity to Baghdad; including Baghdad South, Al Quds to the northeast and Bayji 130 miles north of Baghdad, alongside the main road north to Mosul. Our client was involved with them all and where his engineers went we had to follow. Each base was allocated a project manager and a security team who lived on site. Their first job was to identify the security problems and then draw up a list of improvements, including everything from upgrading the perimeter defences and installing checkpoints to installing safe accommodation and training personnel.

Bayji is a major industrial centre with a population of about 200,000 inhabitants and many of them work at the largest oil refinery in the country or the large power plant. It also has a number of important weapons and chemical plants. The city briefly entered the news in 1990 when dozens of British civilians taken captive in Kuwait were held at the oil refinery as human shields. The refinery was badly damaged during the air attacks which preceded Operation Desert Storm in 1991, and although it was soon back in action after the war ended, subsequent United Nations trade embargoes hindered production.

Bayji is at the north end of the Sunni Triangle, the basis of Saddam Hussein's support, and the oil refinery and pipelines which run north and south from the city were often attacked by insurgents. In common with the rest of Iraq, the city had a tough time following the 2003 invasion and by October the people had had enough. Large groups of rioters focused their anger on the corrupt U.S. backed police force and the police chief was replaced by a local man chosen by the tribal elders. While it was a good move in one respect it did make life far more complicated for us when we moved into the area.

Bayji's power station is a huge affair on the outskirts of the city, between Route 1 and the River Tigris. Italian contractors built it about forty years before and it was coming to the end of its working life. In this age of environmental awareness, the whole complex was a real challenge. Plumes of acrid smoke drifted from the six tall smoke stacks around the clock giving the whole area a pungent smell. Having said that, the power station generated about 60% of Baghdad's electricity, making it a crucial infrastructure site in the C.P.A.'s planning.

Initial assessments made it clear that the power station was beyond repair and the plan was to shut it down and install new generators. That is where our client came in. By this time it was clear that the new insurgency trend was to target infrastructure sites, because they were easier to hit than military bases or government buildings. A determined attack against the power station would have significantly reduced Baghdad's power supply, creating a huge headache for the C.P.A. While there was a military base a couple of miles down the road, they had their hands full with a local civil war and they did not have the resources to secure every site. So that is where we came in.

Just getting to the power station was an ordeal and we did everything we could to keep our moves to and from Bayji to a minimum. The main road from Baghdad to Bayji was Highway 1 or Route Tampa and our teams were subject to random drive by shootings, especially around Samara. The chance of suffering anything more than superficial damage was minute but they kept you on your toes. The drivers forever had to carry out evasive driving to get away from these chancers. You could never open the windows to return fire, all you could do was grin and bear it and hope that they would not damage the paintwork too much.

Route Tampa was also used regularly by the military and insurgents laid IEDs along the route every night. The military used to check the roads for devices every morning and it was unwise to move before they had completed their work. However, they never got them all and one survey we carried out counted three or four detonations every day in May 2004. The bad guys used any explosive device they could get their hands on but artillery shells were their favourite. It did not take an expert to wire a few together and connect them to a battery and a detonation device. The trigger man could then activate the device by wire or radio signal. Some devices were wired together in what were called daisy chains and our drivers always kept a safe distance between their vehicles, so that no more than one would be hit at a time.

You then had to leave the Route Tampa road and drive through Bayji town where insurgents had all the time in the world to plan their attack. From time to time an armed youth would be waiting in an alley, waiting for his dicker to wave as we approached. He would then jump out and spray us with bullets. It was like a game, just their way of letting off some frustration. Having said that the insurgents knew that many of the townspeople were employed on the plant and they did not want to alienate them by carrying out a major attack in the urban areas. So there was no secret to getting through Bayji safely it was just a case of "driving through there so fast it was unbelievable". A real test of your nerves as your driver hit the gas and weaved through the traffic while the rest of the team called out the threats over the radio.

U.S. Army engineers had been working at the power plant for some time when our Forward Reconnaissance Team (FRT) arrived at the end of 2003. The small group belonged to the Corps of Engineers' Task Force Restore Iraqi Electricity, or Task Force RIE, which had been formed in September 2003 to carry out what its name suggests. The group was just one of many our guys encountered carrying out emergency repairs to power installations across the country.

Our client was going to be one of two subcontractors who would be working to install generators at Bayji so it could supply Baghdad. The six original thermal generators were only producing 210 megawatts and the plan was to power four existing gas turbines by tapping into a local supply of sour gas, adding 190 megawatts. The Army engineers had also sourced eight huge mobile generators, each capable of generating 23 megawatts, from as far afield as Mexico, Guyana and Florida and they had been shipped to Turkey. A huge Russian Antonov (An-225 Mriya) air freighter was hired to fly them into Iraq. The final leg of the journey involved escorting the generators through some of the most dangerous terrain in the world while there was a fierce battle raging less than one hundred miles to the south in Al Fallujah. The journeys made by the generators illustrate the lengths that the organizations working on behalf of the Coalition Provisional Authority were making to get Iraq back on its feet.

When the six generator thermal plants, four gas turbines, and eight mobile generation units were working together at capacity it was hoped to produce 584 MW, 10% of Iraq's needs. While the cost would top $300 million, Iraq was fortunate enough to have plenty of oil to cover the costs. But that was all in the future.

Our guys moved into a fort like structure next to the power station, built by the Italians for their head honcho. It looked like one of those old Foreign Legion posts you see in films with high walls and a turret at each corner, but inside there was a villa and a swimming pool. Our huts were also inside and one of the first jobs was to get an excavator to dig a moat on the outside, using the earth to create a low embankment. That stopped anyone parking a car loaded with explosives against the wall. After stringing razor wire around the perimeter, we built sandbagged positions at regular intervals to serve as firing positions. At night we parked the cars behind the steel gates in case a suicide bomber rammed a vehicle loaded with explosives at them. We had to make the fort as safe as possible because our plan was to hold the fort to the last man. We did not have the resources to do anything too technical and the project manager had to be inventive, making the maximum use of the raw materials to hand.

In reality our defences were not much different from the days of the Empire in Afghanistan or Africa when the British Army expected small outposts to hold out against the likes of the Mahdists or the Zulus. We only hoped that Bayji would not be our Rorke's Drift, when a few dozen British soldiers held out against several thousand Zulus.

We did not have the backup to do anything spectacular. We did not have any tanks, armoured fighting vehicles or Humvees on hand. The largest weapons we had were a handful of PKM heavy machine guns mounted in the fort's towers. There were no Apache helicopters or A10 tank buster planes on call if we got into trouble as the U.S. patrols who operated in the area could do. Neither did we have a huge logistic chain like the military, no helicopters making regular resupplies and no convoys dropping off equipment. We shipped everything in ourselves by car until we had enough food, water and ammunition to last for a week. We assumed if a siege lasted longer than that, we could expect to get some airtime on the news.

The official line was that we had to plan to defend ourselves for 45 minutes and all our Standard Operating Procedures (SOPs) were set up to meet that deadline. That was the maximum length of time the U.S. Military reckoned it would take to get to us; well that was if they were anywhere near. I always found it ironic that 45 minutes was the same length of time it had been reckoned was needed to unleash a Weapon of Mass Destruction back when the decision to invade Iraq was taken.

There were ground level guard posts at the three access gates and a similar number of observation towers but they were all concentrated around the accommodation compound next to the main gate. The rest of the perimeter fence was out of sight, particularly during the hours of darkness and it was in a right old state when we arrived. At one time the power station was surrounded by a high chain link fence, topped with barbed wire. That had been more than enough to stop an opportunist thief under Saddam's regime. However, the security guards disappeared after the invasion and looters had had a field day searching for precious metals across the vast site.

The fence had been pulled down or cut through in many places, and not always by thieves. The plant staff had made holes to use as shortcuts to get to work. Although corrugated sheets or barbed wire had been used to block some gaps, the repairs were only temporary and would not stop a determined intruder.

When the plant was built, lights had been installed around parts of the perimeter fence where personnel were likely to work but many were broken, leaving large areas in darkness. The fact they that pointed into the plant worked against us as well. We wanted the area outside the plant illuminated to stop intruders getting to the fence; the internal lights cast the fence line in shadow.

The plan was to employ local guards to watch the perimeter fence so they could fire warning shots if they saw anybody but long grass allowed anyone to creep up to the fence unseen. Fortunately, packs of wild dogs roaming around outside the fence barked at friend and foe alike. I only got close to them once during a drive outside the completed perimeter months later; they were fierce and dangerous, jumping up at the vehicle trying to get at us.

The situation inside the power station was no better because many areas were littered with abandoned equipment, piles of scrap and heaps of rubble. Intruders could easily move around the power station without being seen, particularly at night.

It was going to take time before the client could move in expensive pieces of plant. Fortunately, there was plenty of local labour available to do the simpler tasks. Before long there were gangs of men working all over the site, mending fences, cutting vegetation and moving rubbish. An electrical contractor was also hard at work, bringing the illumination up to a safe standard, introducing low glare lighting around the plant.

Extra fences were added around the key areas including the turbine yard, the accommodation compound and our parking area, limiting access. Plans to build guard towers with overlapping fields of observation around the plant were also put in place, starting in these areas. Eventually there would be two guards in each tower with a coordinated relief system. In short we wanted the power station to become a prison camp, only in reverse. The good guys were on the inside and the bad guys were on the outside.

There were random attacks against the plant virtually every day and most were designed to make our lives uncomfortable. The odd mortar shell would be lobbed in our direction, or someone would pop up out of the undergrowth near the perimeter fence and take a few shots. Every now and again a car would drive up the access road to the bridge. The occupants would get out, fire a few bursts from the AK47s, shout a few obscenities and then drive off in a cloud of dust. They did not bother us because they were beyond effective range and it would have been comical if it wasn't so hot. Of course part of the reason for these random attacks was to check the reaction of the security guards and spot their positions. They also reminded the workforce that they were being constantly watched.

On the occasions I was there, the routine usually started with the sound of distant gunfire or the crump of a mortar round. It was followed by the honk of the air horn or clang of the steel triangle, signalling an attack. You put on your body armour and helmet, got your grab bag and awaited instructions. More often than not, that was it and we went back to work. Sometimes you hoped it was a proper attack, to break the boredom and give everyone something to talk about later.

Only one time was I there when there was a full scale attack. The clients were immediately herded into the bunker and once they were inside we could stop worrying them and man the perimeter. Each of the sangars was numbered and each man went to his allocated position. The project manager then visited each position in turn to assess the intensity of the incoming fire.

The power plant was a huge static target and no matter how much we improved the fencing and security, we could never stop someone firing a few mortar or rocket rounds at it. The insurgents used a mixture of rockets, ranging from helicopter rockets mounted on improvised launchers up to large 122 mm sized rockets which had a range of five kilometres. They also deployed a mixture of mortars varying from 60 mm to 120mm and the largest one had a range of eight kilometres.

Shots would be fired at random intervals on most days and nights and there was little you could do about them. The chances of hitting a generator or the pipeline were very low, but the damage would have caused extensive problems. In six months of daily attacks the insurgents hit the pipeline twice. Each time a specialist team had to drive up from Baghdad and the plant was off line for three days while they carried out repairs. That was three days of no electricity for tens of thousands of people.

If you heard the first round explode you were still alive and all you could do was to hit the deck. It was just a case of pot luck where the round landed and all the guys could do was hope that the mortar crew was poor at aiming. Our guys soon got fed up of having to get out of bed every night and the project manager came up with an alternative approach to a safe night's sleep. He got the guys to fill and stack sandbags against the walls of the dormitory block and the offices. The American security contractors on the camp thought they were crazy for sweating it out in the hot sun. However, they changed their mind once the walls were finished.

Our guys could stay in bed when the mortars began, and as the saying went, they 'pulled the sheets up a bit higher' for protection. That may sound blasé, but when it is happening night after night, what else can you do? All you want to do is sleep and the sandbags stacked against the cabin walls were the best protection you were going to get. We eventually came to the conclusion that the night time attacks were just to stop us sleeping; a nice reminder that we were being watched. And guess what? The Americans were soon building their own sandbag walls.

The whole mortar thing became another game of cat and mouse we had to

Me with a team during the early days, when we were armed with second hand AK-47s.

Iraq's power plants were outdated and polluting the atmosphere.

Setting off from the camp with my Tail End Charlie smiling in the back.

Out on the firing range with my M21 'long' and Glock 17 'short'.

On the Green Zone's training ground with the huge crossed sabres in the background. The ID card around my neck could only get me into a few places.

Car one is through the checkpoint and now it is our turn.

A military convoy eases round craters left by IEQs.

Bayji power plant kicks our plumes of smoke and steam.

A visit to Bayji power plant. Out in the country I wore a cop vest so I had plenty of mags for my AK-47.

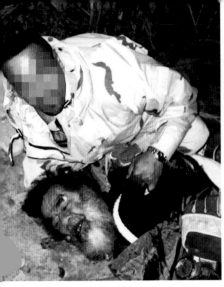

Ace in the Hole; Saddam
Hussein's capture in December
2003.

Stopping to buy petrol and refuel while we can.

A two car team blown up by a suicide car bomber.

The armoured panels and glass protected the passengers while the run flats got us out of trouble.

Crossing the Great Zab Bridge from Kurdistan into Iraq; note the queue of lorries waiting to cross.

Miles from anywhere in the middle of Kurdistan you have to look out for yourself.

A typical traffic jam we encountered on the back roads.

Time to sunbathe after a long day on the road; you are never short of sun in Iraq.

play with the insurgents. They would stake out a new firing spot one night and fire off a few rounds the next day or night. The shell usually exploded harmlessly outside the fence and we could never understand how they missed the compound every time.

During the day mortar teams would set up on the opposite side of the River Tigris, knowing that we did not have time to send patrols across it to catch them. Every time one of our patrols went down to the river bank they would be met by small boats which acted as ferries. The pilots would sling ropes across wherever they were needed and they would always be willing to take you across, using their hands to pull them across the current, for a couple of dollars. Willing indeed but you could bet that they had just taken across one of our tormentors.

It was possible to guess where many mortar sites were by studying the map, and from time to time we sent out armed patrols to investigate them for signs of activity. The same mortar teams were also targeting the U.S. military base down the road and they were as anxious as we were to knock one out. We would send in reports on a daily basis and from time to time we would see helicopters hovering overhead or patrols on the ground, searching the sites we had surveyed.

Vehicle Borne Improvised Explosive Devices or VBIEDs was the technical term but we called them suicide car bombers. They were an increasing threat and a deadly attack on Basra's offshore oil terminal in April 2004 demonstrated what could happen. Since the main military and government buildings were being walled off and protected by heavily guarded vehicle checkpoints, the insurgents were looking for softer targets which had propaganda potential. The fact that you could knock out a major piece of infrastructure, and the problems it caused the C.P.A. were a bonus.

Construction sites were ideal targets because of the large amount of deliveries being made. Any guy who was determined to become a martyr could drive a vehicle loaded with explosives up to the plant entrance. The larger the vehicle the better, and delivery lorries and concrete mixers were ideal. If the driver could trick his way through the plant checkpoint he could drive up to an important piece of machinery and detonate the explosive device. If he was unable to get through the gate he would blow up the checkpoint and the security guards; ours included.

When we arrived the security guards knew most of the delivery drivers and waved them through without checking their ID or their vehicles. Although there was an access control point, it could not stop a large vehicle ploughing through the barriers. Everyone was driving across the compound and parking close to where they worked. The whole system was lax and dangerous and had to be changed.

We only allowed delivery lorries to enter the site and they were searched with metal detectors and mirrors before they were allowed inside. A chicane of concrete blocks stopped vehicles at a safe distance from the main gate and drivers had to wait until their load had been checked with metal detectors and mirrors. A stinger (a chain of linked spikes to burst a car tyre) was placed at the outer checkpoint while a car blocked the inner access gate until the guards gave the all clear. Everyone else had to park outside and walk to their place of work. We eventually issued IDs for all delivery vehicles, drivers and workers; it was a case of no pass, no work.

Later on the bad guys started to lay IEDs along the access road to the power plant. While the military checked the main road every morning, it did not take long for the insurgents to realize that they never checked the road to the power plant. All we could do was trim back vegetation near the road and make our own inspections.

Contractors employed a lot of local labour which made it difficult to contain security leaks and our project leaders were always aware that workers were being bribed to talk about security arrangements. And if they refused to talk they were told not to work on the plant or face the consequences. The bad guys stepped up their game by parking on the nearby river bridge to hurl abuse and fire shots at the main gate. They were too far away to cause any injuries but it did unsettle the labourers.

These attacks were noted by the Americans and, for whatever reason, they decided to act; only they acted without any advance warning. Late one evening we were disturbed by the sound of jets flying low overhead, followed by the sound of explosions. A few ventured out to see that missiles had taken out a span of the river bridge.

It seemed a bit excessive to us and our first concern was what would happen the following morning when the early shift turned up for work. The early starters usually arrived before dawn and there was no way of warning them. Sure enough a few hours later the first three or four cars drove straight off the ruined bridge and the occupants drowned in the river below. That day was a difficult one for everyone on site and the outrage at the deaths increased by the hour because there would be no compensation and no apologies. Our guys were left to pick up the pieces and answer awkward questions. The heavy handedness of the response to a manageable problem had handed the insurgents a propaganda coup.

Another concern was that of protecting the clients while they carried out their work. The plant's remote location and extensive perimeter meant that it was relatively easy for an insurgent to slip inside. While killing someone was the easiest option, the propaganda potential of kidnapping a contractor was well known and worth the risk. Before we arrived, armed men kidnapped one of the labourers working on the site following a personal dispute and if they could do it once, they could do it again.

One recent raid at Fallujah police station had demonstrated that insurgents fired their weapons outside the perimeter to cause a distraction. The snatch team then cut through the perimeter and intelligence provided by one of the workers told them where to find their hostage.

We decided to build an underground shelter in the centre of our accommodation area. After digging a large hole, we shored up the sides with large sandbags to create something resembling a shallow manhole. Railway sleepers formed the roof while a hatch was installed. There were no home comforts inside, our clients just sat inside until the attack was over. By locking them inside, we could forget about them while we concentrated on defeating the attack.

We always had to worry about sabotage because it was easy to smuggle a grenade into the plant unless we carried out full body searches. Almost anyone could get hold of a grenade for a few dollars, and it only needed a limited amount of knowledge to work out where to place one. None of the buildings were locked at night and anyone could sneak in and leave a small explosive device on one of the turbines or control panels. However, the easiest way to cause a major problem would have been to steal or smash one of the computers which controlled the plant.

Every morning the local labourers walked down the access road and queued up by the main gate, waiting their turn to have their identification checked and be searched. At least that was the plan. After weeks of training the Iraqi guards still had not got the hang of the routine and we had to keep a close eye on them.

During one visit to the plant I was watching the routine, to see how it was working. As my driver and I sat in our car, we watched the crowds of Iraqis shuffling over the brow of the hill and down the slope. They looked a typical sorry lot and after what they had experienced in their lives you had to feel sorry for them. After years of living under Saddam's harsh regime, they had probably had family and friends killed or injured during the war. Although they had been told they were free now, freedom had come at a hell of a price. Their only way of putting food on the table was to work for the Westerners, the very Westerners that had invaded their country.

At that moment in time we were not concerned with the plight of the workers though, we were watching the guards as they checked them into the plant. In amongst the crowd, one particular guy stuck out. The typical Iraqi was a skinny, dejected individual with sagging shoulders, who dragged his feet as he shuffled along in flip flops. Not a very complimentary description I know but the man who had caught my eye had a spring in his step and he looked far too muscular and well fed to me. His shemagh was also wrapped carefully to conceal most of his face. This guy was on the ball, a little too much on the ball for my liking.

As he walked closer I eyeballed him and for a moment he did the same to me, just to see what I was doing. That quick glance was enough for me; he was not going into the plant until I had had a closer look. I gave my driver the nod and pushed the car door open as he walked past. "Get on the floor" I shouted, as I shouldered my weapon and pointed it at him. He went straight down on his knees, before lying face down with his hands behind his head. Interesting I thought, he understands English and he had done that before. As my driver covered the guy with his weapon, I knelt down and pulled the shemagh from his face. "Hello what have we got here" we both thought. Pale skin, long ginger hair and ginger beard; it was also clear that he was not happy about lying on the ground either. Only he was not complaining in Arabic, he was complaining in English with an accent I placed around Belfast. Now I knew the job situation in Northern Ireland was tough, but we did not for a moment think that he was here looking for work; he was up to no good.

We cuffed the guy and manhandled him into the backseat of the car where I kept my gun trained on him. My driver radioed the gate to let us back in and also told the office to prepare the client's bunker for a prisoner. It was time to find out what our visitor was doing here and did he have any friends. The project manager also put a call out to the U.S. military to send a patrol over to take the guy into custody. Although we had captured him and we were anxious to find out his intentions, we were not allowed to interrogate him. Well not for long anyway.

We drove up to one of the bunkers and dragged the guy inside, kicking and shouting about how unfair his treatment was. We begged to differ; we had a damn good idea why he was here and what he had been up to. One of the daily bulletins put out by the American military had noted that a small group of Irish paramilitaries had made their way to Iraq. After years of experience fighting the British Army in Ulster, members of the I.R.A. were the world's experts on targeting military convoys. Since the Good Friday Agreement in 1998 they had been out of work and somehow one of the insurgent groups had enticed around ten guys to carry on their work in Iraq. No doubt they were in Iraq in exchange for a sizeable financial reward rather than promise of nice weather and a sun tan.

The British Army engineer teams working in the Basra area had noted that some IEDs were similar to the roadside bombs that the I.R.A. had perfected along Northern Ireland's roads. In places like Armagh, they had been so effective that the army had been forced to suspend road patrols for a considerable time.

So there we had it. After all those years we had served in Northern Ireland, here we were up against one of our old adversaries, half way around the world; a small world. In retrospect it is probably a good thing that the American military police came sooner rather than later. We did try to get some information out of the guy but he was probably used to a lot tougher questioning than we were prepared to give him. We would let the Americans ask him why he was blowing up their guys.

No doubt these guys were giving assistance on how to set roadside bombs, where to set the best ambush and how to rig car bombs. Iraq was a playground for anyone trained in those tactics, and there would have been no shortage of pupils who were backed by rich paymasters. Ironically we were all there for the money I suppose. The Irish guys were not the only foreigners dealing in death in Iraq. Iraq became a centre for terrorists from around the Middle East looking to strike at the Westerners and everything they stood for. We could never really see where Northern Ireland's Troubles fitted into that argument...

We never heard anything back from the Americans about him but we did hear more snippets of intelligence about an Irish team working around Baghdad, but the information was highly classified and it was just another thing we all had to look out for. We also heard rumours that British Army Special Forces teams were out and about in Baghdad chasing after them but we were not privy to the information, we just listened and learned. We just hoped they snatched some before they did too much damage. It was nice to capture one of our own bad guys though.

As much as anyone loathed writing them and everyone hated following them, we had to put in place procedures for everything from access control and evacuation to security and perimeter routines. You name it we had to have it all written down, translated and posted. We also had to train guys to follow them and although the Iraqi guards were willing, our attempts to turn them into a security force often fell short of the mark. It would take a lot more than a company t-shirt and a weapon to turn these guys into an effective security team.

There were regular meetings and our project manager attended to get the security angle on what was being discussed. Everyone had to get on with work as fast as possible but we did not want to compromise safety. At least that is what we thought... At one meeting the client discussed powering up the plant and all was going well until someone asked about the sour gas installation. The technology was beyond us but the basic principle was to extract sour gas, remove all the nasty chemicals and use the clean gas to power the generator turbines.

That is more than we had to know. However, during the course of the meeting it became clear that the sour gas was hydrogen sulphide, which was really nasty stuff. A good whiff of it could do irreparable damage to somebody's lungs and even kill them. Now this was news to our project manager and the pipeline was only thirty metres from our offices.

Questions came thick and fast. What would happen if someone tossed a grenade into the sour gas compound or if a mortar round hit the pipeline? It did not take too long to figure out that there had been misunderstandings which had to be rectified straight away. A couple of days later gas masks and life saving equipment had been shipped up to Bayji while everyone was being put through an emergency drill. By pure luck we had got away with it and the sour gas plant was never hit; it was a good job the insurgents were as ignorant about the evil stuff as we were.

One night when I was visiting the power station we were awoken by the guards who had seen insurgents gathering outside the wire. It was later estimated that there could have been around forty armed men taking random shots at the guard towers, while someone tried to cut the perimeter wire. The clients were soon in the bunker, we were in our sangars and we were not unduly concerned. Normally these attacks ended after a few minutes and the bad guys went home. No doubt to get a good night's sleep ready to work in the plant the next day; you never could tell.

This night they did not stop and every time we thought they had gone, more shots rang out. We had a stand-off and when it looked as though it might go on all night we decided to end the game of cat and mouse. We needed our beauty sleep and out of sheer frustration we took the decision to go on the offensive...

About fifteen of us assembled quietly in the car park and filed out of the gate, forming up in an extended line facing our enemy. Our advance was text book platoon tactics, based on two teams moving in what we called pepper-pot formation. While one team remained kneeling, shooting off a magazine of aimed fire from the shoulder, the other team moved forward a short distance. By taking it in turns we leapfrogged forward, never letting up the covering fire. It was just like the old army days, no different from the tactics conducted on Mount Longdon in the Falklands, over twenty years earlier.

We took the bad guys by surprise and while they took a few pot shots at us, the firing died down as we drew closer. Shadowy figures were seen running for the reed beds along the river bank but we did not follow in case they were enticing us into a bobby trapped area. Instead we took a different route to the water's edge, to see if we could catch them paddling across.

We didn't find our adversaries on the river but we did find ammunition boxes they had left behind. We also found an old boatman waiting there with a big toothless grin on his face. It was obvious that he had just ferried the bad guys across the water and he was hoping to double his money by taking us across. You had to admire his cheek as he graciously asked if we were looking to cross the river for only a few dollars. We declined of course, there was no way we wanted to be sitting ducks out in the middle of the River Tigris. We had accomplished our objective and it was time to get back in our bunks for some beauty sleep.

During a single three week period the project manager logged an astonishing number of attacks on his Threat Assessment Index. The index compared the probability of attacks occurring and the likely outcome of an attack. Mortar teams fired 65 salvoes while 48 IEDs were detonated or discovered on the access road. Three suicide bombers drove up to the gate; all three were killed before they detonated their devices. 33 small arms attacks and 16 RPG attacks against the perimeter were also logged. Four workers were found trying to smuggle hand grenades into the power plant.

During that three week period there were 137 life threatening incidents; around seven or eight every working day. That number does not include the intimidation that the workers were subjected to outside the plant. Many received a knock at their door in the middle of the night, either telling them to stop working on the plant or asking for information. Those figures illustrate how much effort the insurgents put into trying to knock out Baghdad's power. You could say that the lads earned their money protecting the ageing plant and the engineers who were bringing electricity to Iraq.

After six months of hard work, Bayji power station had six generators on line and it was deemed a significant moment, so significant that Paul Bremer, the head of the C.P.A. decided to make a visit. Now you know how it goes when a VIP decides to put in an appearance, everywhere had to look spotless and nothing could be allowed to go wrong.

Nobody had taken much notice of the power plant since we had been there, but all of a sudden the place was flooded with representatives from the U.S. military, the C.I.A. and the press. I had also driven up there to give the lads a bit of moral support and help make sure that everything ran smoothly. There was the usual last minute rush as the military searched the area and put the power station on security lockdown but after a few tense days, it was time for the opening ceremony.

A landing pad had been built a kilometre outside the perimeter because the helicopters could not go near the power lines. All was ready and for what seemed like an age we waited in the sweltering heat, waiting for our VIP. The sound of a Blackhawk helicopter in the distance signalled Bremer's imminent arrival and like everyone else I strained to catch a glimpse of the 'man in charge'. Everyone cheered, the Americans louder than any of our guys, as the helicopter touched down and the great man stepped out; only it wasn't him, it was a double. Despite the security lockdown, the military were taking no chances. If an insurgent had been able to hit the Blackhawk with an RPG, it would have made headline news.

And so we waited again while a second Blackhawk touched down on the landing pad. There was another cheer as 'Mr. Bremer ' stepped out but again it was a double. This was getting confusing and not just for us, you could see puzzled faces everywhere you looked. Believe it or not, the U.S. military landed five Blackhawks with doubles before they were sure nobody was going to shoot. I do not know if it was the same helicopter going round, or five different helicopters, but by the time the real Mr. Bremer stepped out onto the landing pad, the cheers were a bit lame.

After all that build up you would think that he would have stayed a while and seen what all the fuss was about but it was not to be. After cutting the ribbon and a short speech in front of the television cameras, he was back on the helicopter and heading back towards Baghdad. Then, with the excitement over, it was back to work for everyone.

Chapter Fourteen

Home Comforts

WHEN YOU HAVE SO MANY MEN working so far away from home you are bound to have problems and at times it felt like I was their boss, their mentor and their confidante all rolled into one. There was always someone with a problem at home, whether it was a problem with their relationship with the wife or girlfriend or with the kids being ill or not doing well in school. When I joined the army the only contact with home was the weekly letter, nicknamed the 'Bluey' and the odd call when the pay phone gobbled up your change. Back then the enforced separation seemed to make you appreciate your loved ones more. You had your letter or your call and then got on with your soldiering.

Today, in this world of instant communications the guys were constantly in touch with home, either through text messages, emails, internet chatting or webcams. While it increased the amount of contact, the guys were hearing about every little problem and little problems became big ones when they were misunderstood. I used to think that instant communications caused some of the biggest personnel problems we had.

Believe it or not, the more you kept in contact with your loved one while you worked away, the harder it became. Each time you called home, it reminded you how much you missed your family and it reminded you how much you had to lose. Every little thing you said to your wife or kids stuck in your mind and it went round and round your head until you spoke to them again. Usually, it was just your mind playing tricks on you but the insecurities of working in such a dangerous environment played on your fears.

Your loved ones were anxious to hear you were alright and that you were not in too much danger, so you never told them how crazy your life was out there. You loved them too much to give them more worries than they already had. Conversations were often based around a few white lies as you tried to protect your loved ones from the difficulties of living completely different lives. While hers revolved around the house, the kids and your friends, yours revolved around trying to stay alive in one of the most dangerous cities in the world.

My wife and I always agreed to keep in contact by email and our Sunday get together on the internet allowed us to keep in touch. We usually spent an hour chatting away, and most of our conversation was about the kids and the rest of the family. Although she knew I had a hectic routine in a dangerous line of work, we never talked about it. As long as I was looking after myself, eating good food and keeping healthy that was all that mattered.

She had never watched the news all the time we had been married, it was something that stemmed from my military service when I often disappeared on operations without saying a word. She was used to it, or as used to it as anyone can get when their loved one is in danger. I suppose her attitude was to carry on with normal life, it was no use worrying. As long as the phone did not ring I was alright; she would only worry if someone called her unexpectedly. It was our way of coping.

Some of the men were single lads but a lot were married or with girlfriends and separation can do funny things to relationships; it either makes it stronger or blows it apart. Rumours were easy to start, easy to circulate and difficult to stop. Around 10% of the staff on some American bases were women and as fraternization was banned in the U.S. armed services, our lads were happy to move in. All sorts of flirting and more was going on with the secretaries and nurses and there were occasional romantic problems.

Lads being lads there was always a problem cropping up and it was a wonder that we got any work done at times. One small example illustrates the sort of crazy things I had to deal with at times. One guy was on leave in Kuwait when he met a young lady in a bar. Now they hit it off straight away and they agreed to meet the following evening along the sea front where courting couples traditionally went for a bit of privacy, because Kuwaiti society is very strict about all matters sexual. Anyway one thing led to another and, as far as I know, both went their own way happy with the encounter.

All well and good, however, what our guy did not realize was that she was the daughter of a Kuwaiti minister. What she did not realize was she was being shadowed by undercover security guards to make sure that she did not get into trouble. At one point they had disappeared down Kuwait's equivalent of lovers' lane, they did not believe that she had agreed to it and took the view that our guy must have forced her to go there. He had been in prison for three days by the time that we found out he had been arrested. It took some delicate negotiating on the company's part and some serious explaining on the young lady's part before he was released.

Drink could have been a big problem if we had not kept a close eye on it. Although I never had a drink unless it was a nip of something out of my tiny lucky tankard at the end of a hard day, we stuck to the two can NATO limit while on operations. The U.S. military were not allowed to drink at all and when you saw the amount of weapons and the size of some of the egos in the Green Zone, I used to think it was a good idea. If we found anyone drunk they were sacked on the spot; we simply could not afford to have guys drinking on the job. Two guys found out we enforced this rule rigorously when they got drunk in Shaibah camp NAAFI. They were told to pack their bags immediately and were escorted straight back to Kuwait City.

When guys were heading south for a holiday they were, of course, looking for a bit of a blow out to relieve the tension. However, it was well known that the Kuwaiti border guards would target cars driven by Westerners and search them for contraband. Now this was not just a once over, it could involve a complete strip down of the vehicle if they found the smallest thing, like a few rounds, alcohol, pornography or anything else they did not like; and believe me you never knew what the rules were. The one thing I did know was that the fines for carrying drink were horrendous while being found in possession of pornography could result in a prison sentence.

We were forever warning guys not carry contraband but there was always the odd one who forgot or thought he might get away with it. One of the lads was looking forward to his holiday that much, he decided to stash a couple of cases of beer in his car. He had hidden them in the compartment where the spare wheel goes and then piled all his bags on top. It was a poor choice. The border police took no time at all to find them and the poor guy found himself looking at a $10,000 fine. That was virtually all his wages gone, ten weeks of hard work down the drain. I would hate to think what his other half thought of him when he confessed.

Many of the guys had their superstitions, relating to how they dressed or how they prepared for their day's work. Tempers would flare if they could not find a lucky piece of clothing or someone interrupted their little routine. Nearly everyone carried a talisman, usually something small that reminded them of home. The one I always remember was a hair band tied to a guy's weapon; it belonged to his little daughter. Something so special belonging to someone he loved dearly attached to something so deadly. My good luck charm was a tiny pewter jug I had acquired during my days in the army, the same one I had nip of something strong out of after a hard day.

On 11 November 1918 the Armistice came into effect, bringing the First World War to an end. Over 800,000 British soldiers had been killed, many more injured, the majority in the mud and blood of France and Flanders. That day had become a day of remembrance around the world, a day when families remembered their lost loved ones while old soldiers remembered their fallen comrades. It had also been an important day in the army calendar and we as ex-soldiers wanted to carry on the tradition of remembrance.

During the First World War Iraq was known as Mesopotamia, an area fought over by the British Army and Commonwealth forces against Turkish troops of the Ottoman Empire from autumn 1914 to August 1921. Thousands of men fought and died in the area (many from disease) and Iraq had many war cemeteries filled with graves and memorials.

A memorial to over 40,000 members of the Commonwealth forces who had died and had no known grave was built by the War Graves Commission at

Maqil north of Basra, where many of the soldiers landed in Mesopotamia. By 1997 it was surrounded by the main quay of Umm Qasr's naval dockyard and in a sensitive military area due for redevelopment. Saddam Hussein had it taken down and then rebuilt, walls, headstones and remains, at huge expense, twenty kilometres west of Basra, near Shaibah camp.

The British military celebrated Remembrance Sunday at the memorial every year, a particularly poignant ceremony because the officers and men who attended were remembering friends who had been killed in the recent fighting. Even though we were never invited to the ceremony because we were private security, I sneaked in on the two occasions I happened to be in the area. Each time there was a massive military security operation and the memorial was surrounded by a large exclusion zone. On each occasion a few of us turned up, asked if we could pay our respects, flashed our old military ID cards and we were allowed to stand near the back.

There was no British military remembrance service in Baghdad but we always held our own private service in the villa compound on 11 November, to remember the friends we had lost. We then attended the United States Veteran Day ceremony as a mark of respect for our clients, as many of them were ex-military. We were also invited to the after service dinner in the cookhouse, where the cooks spent all night getting it ready. There would always be an empty chair and a place set at the table, as a mark of respect for lost friends and the candle of remembrance flickered as we ate our meal.

As for birthdays I ignored them completely, a lot of the lads did. At most someone would mention it over breakfast with a joke about getting older but everyone still went out to work. While we saw marking the passing of another year as tempting fate, it was different when it came to Christmas. Although we were in a Muslim country, we made the most of the traditional festivities when we could.

If we were in the Basra area, we would head to British NAAFI and join the Christmas celebrations. In Baghdad the Americans really pushed the boat out and we had a right old time in their canteen halls, making the most of their massive spread. But while it was a free for all with the food it was not with the drink. All in all everyone was in a festive mood and it was like Christmas at home only we did not have grandma in the comfy chair in the corner, moaning about there being nothing good on the television. The most difficult part about the day was the phone call back home because everyone missed home the most on Christmas Day.

Our clients did not work between Christmas and New Year and while we were confined to camp we could let our hair down; technically speaking anyway, as most of us did not have any hair. Most of the guys headed up the road to the Presidential Palace where a large gym had been installed inside one of the cavernous halls. We would strip down to our swimming trunks and stretch out by the swimming pool on one of the sun loungers. While we were having fun, having a laugh with other guys and women who had gathered there, it was crazy to think how different life was outside the Green Zone.

But the thing that everyone did look forward to was leave. Tours were either six weeks on and two weeks off or two months on and one month off. Two weeks' holiday was never enough for me because it took me three days to get flights from Kuwait to Spain and then back again. That only left me five days with the wife and kids and it always felt like I was just relaxing when it was time to pack my bag and get going again.

Everyone went through phases when they were on a tour. To begin with they were fresh and focused on cracking on with their work. The family was a long way off and it was just easier to knuckle down and get on with the job. Their mood changed as their tour was coming to end because as much as they were looking forward to going home they tried not to. We had to watch guys who were about to go on holiday as they shied away from the tougher jobs and we tried, when possible to task teams accordingly. These short timers would often be knocking on the office door asking if they could change their duty because they only had a few days left before their holiday started.

A guy's mind started to wander from the job as he planned for his break and many became increasingly superstitious, worried that a little change in their routine would bring them bad luck. Everyone was worried something would happen because you were about to go home. You were starting to pack your kit away and it made you edgy. Then your defences dropped a little, you made silly mistakes and became paranoid because your mind was on other things.

One of the guys was killed only a few days before he was due to go home. He did nothing wrong, he was just in the wrong place at the wrong time. The heart breaking thing was his wife had just had a baby and he was going home to see the youngster for the first time.

As much as guys looked forward to going home, many found they did not get the welcome they were expecting. Some got home to find that their missus had moved on, despite talking about the holiday together for some time. Like any couple living apart, the loneliness drove couples apart and quite a number of the guys returned to work having had to come to terms with a Dear John letter or a blazing bust up. They were earning the money they had always dreamed of but it just goes to show that bringing in the dough was not everything in a relationship.

All sorts of organizations were being set up as we settled in to our villa and over 5,000 officials and contractors would eventually call the Green Zone home. The military established barracks, offices, depots and medical facilities and we made a point of exploring them all to see what we could find out or what we could acquire. The C.P.A. was getting organized in the Presidential

Palace while other private security companies were settling into the villas close to ours.

There were a similar number of Iraqis trapped inside the Green Zone. While many were homeless sheltering in abandoned buildings, there were families making a living out of supplying people like us. These people were virtually prisoners in the Green Zone. Although they could easily get out of one of the checkpoints, it was difficult to get back inside. They had to queue for long periods to get their security checked and had to wait overnight in the Red Zone during one of the many lockdowns.

On top of that they too were viewed by some as traitors for helping the Americans and became targets of abuse, kidnap or death. Most chose to relocate their families inside the concrete walls where they started a new life, rather than face the uncertainties of commuting.

The Iraqis were very resourceful people. They watched us and listened to us, looking for opportunities to make a living. Before long they were all either working directly for the Americans, or running a business servicing the Americans. They say Britain is a nation of shopkeepers but the Iraqis put anyone to shame. They were ingenious entrepreneurs and stalls selling everything from food to clothes, from electrical gadgets to furniture, from cars to apartments appeared wherever there was space. We could get virtually anything we wanted in a short distance from the villa.

Life for many in the Green Zone revolved around the huge market place and it was a pretty random affair, bustling with locals, military and contractors like us. There were equipment outlets that any Western town would be proud of, and there was also a lot of black market military and civilian equipment on sale, some of it stolen and some of it sold by unscrupulous soldiers.

But most of the guys went to the American supplier Blackhawk and came back loaded down with everything they needed; bags, vests, slings, pouches, gun cases, clothing, footwear, holsters, torches, personal hydration systems, knives, medical packs. You name it they had it and the place was always packed with guys looking for the perfect piece of kit.

Food outlets covering all tastes also opened and a couple of villas were converted into a Chinese takeaway and a curry house. One entrepreneur turned his petrol station into a large outdoor cafe, building a large counter and putting out lots of chairs and tables. An awning style shelter shaded the customers from the sun and the garage forecourt was soon jammed with vehicles. It was just like pulling up at any takeaway and within days it was buzzing with armed military and security contractors mingling with civilians.

The owner had created it out of nothing and it was a great place to stop by for a quick coffee and a sandwich. Our guys often popped in while their client was busy and all it took was a quick phone call to be back on the job in minutes. It was also a great place to meet your friends and exchange stories with other contractors.

The place was so advanced that a couple of young Iraqi lads were pimping for half a dozen girls who were working out of small rooms in the petrol station shop. Guys could go up to their desk, get allocated a time slot, and then wait for a call from the pimps. The same system you see at your local supermarket delicatessen; only there was a little more on offer. Although we had not expected to see brothels in Iraq, we came to the conclusion that they must have always gone on out of sight under Saddam's regime.

However, the cafe's success was also worrying. A lot of military and security guys were milling about and anyone could walk off the street into the crowd. In short there was no security and it was an obvious target for a bomber. We warned our guys to stay away but despite the dangers it was still tempting to drop by. And sure enough the worst happened. Two guys walked in with rucksacks one lunch time, the busiest time, and sat drinking tea and talking for about half an hour. One then left and headed into the market. Two blasts filled the sky above the Green Zone with smoke as the two men detonated the explosives carried in their backpacks, committing suicide seconds apart.

The cafe was blown apart, destroying the counter, the awning and the chairs and tables. The second bomb destroyed one of the popular stalls in the market. Ten people were killed and dozens were injured. Four of the dead were Americans who worked for another security company. Only three days earlier I had been drinking tea in there with friends. It could so easily have been us.

While we were settled into a routine, we were also getting into a rut. Briefings followed breakfast and then the teams were on the road while we dealt with the correspondence and phone calls in the office. Contracts had to be won, team leaders needed advice, and logistics had to be organized. We were trying to keep everyone happy; our clients, the military, the Iraqi authorities and, of course, our lads.

To put it bluntly, Baghdad was a depressing place. Every day I read dozens of reports about car bombs, gun attacks, IEDs and casualties in a continual stream of doom and gloom. Although emails kept you up to date, the volume spiralled out of control until they became a nuisance. The guys were seeing events every day on the streets, and they did not need reminding how bad things were. We sifted through the mountains of information looking for new developments but our nightly Prayers were becoming monotonous; a case of 'Same Shit – Different Day'.

It was a non-stop grind for everyone, myself included, and the monotony was getting on everybody's nerves. Tempers were becoming frayed and we needed a morale lift before the depression spiralled out of control. But following the bomb attack on the cafe, we had nowhere to hang out and relax. The guys needed somewhere to chill out and something to focus on. We decided that we needed a bar and when the idea was raised, everyone was in favour. So we set about planning how we would build one.

The plan was to build it on the roof of our annex where we had a gym. It was a secure area with easy access through the main part of the villa. Everyone was in favour so we gave the go ahead to start foraging for material. As if by magic, daily talk turned from the daily dangers to plans for the bar because the guys had something positive to focus on.

Scrounging began in earnest and before long useful items started to appear in the villa compound. A bit of bartering relieved a large quantity of plywood from the U.S. military and night after night, after finishing work, the guys were busy hammering and cutting it into shape. First off we made a counter with plenty of room for the stock and staff and then we topped it off with roof. More sheets of plywood were used to build a low wooden wall around the edge of the roof to stop revellers falling into the compound below.

Discussion then turned to how to equip the bar and furnish the terrace; the only answer was to scavenge and barter. Friendly rivalries developed as everyone started touring the Green Zone, exploring parks and empty buildings in search of something useful. All sorts of abandoned items were being studied to see if they had a use. I suppose some might look on our activities as looting but we believed we were giving items a new lease of life; we were liberating them.

It took several weeks to complete the bar, but the guys had something to take their minds off their work. The daily challenge was to find something useful for the bar, something that everyone could share and enjoy. What to look for next and where it might be found, became the topic of conversation on an evening rather than the latest incident on the streets. Everyone joined in and it went a long way to relieve the tension. Some of the lads took the project personally, devoting all their spare time to joinery and painting to make it look good, while others prided themselves in finding ornaments and pictures to decorate the area.

Eventually our roof top had a bar on one side and an open balcony covered with garden style tables and chairs on the other. Freezers had been acquired from bankrupt electrical shops, and after a bit of rewiring and cleaning they were up and running ready to be stocked. But while we had a bar in Baghdad, the capital of an alcohol free country, we needed lots of tins of beers and bottles of spirits to attract the punters. Fortunately we had an alcohol supply route across the country, and we had been smuggling stocks across the Kuwait border and ferrying them up to Baghdad since the early days. We also had lots of under the counter methods for obtaining drink because we used alcohol as a bargaining tool with the American military. While they had excessive stocks of the hardware and medical supplies we needed, they found it hard to obtain black market alcohol so we resorted to bribery. Soldiers being soldiers, they like the odd drink on the quiet and a regular supply of beer or spirits meant we could source items in Baghdad, rather than having to ship them in.

After a lot of hard work by everyone, the bar was ready and we were all ready to take our turns behind the bar. Opening hours were set at 10:00pm to 2:00am on Friday and Saturday night to limit the impact it had on our daily work. Nobody worked in Iraq on Fridays for religious reasons so we spent our time on administration. After a day of training and maintenance everyone was ready to party.

Invitations to the opening party were emailed and texted to everyone we knew. We also sent out a few to those we wanted to get to know, because we thought the bar might be a great way to meet influential people and we were right. Although we reckoned the roof top area would only hold 200 people, around 250 crammed into the small space on the opening night while another 200 were turned away. Anyone and everyone wanted to be there; contractors, clients, the American military, the press and medical staff. It seemed to us that the whole of the Green Zone had been looking for a safe place like our bar to hang out and relax; even if they did not realize it.

The bar was supposed to have been a small venture for our colleagues in the security business but it took off rapidly and its success surprised us all. The response was unbelievable and news spread like wildfire. As the emails asking for invites poured in, the phone and the radio was always busy with people checking if the bar was open on Fridays and Saturdays. The rules stated that no one was allowed to open a public bar in the Green Zone but ours was an invite only bar and somehow we managed to bypass the rules. The fact that many influential people became some of our best customers might have contributed to our continuing success; we never asked and we were never told. The fact that we ran a tight ship also helped.

We had a dedicated security force of Ghurkhas, ex soldiers from the British Army regiment, maintaining security around the villa. They kept our 'home from home' safe, allowing the security teams to rest when they were not on duty. The eight-man Ghurkha team rotated, four men at a time, around the clock. Two checked deliveries and visitors at the gate while the other two patrolled inside and outside the compound. We knew that it would have only taken one fanatic to walk in with a suicide vest and we would have been wiped out. The Ghurkhas allowed us to concentrate on our work during the day and sleep easy at night. We eventually employed 160 Ghurkhas on our compounds in a similar role and they were all hard working and loyal.

On a Friday and Saturday night customers started arriving, parking their cars on the road outside. Many of our customers were security contractors like us and they pulled up in the armoured cars they used to carry clients around. Many were bastardized vehicles bristling with armour plate, weapons and racks stacked with ammunition; some of them customized by our own mechanics. By opening time the line of vehicles outside the compound looked like something out of a Mad Max movie.

The Ghurkhas would check the invites and weapons of our guests. While military personnel and security contractors carried weapons wherever they went, we did not want problems which could arise if you mixed alcohol and guns in the bar. A small downstairs storeroom had been converted into a secure armoury and one of the Ghurkhas checked in weapons in return for chits, the same way as a nightclub cloakroom. Some locked their guns inside their vehicles but the few who refused to check in their weapons were politely turned away.

After climbing the stairs, visitors walked out onto the roof top bar and joined the party. We did not want our own guys getting drunk because it would reflect badly on the company. The rule had always been to sack anyone on the spot if they were drunk. So we stuck to the unpopular two drink rule and introduced a monthly drinks card. There was a box for each weekend night and the first drink was marked with a dash, a second dash the opposite way formed the sign of the cross and no more alcohol. Everyone else could drink what they liked, as long as they behaved themselves.

Before long the bar was the place to be on a weekend. It was somewhere safe where everyone could relax with friends, share experiences, swop stories and intelligence. It was a bit of normality in the middle of a crazy city. While there might be helicopter strikes going on across the river, mortar attacks in the distance and gun battles on the streets, no one took much notice when they were having a good time in the bar.

It was also a place to meet members of the opposite sex; well a mixture of men, women and alcohol, and relationships are bound to flourish. The ratio of men to women was about ten-to-one and competition for female attention was fierce. The dangerous environment increased testosterone levels to crazy heights and the bar was one of the few places men and women could chat in a relaxed atmosphere. Of course tempers sometimes frayed as the alcohol flowed and our guys were sometimes kept busy maintaining the peace.

As well as raising our profile in the Green Zone, the bar had many useful sidelines, some of them unexpected. We only accepted U.S. dollars and the steady flow of hard cash was useful for buying equipment and food. The bar also became a great place to keep up on the news in the city; it was our very own 'Word on the Street'.

Security contractors often settled down at a table and swopped stories of their close shaves over a few beers, exchanging information and tips on how to stay safe. Although the U.S. military banned their personnel from drinking, we had a lot of high ranking officers and even C.P.A. staff dropping by for a drink and a chat. They should not have been there but it was so tempting and I suppose they felt free to speak off the record. All we had to do was serve the drinks and take in what snippets of information we could. Of course it was a case of what was said in our bar stayed with us.

But at two o'clock in the morning the bar closed and the customers started to head home. They paid their bill, collected their weapons and jumped back in their vehicles; sometimes the worse for wear. Hopefully they had just had another good night in our bar.

Although we normally only opened on Friday and Saturday nights, we had a special party one night in March 2006 when some of our old friends dropped by. About 90 guys from the Regiment to be precise; all of them on a high after a successful rescue mission.

Professor Norman Kember was a British peace activist and he had travelled to Iraq on behalf of the Baptist Peace Fellowship and the Fellowship of Reconciliation, to demonstrate against the invasion of the country. He was working with Christian Peacemaker Teams across Baghdad and while his relief work helped Iraqis across the city, the trend for kidnapping and executing Westerners was increasing at a worrying pace. Despite warnings from the American military, the Peacemaker Teams continued their work and on 26 November 2005 Kember was taken hostage along with three other Western CPT peace workers; American Tom Fox and Canadians James Loney and Harmeet Singh Sooden, by a new group calling itself the Swords of Righteousness Brigade. The kidnapping was frontline headlines within hours.

On 5 December Kember's wife made an appeal on the Arab satellite television station, Al Jazeera. The kidnappers answered five days later, giving a deadline for all Iraqi prisoners to be released; an impossible request to carry out. Although they did not mention the four prisoners by name, they made it clear they would be executed. The days passed, vigils were held and the deadline passed. But the first news came seven weeks later when the kidnappers' final demand was aired. A new tape featuring Kember was aired on Al Jazeera on 7 March but hopes were dashed three days later when Tom Fox's body was found.

No one except the military forces on the ground knows what really happened next but on 23 March multi-national forces swept the area where the remaining hostages were held. British Special Forces led the combat teams through the maze of streets and as they approached the building where the other hostages were being held, the captors fled. No shots were fired, no-one was injured and the hostages were released.

However, the story was far from over. Once Kember was back at home in the United Kingdom, many thought his written statement and video appearance were vague about his rescuers. Senior military officers went as far as to give press statements referring to the lack of gratitude shown towards the soldiers who had risked their lives to rescue the hostages. Some even stated that individuals who made efforts to help Iraqi citizens were a liability, especially when they ignored advice from the security services and the British government. Kember's refusal to testify against the suspected kidnappers when they were captured by Iraqi government troops over six months later did nothing to heal the rift.

Some of the Special Forces commanders were good mates of ours and they asked if they could celebrate in our bar. We said of course and the lads gave up their beds for the night so everyone had somewhere to crash out. We were pleased to open up the bar for them because we knew full well they would be more than ready to party after weeks out in the field; and our place was ideal.

And party hard they did – they 'caned it' all night long and a few were still at it when we were getting ready for work in the morning. We caught up with a lot of old friends that night and it was good to see them relaxing and enjoying themselves after a long and hard operation.

Over time our bar got itself a name across the Green Zone as a place to hang out. After the madness of driving through Baghdad's streets, being shot at, mortared and generally permanently stressed, it was a place to relax. Having said that it was always a surreal experience to be stood in the bar talking about normal things over a drink with your friends after yet another mad week in Baghdad.

Chapter Fifteen

Raising the Stakes

MOSUL FELL 11 APRIL 2003 when the Iraqi Army's V Corps abandoned the city, allowing Kurdish fighters to move in. The new arrivals did not have the means to control the city and looting became widespread as the citizens took advantage of the chaos. The arrival of the U.S. Army's 101st Airborne Division in the area soon restored order. The city next hit the headlines in July 2003 when Saddam Hussein's brothers, Uday and Qusay (the Ace of Hearts and Ace of Clubs in the U.S. military's most wanted playing cards) were killed during an attempt to capture them.

The 1.7 million inhabitants of Mosul soon became accustomed to seeing troops patrolling the streets, while U.S. Civil Affairs units began working to restore the infrastructure. Roads and bridges had to be repaired, water supplies had to be restored, and rubbish had to be removed to reduce the spread of disease. The city also needed electricity so it that it could function.

The insurgents also knew how important the work on infrastructure was and in March 2004 a visit to the town of Dohuk, north of Mosul, by the Public Works Minister had not gone unnoticed. Nisreen Mustafa al-Burwari was a member of a U.S. appointed Governing Council and she was high on the insurgents' hit list. Her convoy was ambushed as it drove back through Mosul's Karama district, on the east bank of River Tigris. Four guards were killed in the crossfire but their colleagues managed to get the Minister to safety.

Our client had a contract to restore the electricity in Mosul and we had to organize the security. The area was considered to be safe compared with Baghdad because the military presence and Kurdish influence restricted unlawful activities. The electricity station we had to visit was situated in a busy area on the east bank of the Tigris. While the compound was surrounded by commercial buildings, a high concrete wall stopped anyone shooting at the generators. It was also doubtful that insurgents would be able to find somewhere to set up mortars in the narrow streets.

The first thing we had to do was set up a safe area to live inside the compound. Then our team could train locally employed guards to patrol the perimeter, so our guys could concentrate on protecting the engineers. Our team had taken our client on several assessment visits and, apart from the occasional guy taking a pot shot, it had not experienced any problems. Compared to the work in Baghdad, Mosul promised to be straight forward.

Life at the camp would soon settle into a steady routine and the scheduled trips back and forth would slot easily into a regular pattern of deliveries and personnel changes.

It was always important to regularly join the teams on site to check the routes, the camps and the routines at first hand. A mental picture of a situation is never the same as the actual situation and site visits allowed us to make informed assessments of potential requirements and problems. It was important to show our face on a regular basis so we could judge the guys' morale and address any issues face-to-face. It also showed the client that we were a proactive company.

So far I had not been to Mosul because the long journey involved an overnight stay, taking me away from my office in Baghdad for two days, leaving my partner with two shifts to cover. Going out of Baghdad also limited my mobile phone coverage, cutting me off from the office. I dreaded returning to the inevitable backlog of paperwork and emails.

Two new guys were due to go to Mosul and we wanted to see how they fared on their first run into bandit country. The five hour journey involved a long drive north through the Sunni Triangle, passing Tikrit and Bayji, before driving the final stretch to Mosul. Then we switched on as we entered the sprawling suburbs of the city and drove across the huge arched bridge over the Tigris. The electricity compound we were using as a base was close by but it was not easy to get to.

Our reconnaissance team had located three routes but each one had its problems. The first route took us past Al-Tawba mountain and the huge mosque where the prophet Nebi-Yunis (also known as Jonah, who was famous for being swallowed by a whale) was buried, the second route would have given us the chance to see Saddam's Big Mosque with its many domes. Both routes went through built up areas where traffic jams were likely so we were sticking to the fast moving three lane highway which skirted the ruins of the ancient Assyrian city of Ninevah, one of the oldest cities in the world dating back over 5,000 years. But we were not interested in Iraq's history, we were interested in getting to the power plant safely.

After leaving the motorway, we headed south on the home run; all we had to do was cross one more intersection and the compound was in sight. The final approach along a dual carriageway ran parallel to the camp wall and then we had to drive 200 metres past the camp to a set of traffic lights. The final U-turn into the gate took some doing and while the road junction was a dangerous choke point, it was the only way to get into the camp. While we did not think the place was under surveillance, teams arrived at random times in case anyone was watching the gates.

So after an uneventful journey, it was heads up as we drove the final stretch up the traffic lights. We put a call into the camp so the Iraqi guards could open the huge steel sliding gates and take up positions on the walls above. Although the concrete wall around the camp was three-metres high, steps and platforms allowed them to give covering fire if necessary. If it all went to plan we could drive straight into the compound as the door shut behind us.

Our driving became defensive as we approached the traffic lights, looking to time our move just right. The manoeuvre involved car one making a tight U-turn while the lights were red, heading straight for the gate. Car two would drive defensively on the outside of the turn stopping traffic getting in the way; it then followed car one into the camp. Even by Iraq standards it was a crazy manoeuvre and the two drivers had to keep both cars moving together.

But this time the traffic was a nightmare and we could not move slowly through the junction as planned; we would have to wait in the traffic. We kept our eyes peeled, and while the drivers concentrated on the cars in front, we (the passengers) focused on the buildings overlooking the intersection. Nudging forward, there was nothing we could do except sweat it out.

As luck would have it, our car ended up at the front of the queue with the second car close behind. But as we came to a stop, we noticed half a dozen flashes straight ahead and heard thuds on the car bodywork. For what seemed like ages (but was actually only a fraction of a second) we sat there thinking what is going on? There were rounds coming in; we were in the middle of an ambush.

You are rarely looking straight at your enemy when they open fire at close range. Usually you hear the crack of gun fire, hit the dirt and then look for them. The situation threw us, but only for a moment. We had half a dozen or more automatic weapons firing at us and had to get into the compound fast.

The driver took evasive action in response to the call over the radio; "Contact front... Drive... Drive... Drive". As he hit the gas and spun the wheel, the car lurched forward in a tight circle. Calls were made on the direction of the firing and instructions barked out on how to escape the situation. We had no idea who or what we were facing and could not afford to get caught in a prolonged gun battle, we needed to get our client into the compound as quickly as possible.

So far so good, no one was hurt and the team were only moments from safety. Or so we thought because the gate was closing. The Iraqi guards had heard the gunfire and they were only concerned about their own safety. The gun fire caused chaos and there were cars everywhere, blocking all our escape routes so I took the decision to ram the gates.

We were in a real predicament. We were being shot at and could not return fire. Cars were randomly screeching to a halt and driving off as drivers panicked. The client was hugging the floor of the car while the radio was busy with calls. Total mayhem.

More insurgents appeared around the crossroads and we were being hit by a hail of bullets. As we drove close to the closed gate, we could see guards peering over the top of the wall but they were not returning fire. They were not opening the gate either, leaving us to the mercy of the gun men. The driver responded to the instruction "ram the gate", in the hope that we could smash through the gate, into the compound. We braced ourselves for the impact and the car slammed into the gate with a sickening crunch of metal and breaking glass. We nearly head butted the windscreen while the client rolled uncomfortably around on the floor behind; our plan had failed. The gates were the sliding type and the runners at the top and the bottom held it shut. It would have taken a tank to get through. The door was still intact and we were sitting ducks in a badly damaged car. I had to open it so the driver could drive inside.

As I clambered out of the car, we both looked back at the horror unfolding a short distance away. Car two was still on the far side of the road, smashed into the low concrete wall which formed the central reservation. The driver was dead, slumped at the wheel. The rear door of the car was open but our Tail End Charlie was nowhere to be seen.

As we absorbed the chaos going on around us, we could see about ten men walking towards the stricken car across the road, pumping bullets into it, shattering the glass and turning the bodywork into a colander. There was nothing we could do to save our two men. The insurgents would soon be turning their guns on us.

The steel gates into the compound were jammed firmly shut, even more so now thanks to our attempt at ram-raiding. But I could get through the pedestrian side door, hoping the guards had forgotten to lock it. Grabbing the handle and shoving hard against the steel it swung open.

Inside the Iraqi guards were in a state of chaos. Some were arguing in the courtyard while others were up on the walls, shouting out a running commentary of the events while they ducked the bullets. The only thing they were not doing was putting down covering fire. There was no point asking for help, they would have probably objected to opening the gate. Instead I freed the locking bolt and pulled the gate open while the guards shouted to stop.

As the gate slid open the driver nudged the damaged car into the compound as bullets sparked off the steel doors. Once inside he helped close the gate and manhandled the client to a safe place at the foot of the wall while he parked in front of the gate to stop anyone else trying to ram through. We were safe for now – or were we? There were only two of us willing to fight while twenty or more insurgents were gathering on the far side of the wall. Surely they would try and finish us off?

Running up the steps onto the parapet, we peered over the top of the wall to see what was happening outside. Shouts, gun fire and car horns filled the air and while some drivers tried to extricate their cars from the chaos, others milled around waiting to see what happened next. What had started as an ambush by a small number of insurgents was quickly turning into a general public protest as the crowd bayed for our blood. All we could do was to wait for the bad guys' next move.

The main group gathered near the foot of the wall, shouting and jeering at us. While some fired into the air, a few fired badly aimed shots at us. While they had little chance of hitting us, they were trying to provoke us into returning fire. We only had half a dozen magazines each, enough ammunition for three minutes of sustained fire; then we were out of ammunition. Although there was a stash of magazines in the car, it would have been unwise to run down and get them. The Iraqi guards were not going to fetch them either. They were wishing they were somewhere else; we felt the same.

Across the street where another group had gathered round our wrecked car we could see what had happened to car two. After the driver was killed, the car crashed into the central reservation. Our Tail End Charlie had climbed out to return fire, drawing the insurgents' attention from us. But he had taken aimed shots at the insurgents rather than taking cover behind the wrecked car. His magazine only had thirty bullets and the moment it was empty, he was a dead man. He had forfeited his life saving ours.

As much as we wanted to exact our revenge, there was nothing we could do for our two mates out in the road; we had to protect the client. We had to sit it out and save our ammunition. As the mob pushed forward hoping to see a macabre spectacle the ring leaders drove them into a frenzy with their jeers and shots. They knew we were heavily outnumbered and were goading us into wasting our ammunition.

While our blood boiled with hatred, all we could do was stare them out with our fingers on the triggers. Happy with the result, the ringleaders withdrew from the foot of the wall and melted away as the crowds went mad, chanting, cheering and blowing their car horns. As the full horror of the situation sunk in, the driver kept a watch on the street while the call was put out to our Baghdad office on the satellite phone. There was nothing they could do, they were four hours away. We were on our own and the only consolation was we were in a secure compound. All we could do was wait and hope we could get the Iraqi guards to bring our ammunition up to us. Then we could keep the bad guys away from the gate. The situation was turning into our own personal Alamo and neither of us felt like being John Wayne. Whichever way you looked at it; we were facing a long and difficult afternoon.

While the insurgents had disappeared, we doubted they had finished with us. They had either gone for ammunition or to inform their friends. The crowds were still milling about, discussing the afternoon's events with lots of arm waving and loud chatter, but the general mayhem had died down. Eventually we managed to get some of the Iraqi guards to man the top of the walls, allowing us to collect ammunition and water from the car and check on the client.

As we discussed plans around the car, shouts from the Iraqi guards on top of the wall warned us that something was happening outside the compound. Surely the insurgents had not returned already, we thought? After a quick glance at each other and the client, we grabbed an armful of magazines and headed back up the wall, to see what was happening. As we climbed the steps it became clear that the guards were shouting the word "Americans, Americans" over and over again. Peering over the parapet, we could see that the cars were leaving and the crowd was dispersing. It did not take us long to work out what was happening.

Looking north we could see a long line of military vehicles stretching into the distance. A large U.S. military convoy was driving slowly towards us and for once we were overjoyed to see them. We had to stop them and see if we could hitch a lift to safety. In a flash we were down the steps, out of the pedestrian gate and in the middle of the road waving our arms. As the lead Humvee rolled to a standstill, we could see the crew were puzzled. Behind a queue of around forty Humvees, lorries and low loaders carrying battle tanks, came to a halt.

As I explained our predicament to the officer in the lead Humvee, soldiers were debussing all along the road, forming a defensive perimeter around their vehicles. While tanks are a formidable adversary in battle, they are sitting ducks when they are sat on the back of a lorry. The convoy commander asked what the hell was going on in his forceful military manner when he joined the conversation. He had a schedule to keep and we had stopped his convoy in the middle of a potentially dangerous built up area.

To make matters worse, several press teams operating in the city had picked up news of our contact by listening into the military net. They were soon hovering around, shouting out questions while taking photographs of the bodies and the damaged vehicles for their next scoop. There were also hundreds of Iraqis, many of them stuck in the traffic, straining to see what had happened.

The place was turning into a circus, we were in the middle of it and it was time to clear it up. While soldiers covered the ambush site, we carried our mates' bodies inside the compound out of sight of the gawping crowds. A Humvee towed our wrecked car off the road, parking it alongside the other inside the compound. I would have to invent a story for the hire car company because they thought we were on a sightseeing tour of Kuwait, not driving around war torn Iraq. The problem was not at the top of my list of priorities. We had to get ourselves and our client back to the safety of the Green Zone, 250 miles to the south.

The military commander made it very clear that he wanted his convoy moving before the insurgents returned. The commander then told us the area was too dangerous to call in a helicopter to take us to safety. After a brief conversation we were told to join the convoy in our battered hire car. We had no other choice. So as the convoy mounted up and drivers revved their engines, we climbed into our car and drove out of the compound, slotting ourselves in between a Humvee and a low loader. As we moved off, we knew we were in for the longest journey of our lives.

The convoy could not drive faster than 20mph and they had to stick to the main routes. As stated earlier, they were a prime target for the bad guys and easy to hit. Anyone could dick them and call up ahead on their phone, giving their mates time to set an ambush. But while everyone else was tucked up inside an armoured cab or sat behind a 50 calibre machine gun, we were stuck in our beaten up Pajero with only our AK47s and pistols to protect us.

Despite the risks, we had no other choice, particularly as our car could break down at any moment. With dusk approaching, we were in no position to drive off alone, even if the convoy commander might have liked us to. We just had to take our chances and sit it out. The only consolation was that we were surrounded by a lot of weaponry.

The long journey south was endless, crawling along behind a Humvee, with the sight of a huge truck in the mirrors. As the sun disappeared behind the horizon and the shadows lengthened, we said little to each other in the front of the car, while our client in the back was still in shock. All we could do was to endure the monotony and watch the horizon for threats. All three of us had too much time to think about what had happened and contemplate what might have happened. We had stared certain death in the face and only luck had saved us; but it had not saved our two friends.

As we drew closer to Baghdad, my phone started to ring continuously. The press had been bombarding our office for information and a small story had already appeared in the media. Phone calls asking for details of the deceased were being made and we still had to deliver them to the mortuary. In this world of 24/7 news, incidents like ours were just what the media wanted to hear about. One press team excelled themselves in getting their story to London and pictures of our bullet riddled car appeared in the papers the following morning.

Our guys in the Green Zone and the outlying compounds were learning about the incident on the television, rather than from the company, and it was bad for morale. Everyone wanted to know who had died and while mobile phones are great for keeping in touch, they were a nuisance at a time like this. Call after call was being made to my phone and while I wanted to keep everyone informed, I had to make the necessary arrangements first, without interference.

We cut away from the convoy on the outskirts of Baghdad and were relieved to re-enter the Green Zone. The U.S. military let us place the bodies in their mortuary and then it was back to the villa. Then there was a list of questions to be answered by the employer, the military, the press, the hire car company and everyone in the company. I also had to make arrangements with our London office so that we could arrange for the repatriation of the bodies and inform their next of kin.

It was time to prioritize. The employer had to be informed first and they were shocked by the incident because they had been led to believe Iraq was safe. While the rise in insurgent activity had been reported in the media, the intensity of it had been played down between Baghdad and Washington D.C. After all, four ministries with members on the U.S. appointed Governing Council were about to be handed back to Iraq control.

One of the reasons we had been successful during the early days in Iraq was our ability to blend in with our soft-skinned vehicles. Armoured SUVs cost a lot more and no one had wanted to consider using them when we went into business. Contracts for new security companies insisted on armoured vehicles and contracts had been priced accordingly. But the fact that the huge SUVs stuck out like a sore thumb on the streets of Baghdad did not appeal to our covert mentality.

There were arguments in the telephone conversations and emails that followed but nobody could turn back the clock. We had escorted a senior employee to Mosul and he fully backed how we had dealt with the situation. He had nothing but praise for the way we had protected him, the two guys who had lost their lives during the ambush and the way he was extracted to safety. But it was time for all of us to reassess how we conducted business in Iraq. We either had to reassess it or get out because the stakes were getting too high.

While we were notifying the next of kin and organizing the repatriation, the press were calling for details. Despite many guys serving over twenty years' service in the Army there was going to be no hero's welcome through the streets for our guys. We were there for the money; it was as simple as that. Not many people had any sympathy for us in that respect and I cannot say I blame them.

In this job, like any, you have to continually assess how you conduct your business and how your competitors are doing. Only in the world of security, the competitors have guns and explosives and they are intent on killing you. It was clear during the Mosul attack that the insurgents had targeted our driver and on reflection, it made sense. Our usual response to an ambush was to drive aggressively away rather than engage the gun men. We only returned fire if the car stopped. In Mosul the gunmen aimed to injure or kill the driver, making the vehicle go out of control and crash. They could then move in to finish off the passenger. That is exactly what they had done to us in Mosul.

As usual, we wrote up an account of the incident and circulated our conclusions to the rest of the security companies working in Iraq. It was then time to look for a solution to the problem. We needed to find a way of being able to control the speed and direction of the car if the driver was put out of action. So we devised a dead man's system to allow the passengers to take over the controls. The driver's seat was rigged to collapse backwards into the foot-well so either the front seat or the back seat passenger could lean across the injured driver and grab the wheel with one hand. His other hand pulled on a cord attached to the accelerator to control the speed; gears were automatic. As long as the car did not stall, the passengers could keep the car moving and with a bit of practice and a bit of luck, steer themselves out of trouble. It took less than an hour and a few dollars to rig each car. It was then time to practise the drill over and over again. We also circulated our invention to the other security companies.

The attack changed how we conducted business for the rest of our stay in Iraq. Although we did not know it at the time, it would also change our futures. Our client recognized that he could have easily lost his life on the streets of Mosul and while he promised to try and repay us we could not see how. Maybe he would, but for now it was back to business.

Two months later the attack merited a mention by Brigadier General Mark Kimmitt, Deputy Director for Coalition Operations, during his daily security briefing. He reported that coalition forces had conducted a cordon and search operation in the northwest suburbs of Mosul, and taken Mohammed and Marwan Sabri Salih captive. The two brothers were suspected of organizing the ambush which killed our two guys. We were sure there were many more ready to take their place.

Chapter Sixteen

Getting Tougher

AFTER THE MOSUL ATTACK the client sat up and took notice of the risks we were taking. They could not afford to lose one of their members of staff and the rules suddenly changed. The new insurance policy meant we were not allowed to use soft-skinned hire cars anymore and instead we had to move the clients around in armoured vehicles. This caused the company a number of big headaches.

We were faced with the problem of acquiring nearly 70 armoured vehicles and each one cost a huge amount of money new while second hand ones were a small fortune. We were a small company which had been trading only a little over a year and we were working in a risky business. There was no way we could get credit to purchase them and we definitely did not have the cash to buy them outright. Pure and simple, if we could not source armoured cars we had no income, so it looked like our business was dead in the water.

We had no option but to come clean with our client and explain the situation to them, making it clear we would have to part company unless they had any ideas. Well they say you never know until you ask and as it turned out they did have a plan to help us. They were more than happy with our work so far and they did not want to get rid of us. Their order book was booming, problems across the country were increasing and now was not a good time to change security companies.

The client offered to acquire armoured vehicles, either by sourcing them from their other contracts or by buying new or second hand ones. We would then use them on a lease to buy contract. And there we had it, our get out of jail free card. We still had a business.

Our client had already sourced a lot of armoured cars across the Middle East and they started moving them to Kuwait where we had to pick them up. This left us facing a huge logistical nightmare. We had 69 soft-skinned cars to round up from all over Iraq; it would have been 70 cars but one was riddled with bullet holes in Mosel and it would never move again. We had to return each one to the car hire company in Kuwait City and the guys had to travel in four man teams or more for safety. It was not going to be easy and it was going to be difficult to limit the impact on business.

The hire car company was disappointed to hear that we were returning all their cars. They had guessed we were using them in Iraq and when they saw their smashed car up in Mosul on the television news, it confirmed their suspicions. They did not want to lose the income and they offered a deal to continue hiring them on condition that we paid for any we destroyed or damaged. However, it was not to be and they faced losing a lot of money. And they were not the only ones. While the client reduced the contracts around Basra and stopped work around Baghdad for three weeks to help us move the cars, we had no money coming in.

Our only saving grace was that many of the cars were in the Basra area where the handover trip only took about three hours. Our Shaibah office started moving six cars a day to the border and within a week all the Basra cars had been exchanged. But we still had more than twenty scattered around in the Baghdad and Al Nasiriyah sites and the clock was ticking. So guys going on leave were used to make the long drive from Baghdad to Kuwait.

As the nightmare came to an end, our final problem was how to move three Pajeros from Al Quds power station, northwest of Baghdad. The hire period was nearly up and the hire car company kept asking if we wanted to extend it. We did not want to but there was so much to do that the hire period expired before we could send the cars south. We were facing a fine if they were not returned immediately and being a tight Yorkshire man I did not want to hand over any more money. So I came up with a plan. We would return the cars first thing in the morning.

First off I needed a driver and a co driver for each car. I was going as it was my idea but my driver was far from pleased when he heard my plan. I just needed another four volunteers to take the other two cars. I must say all sixty guys were consistent when I asked; not one of them wanted to do it. Fair enough, so I did the only thing I could, I offered them an incentive, or rather I bribed them. I offered a week's leave in Kuwait where they could chill out and spend time briefing newcomers arriving at our base camp. Eventually four took the bait and reluctantly volunteered.

The three cars reached the villa late in the afternoon where the plan was to stay overnight and head off at first light. Unfortunately, all the beds were taken and the lads were unhappy about sleeping on the floor. So I suggested cutting loose and heading for Camp Striker, a huge U.S. military base southeast of the city where there were always spare camp beds. We could grab some breakfast the following morning and head south early, avoiding Baghdad's morning rush hour.

It was a plan and after briefing the operations room, we headed off as the sun began to set, reaching Camp Striker as the skies darkened. As the guys looked forward to a night's sleep, I took a look at the dormitory area and found it full to the brim with young GIs preparing for an operation. While we could have found a corner to get our heads down in, the chances of getting any sleep in that noisy hangar were minimal. All eyes were on me and I could tell that they were unhappy. Maybe this was not such a good idea after all.

Time for another change of plan and while the guys called me a few choice names, I phoned our Shaibah office. If we could get down to them by the early hours of the morning, we could get a few hours' kip on their spare beds before setting off early for the border. If everything went to plan we would be in the swimming pool outside our Kuwait apartment before lunch time. At least that is how I sold the plan to the guys.

By now it was dark and we should not have been moving outside the controlled zones. The Americans never went outside their camps during the night unless they were forced to; they considered it far too dangerous. The guys were far from optimistic. They were prepared to do a lot of things but they believed that driving at night was just a step too far. I reasoned that the insurgents were not expecting anyone moving at night and would be too busy preparing ambushes and IEDs for the morning to worry about us.

Our journey was a straight run of 300 miles down Route Tampa and it was motorway all the way; except for the dirt road stretch south of Al Nasiriyah. We could drive at high speed because there would be no traffic on the road. I reasoned "what could go wrong?" "A lot of things could"; was the answer. The reason there was no traffic was because it was too damn dangerous.

It could have been the thought of an extra day's holiday that convinced them, or maybe it was the thought they might get a few hours' sleep down in Shaibah. Whichever it was they agreed to go for it and after eating and fuelling the cars up off we went.

Security stopped us at the main gate and looked shocked when we told them where we were going but while they advised us to wait until morning, we were on our way. The lights from the camp soon dimmed in our rear view mirrors until the sky was totally black. As soon as we joined the three lane Route Tampa, we turned out our lights because we wanted to do as little as possible to draw attention to ourselves.

As our eyes became accustomed to the darkness, all three drivers manoeuvred into the middle lane, spaced out and then hit the accelerators until we were travelling at 80 mph. At this rate we would get to Shaibah a couple of hours after midnight, leaving time for about four hours' sleep. As we settled down for the long drive the moonlight cast an eerie glow across the desert and the only bright light was the Sat Nav blinking away on our dashboard. As expected the motorway was deserted apart from the occasional Iraqi driving home after a hard day's work. While we settled down for the surreal journey, everything was looking good.

I had noted four Iraqi checkpoints along our route and they were easy to locate. The guards always set them up under overpasses, so they had shade in the day and overhead cover at night. As my car approached the first one, we all slowed down not knowing what their reaction would be. After flashing the lights to get their attention, my driver edged forward slowly and waved our

ID as we drew alongside the checkpoint. The armed guards looked shocked but they did not force us to stop and one by one we rolled through, speeding up once we were clear.

As we approached Ad Diwaniyah, I was pleased to note that we had covered a third of our journey without any problems. The map indicated that we had to drive under several bridges as we passed the town and I gave the warning over the radio to keep a look out because they were great places for ambushes. The bad guys often waited on the bridge and after detonating IEDs at road level they fired onto the damaged cars below. They then drove off into the town to hide. Night time was the only time that the insurgents could prepare their IEDs undisturbed and they would have look outs watching for traffic. The last thing we wanted to do was drive blindly into an ambush team, so it was time to be alert.

We did not have to wait long. The map said the first bridge was approaching but a much darker silhouette was looming out of the darkness. While I was puzzled, it would not be the first time the GPS had been wrong. I could see the gap under the bridge was getting darker and darker; in fact too dark. Although there should have been a shadow, we should have seen the outline of the bridge deck and the abutments by now. The whole situation did not look right, but we could not work out why.

As we strained to see signs of movement I called over the radio "Slow down… Slow down" until we stopped. As the rest of the guys set up a perimeter around the cars, I edged forward to investigate the dark mass stretched across the road. With my nerves on edge and my eyes straining, my pounding heart seemed to echo through the still night. But it was the only noise I could hear as I walked closer.

As I become accustomed to the darkness, I could make out the outline of an articulated lorry parked across all three lanes of the motorway. Well that was that mystery solved. If we had not slowed down, our car would have slammed into the lorry at 80 miles an hour, at best leaving us injured and stranded in Iraq in the middle of the night. As I counted my blessings, I did consider the next problem; were the guys who had left it there still about?

Strange things often happened in Iraq and two ideas immediately came to mind. The lorry might have been hi-jacked and the robbers had forced the driver to stop across the road. After robbing the trailer, they had headed off before the police or the military turned out to investigate. That was the best situation for us.

More likely however, was that insurgents had stolen the lorry and parked it on the motorway to form a roadblock, no doubt booby trapping it before they left. They would then wait for the dawn patrol to appear, knowing full well that it would have to deal with the traffic jams until the recovery team turned up. They would then ambush the patrol and cause a few casualties before they drove off.

Edging forward, my driver and I investigated the area around the lorry, checking for signs of movement, while the rest of the guys watched our backs. They were tense moments in the dark, still night, but we could see nothing and it was time to get the hell out of there. We made as wide a detour as possible around the lorry, driving along the verge to get past, and then it was back up to speed and on our way again.

The next town along the route was An Nasiriyah another 100 miles to the southeast, in the heart of territory controlled by the Italian military. Normally the area was quiet compared to Baghdad but there were enough attacks to keep the Italian soldiers on their toes. Only six months earlier insurgents had fired on the check point outside the Italian military police headquarters, scattering the guards. In the confusion that followed, the road block had been dragged aside, and a suicide bomber drove a tanker truck rigged with explosives up to the three storey building. The explosion demolished the facade, killing at least 28 and injuring over 100. The Italian Army suffered 17 killed and 19 injured on 12 November 2003; its greatest losses since World War II. Two Italian civilians were also killed in the blast.

The motorway crossed the Euphrates River just before An Nasiriyah but the bridge had been destroyed during the war. A pontoon bridge now spanned the abutments and guards were posted to check traffic heading into town. The map and the GPS were spot on, on this occasion and as I came on the radio, we all slowed down to a stop some distance from the checkpoint.

Stepping out of the car, I walked towards the bridge on foot, straining to see the roadblock. A shout in Arabic and English of "Halt who goes there", stopped me in my tracks. I felt as if I was in a scene from Dad's Army... I shouted back "a British security team" and a torch flashed into my face, half blinding me. So far so good I thought as the guard gave me an order to switch on the cars' side lights so he could see where we were. The dim pool of light revealed what we were facing; dozens of armed guards with their weapons pointing straight at us.

The Italian guards had heard our cars approaching and, thinking they were about to be attacked, they had alerted the entire garrison checkpoint. There was no way they were going to let a suicide bomber drive straight into their roadblock and they were bracing themselves to shoot at us. Understandable behaviour under the circumstances but for a second time we were breathing a big sigh of relief. If we had driven for just a few seconds more our cars would have been riddled with bullets and maybe even a rocket or two.

Not surprisingly, the Italians had quite a few questions for us and as they listened carefully to our answers, I think they came to the conclusion that we were mad. They wanted us to stay until dawn, but after a prolonged discussion with my mate running the office in Shaibah Camp, they reluctantly let us continue on our journey.

As we drove away from the Italian checkpoint we reckoned we only had another 100 miles to go and by rights it should be the easy bit but none of us were ready to relax as the drivers hit the gas. South of An Nasiriyah is the section of road that Saddam refused to tarmac to keep the Shi'ites around Basra at bay. The sound of crunching gravel under the tyres meant it was time to slow down because now was definitely not the time to get a flat tyre.

Even though it was the dead of night, the horizon in front turned from a low dull orange glow to a bright yellow, a sign that we were entering the Basra oil and gas fields. You did not notice the flames leaping from the flare stacks, burning off surplus gas from the oil and gas fields, during the day but at night they lit the desert with a surreal light.

As we drove on the silence was suddenly broken by the crackle of the radio. "Can we stop, I cannot see where I am going" one of the drivers asked. His window had become encrusted in sludge thrown up off the road and his windscreen wipers could not clean it. Brilliant we thought aloud. Here we are in Iraq, in the dead of night and his bloody windscreen wipers do not work. Well there was nothing for it but to stop and take our chances. After all anyone creeping around at this time of night was going to be more surprised than we were.

One after another the three cars came to a halt, and out we got and formed a defensive perimeter, guns at the ready. There was no one around and while all the drivers checked their windscreens in turn, I gazed at the orange horizon and the flames leaping into the sky, casting an eerie glow across our cars. It was just like something out of a post-Apocalypse movie.

"It's funny isn't it", one of the guys called out, "we have the weapons, the sat navs, mobile phones, everything technology could give us, but here we are stuck because of a bloody faulty windscreen wiper". Well that just broke the tension and we were all giggling away like kids as we climbed back in the cars and headed off. The journey was nearly over and the mood relaxed. It was half enjoyable by now and the banter increased as we approached our destination.

We were again greeted by surprised faces at the entrance to Shaibah Camp, but the security guards had been warned of our arrival, so we were soon pulling up outside our office. And there he was, the office manager waiting for us with a big smile, a handshake and a mug of tea. We had made it. As we settled down and relaxed he told us how everyone had been listening into the radio net and watching our progress across the country. Some were even placing bets on whether we would make it or not. Charming I thought; we were always going to make it, weren't we?

There was not much time for banter and we soon got our heads down because we had to be up early. As dawn was breaking, it did not seem like two minutes since we had left Baghdad but we still had the last stretch to cover. We headed south across the border and we were soon pulling into the petrol station on the Kuwait side where we were reminded of the luxuries that lay ahead. After getting a coke from the vending machine and an ice cream from the shop, the guys sat there relaxing and chatting about what they were going to get up to during their holiday, while I called ahead to the Kuwait office to let them know we were nearly there.

Down at the car rental they were sad to see us go. We had been hiring cars off them for a year and the numbers had increased from half a dozen to seventy. That was a serious amount of money they were making out of us every month. Although one had been destroyed in Mosul and another four or five had been smashed in traffic accidents, we always paid for the damage or replacements. The rental firm had had a good deal and they knew it.

After the goodbyes it was time to pick up the armoured vehicles our client had arranged for us and then drive down to our apartment. In no time at all the guys had their swimming gear on and were diving into the pool. Of course I had to call the Baghdad office to let them know we had arrived safely and, oh yes, we were having a lovely time as they could tell from the laughter in the background. Again it was surreal to think that only a few hours earlier we had been facing all sorts of dangers as we drove across Iraq in the dead of night.

I let the lads enjoy their swim while I caught up with the operations guy in Kuwait. Although I spoke to him most days it was good to see him and we both took the time to iron out a few outstanding issues. You can only say so much on the phone or by email, so we were both grateful for the opportunity. That is when I found out there was an extra car and it had to be taken straight back to Baghdad. As I looked at the lads chilling out in the pool, I thought I could not go back on my promise. They deserved their holiday for volunteering. As drained as I was, I loaded up the vehicle and prepared to head back north to continue where I had left off.

The armoured cars we acquired were a mixture of purpose built Toyota Land Cruisers, GMCs, Ford Explorers and Pajeros. The cars were mighty beasts with a bullet proof chamber around the passenger compartment. They were built to order and came with a hefty price tag. For example the style of BMW we used cost $75,000 off the production line and another $100,000 to upgrade them. Even second hand armoured cars cost $100,000 each.

Once the doors were closed the passengers were sealed inside a safe compartment. The design principle was that the car absorbed small arms fire long enough for the driver to take evasive action and drive away from the scene. There was no point stopping and opening the doors to return fire because it broke the armoured seal. The compartment gave protection from bullets and shrapnel while the tough body frame would protect passengers if the car rolled over. It would also absorb some of the blast from an IED.

The Kevlar armoured plates in the doors and roof could also stop bullets while the anti-blast panels in the floor gave protection against mines. The windows had four inch (100mm) thick glass and they would stop a few bullets, shattering but not breaking from the impact. Armoured plates also protected the engine block and the fuel tank. Insurgents often shot out our tyres to try and make a car crash or stop but these beauties had run flat tyres. The bad guys would aim at your tyres, hoping to slow you down or lose control and these tyres were designed to remain intact for about three kilometres after they had been shredded by bullets; then they disintegrated. It was enough to get you away from the ambush and to a safe place where you could change the tyre.

One drawback was that these monsters weighed up to three tonnes each. While the armoured plates and bullet proof windows stopped bullets, they also stopped rapid manoeuvres. Acceleration and braking were slower while turning circles were bigger. So we had to allow our guys time to become accustomed to driving them out on the training ground.

If you thought we were safe against anything the insurgents could throw at us, you would be wrong. These cars stuck out like a sore thumb compared to the old hire cars and it did not take the bad guys long to work out that their bullets were not having the desired effect. They acquired heavier guns which could fire armour piercing rounds and they bought shaped charges and rocket propelled grenades to take us on. These weapons were designed to take out tanks, Humvees and armoured personnel carriers, so our armoured cars did not stand much of a chance against them. There was a good chance that they would disintegrate if they suffered a direct hit.

It was not the first time the insurgents had taken a step back when we changed how we conducted business. It did not take them long to change their tactics and their weapons in the ever increasing circle of violence that was becoming rife across Iraq.

The 4x4 armoured cars were not the only beasts we used on the road. One contract we took on involved escorting United Nations food convoys to rural areas. At the same time as helping the poor and starving they hoped to win the Hearts and Minds of the people still loyal to Saddam Hussein.

The convoys were long lines of lorries stacked high with food and they had to follow regular routes, driving at slow speed to their destination. The route we took on was the one to a guarded warehouse at Samarra, 120 kilometres north of Baghdad in the notorious Sunni Triangle. The food could then be distributed to the villages either side of the road to Tirkit, Saddam Hussein's area where he had been found hiding in a hole on 13 December 2003.

The convoys were easy targets and the bad guys knew there would be riots if they could stop them reaching their destination. In our infinite wisdom we decided to buy two armoured personnel carriers called Mambas from the South African army and had them shipped to Iraq. They were serious pieces of kit and cost $175,000 each but we expected them to make any insurgent think twice before taking them on.

The Mamba is an eight wheeled armoured vehicle which could carry 12 people. The armoured hull had firing ports along the side so the guys inside could engage their enemy while a machine gun position on top of the cab and a turret at the rear gave extra fire support. The body also had a V-shaped floor designed to deflect the blast of an explosion. They were serious machines designed for patrolling South African townships and we thought they would be perfect for protecting the food convoys.

We tried the Mambas out on Route Irish to begin with and they worked well because drivers quickly got out of your way, thinking they were military or police vehicles when they drove up behind with the horn blaring. We also painted them white so they looked like U.N. peace keeping vehicles or police vehicles on patrol. If anyone was stupid enough to open fire, the roof top PKM and GMPG machine guns could return fire over the traffic. It was usually enough to make the bad guys run for cover, after all there were far easier targets to engage. They could never penetrate our armour and they never stuck around long enough for us to hit them.

Before long it was time to escort our first convoy and the Mambas rendezvoused at the United Nations aid warehouse. The line of lorries was about a mile long and we planned to put one Mamba at the front manned by a British team. The other at the rear was manned by a South African team and it would stop any bad guys trying to overtake. Half a dozen two man teams in armoured cars would act as outriders, driving up and down the convoy to check on the lorry drivers. All together it was a big operation.

The first run went to plan and more followed and the escort team had soon settled into a routine. Although it was only 70 miles north along Route 1 to Samarra camp, the convoy took eight hours to make the journey. It then took all night to unload them with fork lifts. The following morning they came back down to Baghdad and our security teams rested while the lorries were loaded up again. As we were working for a charitable organization, the military had no obligation to protect the convoys and the aid company had to pay for its own security. Occasionally a few Humvees joined the convoy, but the military was usually overstretched and could not spare any resources.

All went well for three weeks and we were making good money but there was no doubt the insurgents had the convoy in their sights and were trying to work out how to stop it. You could shoot small arms all day at a Mamba and the bullets would just bounce off. You could fire RPGs or shaped charges at them but the sloping armour would deflect the missile. The same happened if you detonated an IED underneath one; the V-shaped armoured floor would protect the crew inside.

But the insurgents watched and waited until they had found the chink in the Mamba's armour. They had correctly assumed that the guy in the front passenger seat was the convoy's team leader and had decided to set a trap to take him out. They had calculated the height of the cab window and fixed a steel tube into the wall of a building at the same level. They loaded the tube with a shaped charge and stuffed a large lump of steel inside to act as the projectile.

As the convoy rumbled slowly past one afternoon, the bad guys detonated the charge, firing the lump of metal like a rocket at the Mamba's cab. It went straight through the six inch thick window, instantly killing the convoy leader. The explosion blew the top gunner out of the turret. He bounced off the side of the Mamba before landing in a heap on the road with shrapnel in his legs. The driver was also hit in the stomach by shrapnel but he managed to bring the huge vehicle to a halt safely covered in his mate's blood. He usually worked as a turret gunner but had been injured by an IED only a few days before. Although he should have been resting he kept asking for work, so I let him drive the Mamba; his persistency had nearly cost him his life.

The roar of the explosion and the squeal of brakes shocked everyone in the Mamba hull and they braced themselves for the small arms fire or RPGs that usually followed. This time there was none; just the noise of the running engines and the shouts for help from the driver and the gunner.

The guys in the back dismounted and checked on the state of the guys in the cab before moving along the queue of halted lorries, reassuring the drivers. They also put in a call over the radio to the office in Baghdad asking for help. We scrambled the Quick Reaction Force and within minutes they were heading north to give assistance. They would have to secure the convoy and escort it back to Baghdad, just in case the insurgents had set an ambush further along the road.

We also informed the U.S. military about the incident because a stationary food convoy in such dangerous territory was a major concern. They scrambled two helicopters and before long, American soldiers were helping set up a perimeter around the lorries while their medical personnel attended to our casualties. They also brought the injured men and team leader's body back to their medical facilities in the Green Zone.

The driver had the two pieces of shrapnel removed from his stomach and the hospital patched him up; he was back working with the convoy after only a week off. Despite his fall from the turret, the top gunner was off work only two weeks, spending his time resting in the villa. There was just no stopping them.

We then tried putting a South African team at the front and the back of the convoy on the assumption the insurgents did not speak Afrikaans. No one understood the language, neither us nor the insurgents, and it was good for security. The South Africans liked to work together because they had often served together in the army; they also had the same unusual sense of humour, the sort that only South African soldiers understand.

The convoys were back on the road and everything was back to normal, or so we thought. The insurgents had located three flood culverts under the road and decided to use them to knock out the other Mamba. They packed them solid with explosives, hard wired them and then sat back and waited for the convoy.

Within a week of the first incident there was a second. As the Mamba crawled over the culverts the insurgent flicked the switch, setting off a huge explosion. While the vehicle armour protected the men inside from the blast, the blast was so fierce that it flipped the Mamba onto its side, shredding the tyres. The battered and bruised men inside managed to crawl out and form a perimeter around the stricken vehicle. The turret man was lucky enough to jump clear as the Mamba toppled over but the two inside the drivers cab were trapped by their seatbelts.

It was dark when I got to the scene. This time we had not lost anyone and there were no life threatening injuries, however the vehicle was a write-off. We had lost $350,000 of vehicles in only four weeks. It just went to show how the insurgents adapted to our defensive tactics with new offensive tactics. It appeared that the heavier the armour, the greater the challenge was to stay alive.

Chapter Seventeen

Iraqi Roulette

YOU NEVER KNEW WHEN you might have a problem on Iraq's roads and the randomness of the violence would have freaked us out if we thought about it too much. At times we felt we were involved in a deadly game of Russian Roulette; Iraq style. But while no amount of SOPs or training would save you from getting into trouble, they sure as hell helped you get out of it... A few examples illustrate how being in the wrong place at the wrong time could end in disaster.

Crime had soared across Iraq since the invasion. A lack of a functioning police force and the lack of money meant many young men turned to crime to make a living. The huge amounts of weapons and ammunition lying around meant that armed crime was rife, including car-jacking and kidnapping. Everyone from organized war profiteers and black marketers down to out of work soldiers and random opportunists had realized that crime did pay.

Hi-jacking lorries was a popular pastime, particularly on Route 6, heading northwest out of Basra towards Baghdad. This area was the base of the Geramcha Gang, a group of around 600 displaced Marsh Arabs who were heavily involved in crime. One day my team was driving past a lorry while armed gunmen were dragging the driver out of the cab. They were clearly hi-jacking the vehicle but we had no authority to stop them and we might find ourselves in the middle of an investigation if anyone got shot.

The rules stated that we could only use force if somebody's life was in immediate danger and while the driver had a gun pointed at him as he was dragged from the lorry, he was more likely to get killed if we had stopped. In a lawless society like that we had to remember that we were not the upholders of the law; we had to stick to our objective and keep our clients safe.

So we drove past at speed, ignoring the situation. But the sight of our vehicles roaring past upset at least one of the gang because he took a few pot shots at us. There were a couple of loud bangs and the windscreen shattered, making us duck down in our seats. A quick look round confirmed no one had been hit but I wanted to stop. The drill was to find a bridge because it provided overhead cover while we checked the car for damage.

When a bridge appeared on the horizon, I told my driver to pull over but he did not acknowledge my instruction. I asked again while looking at him, but it was clear that he was not listening. He appeared to be in a trance, staring forward with a blank expression on his face. What have I done to upset him I thought as I yelled in his ear and shook his shoulder.

I called over the radio, "pull over in 100m... pull over in 50m... stop now..." and the cars rolled to a halt. But while three of us were out of our cars and watching our corners, my driver was still in his seat with his hands tightly gripping the steering wheel. As there were no immediate problems, I called for the guys to stay where they were while I had a word with him. After opening the door, I could see that he was frozen in his seat and still ignoring what I was saying. As he had no obvious injuries, I concluded that he was in shock. The question was why?

A quick check of the car located the two bullet holes in the boot and two exit holes in the front. Only then did we realize why the driver was in shock; the bullet which hit the windscreen had passed through the gap in his headrest. It had missed his neck by millimetres before smashing the windscreen. An inch to one side and he would have been paralyzed from the neck down; two inches and he would have been dead. He later told us that he had felt the burning sensation of the round going past his neck a fraction of a second before the windscreen shattered. No wonder he was in shock.

The guy had served over 20 years in the army but after only three weeks of working for us, he had seen enough and left the company soon afterwards. A close shave like that was enough to make anyone think twice about working in Iraq. It was all down to luck, nothing more and nothing less, but when you are that close to getting killed it must change your focus on life.

You never knew who was watching the streets when you drove through Baghdad. Although the dickers were often easy to spot, you never knew who they were talking to on their mobile phone. During one run through the city my team stopped at a large crossroads where the traffic lights were working for once. As we watched the long line of cars and vans moving through the junction, the driver's windscreen shattered and the interior of the car was splattered with blood. "Contact... contact..." I shouted over the radio, waiting for more shots to hit the car; but there were none. However, the single gunshot had caused panic on the street. While screaming pedestrians hid behind anything they could find, cars stopped with their horns blaring.

"Debus and check for targets..." was my next instruction because we needed to be ready to return fire if any more bad guys were heading in for the kill. But as the team took cover and checked everywhere for armed men; there were none. We had been the target of a one-shot sniper who had been watching the traffic lights from a hidden perch. He would be long gone by now, believing that he had killed one of the 'infidels'.

So it was time to check for injuries because someone had been hit and from the amount of blood all over the car it must have been a serious wound. It turned out the sniper had targeted our driver and the bullet had split his nose and when I say split, I mean split, because the wound started at his forehead and ended at his top lip. As our medic patched him up, I checked the car to see where the high-velocity bullet had left a hole in his side window. We reckoned that the sniper had been aiming at our driver's head and he had been spot on. However, the four inch thick glass had deflected the round so the bullet hit his nose. Again it was pure luck that he had been targeted and it was pure luck that he was still alive, although he faced months of surgery and a lifetime of disfigurement. I hate to think what would have happened if I had been leaning forward in my seat to check the traffic; I might have got the ricochet in the back of my head; who knows.

As often happened in Baghdad, the U.S. military came to investigate the traffic chaos and they were kind enough to evacuate our injured driver back to one of their hospitals. That left us having to drive back to the villa in the blood splattered car.

Another day my team was visiting Al Quds power station northwest of Baghdad. The route out of the city was a tricky one, through dense, urban suburbs and the insurgents had their pick of tall buildings and alleyways to hide in. The road was also a nightmare of choke points and check points, which often resulted in random traffic jams.

While the drive out to the power station passed off without incident, there was a huge traffic snarl up where we turned onto a dual carriageway on the return leg. Stationary vehicles were parked along the slip road so I took a snap decision to change the route home. After letting the guys in the second car know, both cars side-slipped the traffic jam and joined the dual carriageway at the next slip road only a couple of hundred metres further on.

Like all good drivers, mine looked over his shoulder to check it was safe to merge into the traffic. He gasped as he did and came out with a few choice words. So we all looked back and saw the reason for the traffic jam. Another security team was in the middle of a big fire fight at the end of the first slip road. The two cars were stationary and the four guys were returning fire, trying to protect their client. There were several car loads of insurgents giving them hell and it looked as though the security guys were having a tough time of it.

We all said "bloody hell, that could have been us if we had been a minute or two earlier", or words to that effect. As much as we felt sorry for the guys under fire, we were travelling at speed away from them amongst two lanes of busy traffic. The central reservation stopped us making a U-turn even if we wanted to while driving back through against the traffic flow was not what the client was paying us for. We just had to keep heading back to the Green Zone and hope they had help coming out to rescue them. That day it was not our turn, but it would be another day.

Another random incident occurred on Al Qudos power station. A lot of local labour was employed and they worked hard to help our clients, cooking and cleaning as well as unloading and moving equipment. Others built fences and checkpoints while they were trained to carry security duties. On the larger sites we employed locals to cook and clean in our compound.

Tankers regularly delivered the petrol needed to start the Al Qudos generators and we knew that they were controlled by the Wahabbi tribe; Osmana Bin Laden's tribe. We were also sure that the insurgents would be looking for an opportunity to get a bomb into the plant. Although our guys kept a close watch on all the deliveries, they kept a particularly close eye on the tanker drivers.

Every morning the labourers walked from their village and waited in line to be body searched at the plant gate. One morning I was in the office when the guy supervising the gate came on the radio. He had a big problem. A young lad who worked in our kitchen had let the security guards know that he was wearing a suicide vest; just what you do not want to hear at the start of the working day.

It later transpired that insurgents had found out that he worked in our camp kitchen and had forced him to become a suicide bomber. They visited his home one night and held his family hostage while they strapped explosives around his skinny torso. The deal was that if he detonated the bomb in our mess and killed a few Westerners, his family would be freed. They would also receive a substantial financial reward for their loss.

The lad knew that the guards would probably find the suicide vest and decided to confess in the hope that they would help him. As soon as I got the call I told the guards to push the kid away from the gate and then force him to walk to a safe distance. We did not know if he was looking to sucker us with his plea for help and then detonate the vest as our guys gathered around. You never knew what went through people's minds in these situations.

We needed to reinforce the gate and half a dozen of the guys were soon jumping into cars and driving down there to see what was happening. We found the kid was standing, bemused and frightened, about one hundred metres away from the gate. We all trained our guns on him in case he decided to run at us, but he was just standing there shaking. It took some time for him to understand that we wanted him to take the vest off. We did not know if it had been booby trapped to detonate if it was removed and we were not going to go over and find out. Everyone went silent and I could feel my heart was pumping as he slowly unbuckled the straps around his body. I winced as he pulled the vest over his head, expecting an explosion as he threw it on the floor, but nothing happened. Everyone then began shouting for the kid to come over but he ran the opposite way.

As I called the military and asked them to send a bomb team out to destroy the vest in a safe manner, the hunt for the kid was on. His friends kept calling but they never got a reply, leaving us wondering where he was hiding. We did not have to wait long before we found out. Around lunchtime a car stopped near to the gate and the kid was shoved out onto the road, dripping with petrol. What happened next left us chilled to the core... The bad guys set his clothes on fire and he screamed in agony as flames engulfed his body. The bad guys had made their point and they drove off.

There was a mad rush to get to the boy but a few Iraqis got there first. We could not believe it as they threw a muddy wool blanket over him and knocked him to the ground. The melting blanket stuck to his burning flesh as they rolled him around to put out the fire, adding to the kid's agony. Our two medics tried to push through the crowd to help him but the Iraqis would not let them. There was nothing we could do. Although our guys knew the best way to deal with the boy's injuries, we would have had to threaten the Iraqis with our weapons to get at him. The only thing we could do was to stand back and try to calm everyone down. It was heartbreaking to see the poor kid being thrown into the back of a car and driven away to the nearest hospital.

Although we hoped for the best, the kid died a few days later; he was only fifteen. His self sacrifice had saved us from being killed. We did try to contact the family but they were frightened of what might happen to them. After discussions with the local sheikh we eventually managed to get $500 to them as compensation. You will think that is a paltry sum for a son's life. We did too. But the sheikh warned us that the family would have been seen as collaborating with us Westerners if they took any more money. We were caught between a rock and a hard place. $500 for saving our lives, it was so wrong.

The final example of Russian Roulette involved a two car team moving supplies from Basra up to Baghdad. Although most of the four-hour drive was through open countryside, it was necessary to make a detour through the town of An Nasiriyah to cross the River Euphrates.

When the team stopped at a set of traffic lights, nothing looked untoward and the traffic was moving normally. The team leader and his driver had clocked a coach waiting at the red light and wondered how something so battered was still on the road; like many of the vehicles in Iraq.

As the lights changed to green, the lead car set off across the intersection... At the same moment, the coach lurched forward. It all happened so fast there was no time for evasive action. While everyone initially thought the driver had hit the accelerator by accident, it was no mistake; he kept going. The driver slammed into the lead car, rolling it on its side as the coach reared into the air.

After the shock and noise of the crash, everyone was stunned for a few moments. The coach driver had been catapulted through the windscreen and his lifeless body hung down over the engine grill. The second car pulled up alongside and the guys formed an all round defence, waiting for someone to spring an ambush. Only there were no bullets, just the blaring of horns as the traffic backed up.

The guys then checked on the team leader and his driver. While the driver was concussed and still strapped in his seat, the initial assessment was that his injuries were minor, considering the force of the impact. However, the team leader had been thrown half out of the car and his arm was trapped underneath; while he was breathing, he was unconscious and losing a lot of blood.

This is where your team work and training can make the difference between life and death. You could not call 999 or 911 in Iraq and there were no roadside recovery companies. The local traffic cop would not be dropping by to see what the holdup was either. All you could do was assess the casualties and keep them alive until you could get them out of there.

The medic put in a call for assistance to the office, reporting the injuries of what appeared to be a straight forward traffic accident. As one of the team checked that the coach driver was dead, he noticed something that made his blood run cold. A couple of dirty old sheets had been hiding something behind the driver's seat until the collision had thrown them onto the floor. They were hiding a stack of artillery shells and the detonator was rigged to a mercury switch. This type of switch involves a tube half filled with mercury and it has two contacts at one end. The plan was for the impact to tip the tube, swilling the mercury over the contacts, completing the circuit and BOOM.

Either the impact had not been hard enough or the circuit was faulty. However, the phone call for help could have cost them all their lives. If the detonator had been a radio activated type on the same frequency, it would have blown up the coach, both cars and all the team members. As it was the team now faced a huge dilemma. Although the medic had freed the driver and pulled him to a safe distance, the team leader was still trapped beneath a couple of tons of twisted steel and a huge unstable bomb which could go off at any moment.

As the medic checked the team leader over, it was clear that he was losing blood rapidly and there was no chance of getting him out from under the car without amputating his arm. There was no way the medic was able to carry out anything as drastic as that in the middle of the street. All he could do was put a couple of IVs into his injured mate and then move back to a safe distance from the bomb and hope something turned up.

What an awful dilemma to be in, having to watch the life ebb out of your mate in the middle of the street, knowing that there is nothing you can do for him. That was what the team faced until luck intervened. An American military convoy was seen forcing its way through the traffic, looking to investigate the reason for the traffic jam and their curiosity was about to change the team's fortunes.

The team waved down the lead Humvee and gave the commanding officer a brief summary of the complicated situation. He retired to a safe distance and put in a call for an Explosives Ordnance Disposal team (EOD Team) to defuse the bomb. In the meantime his soldiers forced the traffic and sightseers back to a safe distance so they could cordon off the area.

Our guys could only stand back and watch as the Americans went to work and you had to hand it to them, they did everything in their power to save our man's life. As the EOD Team worked to disarm the bomb in the coach, the medics tried to stabilize our man down below. He was drifting in and out of consciousness and the only thing he remembered was a young Iraqi boy, about ten years old, sneaking under the vehicle to steal his wrist watch; talk about opportunism. He had just spent a lot of money on the watch and was more concerned about losing it than the extent of his injuries when he came round. It is amazing how trauma drugs can change your perception of a situation.

The EOD Team found a crude explosive device consisting of a stack of around fifteen 150mm artillery shells strapped together. They also found a block of C-4 which would have detonated if the mercury had worked. The small blast would have set off the shells and the explosion would have killed and maimed anyone in range as well as damaging the buildings around the junction.

Once the EOD guys gave the all clear, the recovery team could start work on releasing our man from the wreckage. They cut away the car's back door and dropped the front seat level, releasing him from his cramped position. The whole operation was similar to what happens following many road traffic accidents, only the soldiers were carrying out the tasks usually done by the fire brigade and ambulance services.

After four hours of cutting the medics were able to slide him out of the wreckage onto a stretcher. As they assessed his injuries, a Blackhawk helicopter was called up and in no time at all he was on his way to the U.S. military hospital in Baghdad. The Quick Reaction Force reached the scene and had taken the rest of the team back to Baghdad. That left us with the problem of extracting the smashed up car from the scene. I could also look forward to all the forms the U.S. military would need filling in, and believe me there would be lots of them.

As a side note, our team filmed the medics, not for some gory download on the internet or as a keepsake for our man, but as a training video. The incident had all the elements of a road traffic accident, and the film footage was shown to all our new medics, as an example of what they might have to face one day.

The Blackhawk delivered our guy to one of their hospitals in the Green Zone where the procedure was to hand a British citizen over to the British military as soon as they have been stabilized. Although he was in the best possible hands, everyone was naturally concerned about his condition and it dominated conversations in the villa as we all waited for news that evening. I was more affected than most because I had known the guy for 20 years and I was the one who had contacted him in the first place. He was my best mate but I was not able to be at his side, because I was inundated with phone calls and emails.

That was until I got the call from the hospital later that night. While our guy had been drifting in and out of consciousness, the doctor at the other end of the phone was concerned that he would not make it until morning; I had to get to the Baghdad hospital as quickly as possible... I do not remember much about the drive across the Green Zone, or being escorted through the hospital but I do remember the shock of seeing my mate unconscious on a hospital bed pumped with tubes, with his mangled arm all bandaged up. No matter how you looked at it, he was in a bad way...

Despite wanting to stay at his bedside, I had to alert the London office with the news so they could contact the family. One thing was sure, his life threatening condition would not be on the world news; a few body bags had to be filled before the press took note of security companies like ours. And then we all faced a long night, wondering if he would make it. Time goes so slowly in traumatic situations like this and all you can do is sit and wait; and think how the hell had we got into this. It was at moments like that when I really questioned why I was in Iraq. But you just could not hand in your notice and walk away because you were in too deep. You just had to dig down into your reserves of determination and deal with the situation.

By morning the doctors were in a far better mood; against all expectations our mate had survived the first difficult night and was responding to the treatment faster than anticipated. I had no doubt that his excellent physical condition helped pull him through; I doubt many others would have survived...

But that is not the end of the story. You will have no doubt seen what happened when soldiers killed in action were repatriated to Britain and the spontaneous guard of honour which gathered in the village of Wootton Bassett. Have you ever wondered what happened when injured soldiers were brought home? And do you know how their treatment differed from that given to injured guys working for private security companies? Well it was not as you might expect; it was not what we, who were working in the business, expected.

Over the next few days our guy was moved around different hospitals in the Green Zone until the doctors were happy he could be transferred to the British military hospital in Shaibah Camp. The next stage of the journey was to Kuwait and then it was possible to fly him to the British military base in Cyprus. By then, the doctors were concerned about the state of his injuries and he stayed a week while specialists grafted tissue from his leg to his damaged arm. Once he was fit to fly he was transferred to a British military base in Germany en route for the United Kingdom. His journey courtesy of the British military ended in the National Health Service hospital nearest his home.

In just over a week my mate had gone from driving around the streets of Iraq to lying in a hospital just down the road from his house. There he was attended to by the nursing staff exactly the same as if he had been involved in a car crash on the way to work. As you can imagine, the whole experience had been surreal. He stayed until he was fit enough to go home but it was not the end of his recovery. He faced another two years of painful operations before the doctors completed work on his arm. Only his high level of fitness and fierce self determination eventually gave him partial use of his arm.

As chance would have it, there was an injured Royal Marine who had recently been evacuated from Iraq in a nearby bed. They began talking and were soon exchanging war stories to pass the time. The Marine had been injured by an IED near Basra and because he was fighting for his country, his journey home had been quite different...

The Marine followed the same route home across Europe but landed with several other casualties on a small commercial airfield in the Manchester area. They were not flown to one of the usual R.A.F. bases because of the adverse press coverage about casualties. At that time Selly Oak Hospital in Birmingham, where many soldiers were treated, was in the news due to the growing number of casualties. Although the number of men killed in action in Iraq and Afghanistan has always been publicized, the number of soldiers injured had always been harder to determine.

Despite being bandaged from head to foot, the Marine was picked up by a private hire minibus which was booked to take him to Birmingham. As always, the traffic south along the M6 motorway was horrendous and as the hours ticked by, the minibus driver explained that he could not complete the journey because he would go over his driving hours for the day. Their journey times were logged on a tachograph and he faced losing his licence if he was stopped by the police. So the Marine was dropped off in a service station, even though he was virtually immobile due to his injuries.

It was late in the evening and he was unable to contact his unit headquarters, so called his wife to let her know about his predicament. She eventually tracked him down and drove him in the family car to their local hospital where he was admitted by the Accident and Emergency department. That is how he ended up being in the same ward as our guy. What a great welcome home after fighting for your country.

The two guys became good mates during their stay in hospital and they continued to stay in touch. The aftercare was again, completely different for a member of Her Majesty's Armed Forces and an employee of a private security contractor. The Marine's commanding officer told him to stay at home until the consultants' reports were ready. When the final assessment was made, it was clear that he was unfit for duty, so he was discharged and given a sum of money as compensation. It was a fraction of what you regularly see in the news been given to civilians for accidents or harassment at work... It seemed that while it is all talk of war heroes in the Houses of Parliament and in the newspapers, they want rid of you once you are injured.

Our guy had to wait several months before the insurance company paid up, and our London office took steps to get some money to cover his bills in the meantime. They did not have much luck. Because he had put his Iraq wages into the bank and he had savings, the dole office was unable to help. He had also paid into the Special Forces Regimental Association for years but the hardship fund was unable to provide any money because he had sustained the injury as a private security contractor not as a serving soldier. In the end he had to use his savings to live off until the compensation money came through.

The reason for the wait was that the insurance company wanted to see the consultant's reports. While the figure was far higher than the Royal Marine received, they still reduced the payout because the consultants believed he could get the use of his arm back. The callousness of such decisions does make you wonder what makes these companies tick sometimes.

All in all, it was an experience none of us wanted to go through again. Only the carelessness of the bomb maker saved our guys from untimely deaths on a dusty Iraqi street. The only good thing to come out of the incident was that we knew that the evacuation system worked. The question was, how many more times were we going to have to use it?

Chapter Eighteen

Can It Get Any Worse?

ONE CONTRACT WE TOOK ON was to ferry clients from the Green Zone to meetings at the Ministry of Finance on Rasheed Street, Baghdad's equivalent of Wall Street. While the distance was just over a mile, it was all through dangerous territory. The journey started at Assassin's Gate, the exit on the east side of the Green Zone, so named because of the many assassination attempts made outside it. Then the team drove over Al Jumhirya Bridge, across the River Tigris, and round Tahir Square (Liberation Square), a large roundabout with underpasses. Then it was only a short distance through downtown Baghdad to the Ministry.

Although it was impossible to get lost, there were only two realistic routes to the Ministry and both were direct. We had identified half a dozen bottlenecks where the traffic slowed down and there were plenty of places where dickers could watch you pass. The Ministry's main entrance was on a busy road and there was no way we wanted to head into the narrow back streets to get to the rear entrance. To make matters worse, most meetings were held at the same time each day and there was no way of changing it. So it was impossible to vary the routine and as we used to say; "routine kills in our business".

Recent intelligence had told us that half a dozen suicide bombers were driving around Baghdad looking for targets. These 'Vehicle Bourne Improvised Explosive Devices', or VBIEDs for short, were driving cars specially adapted in makeshift garages to carry explosives. The first suicide car bombers had driven around in unmodified cars and the military soon learnt to watch out for cars with their rear ends scraping on the ground. The bad guys learnt from their mistakes. Mechanics would jack up the suspension, lifting the rear of the car high in the air, and then stack artillery shells inside until the rear of the car settled back to its original level. The bad guys had also worked out that taxis were ideal vehicles to use because the driver had a legitimate reason to wait around for long periods; only he was not looking to pick up a fare.

The insurgents had various ways of encouraging volunteers to blow themselves to smithereens. The word on the street was that the price was $5,000 to the driver's family for each Westerner killed. While that is only the price of a second hand car in the West, it was a lot of money to a poor family living below the poverty line; especially as it would be paid in dollars rather than Iraqi dinars.

Sometimes the driver had been forced to become a suicide bomber because the bad guys had taken his family hostage. He then faced the horrifying choice of trying to blow up as many Westerners as possible or returning home to find his family dead. Either way he would never see his wife and children alive again. Such was the cruelty of some of the bad guys.

Our security team usually escorted three clients to the Ministry. Urban style security requires a heavy presence when the clients were being escorted from their cars to the building, so we had a four man team in each vehicle; with two in the front seats, two in the back and the client in the middle of the back seat. While it was cramped, the journey was only short and doubling the number of cars would have resulted in an unwieldy convoy and additional expense.

While each team had their short and long weapons in their cars, we sometimes sent the camper van out with its hidden 0.50 calibre machine gun. The van could shadow the convoy, ready to move in if some heavy fire support was needed.

So the daily routine was to make a quick run into the city in the morning and then return in the afternoon when the meetings were over. The clients' daily routine often revolved around the baseball back home in America and they watched the games at night and talked about the highlights over breakfast in the morning before heading off to work. And then one morning they asked if they could all travel in the same car so they could carry on their discussion. We refused because too many clients in one car meant too many guards in another; and it was a risk we did not want to take. The cars occasionally became separated when there was a snarl up in the traffic and they could have been left exposed. But it did not end there.

Somehow, they got their manager in America on their side and he called the office to authorize their request. After a round of emails in which we put our concerns across, a signed instruction arrived on our fax machine approving their request; our security advice had been overruled. While we believed their manager misunderstood the seriousness of the situation on the ground, we had his instruction in writing. All we could do was rearrange our drill ready to accommodate the new seating arrangement the following morning.

So off the team went, with two security guys and three clients in vehicle one and four security guys each in vehicle two and three. While everything went to plan after a few days I sat down with the team leader to review the situation. I considered him to be one of our top blokes and after working together with him for 22 years in the army, he was also one of my mates.

The route concerned us both. Most days there were problems at Assassin's Gate and it was only a matter of time before our team was caught in one. But while we were doing everything right, we were both concerned about having the three clients in the first vehicle. As usual the talk ended with a bit of banter and a childish argument over how I had eaten the last portion of his favourite breakfast cereal. While it was something over nothing and forgotten about by the time his team was ready to leave, it stuck in my mind.

The client's meeting was scheduled for nine o'clock and the cars left the compound before eight, heading for Assassin's Gate. As I settled down to my computer the team was waiting at the checkpoint only two miles away; ten minutes later they were crossing the River Tigris. As I concentrated on my screen, I heard a loud bang over the usual hustle and bustle of the Green Zone. I froze and looked up; the bang had come from the east bank of the river. My heart was pounding because I had a gut feeling that something terrible had happened to our guys. I knew our team had been hit... So did the operations manager and his repeated radio calls had failed to raise a response. The convoy had not put out a contact call either which meant that all three cars were in difficulty. It was all looking very ominous.

There were plenty of lads waiting around the villa, so it took no time to scramble a Quick Reaction Force. Eight of us grabbed our weapons and jumped into two cars but as we drove out of the villa gates, the radio crackled into life. We listened anxiously as one of the guys confirmed the convoy had been hit and they needed help. He sounded in a bad way and said there was no time for details; they needed help as quickly as possible. As we drove away from the compound at top speed, none of us had a clue what to expect. I just sat grimly looking straight ahead as the driver drove fast through the Green Zone; it sounded like this was going to be bad.

As Assassin's Gate came into view, we could see a cloud of dirty smoke hanging over the buildings across the Tigris. It looked as though the explosion had been just across the bridge in Tahir Square. The checkpoint guards were straining to see what was happening and they initially refused to let us through. They explained the exit was blocked because there had been an incident. We screamed back "We know, it's our guys over the river; so let us through, they are calling for our help".

The guards let us go and we cut through the traffic across the bridge, straining to make sense of what was in front of us. Tahir Square was a scene of devastation, the likes of which you would expect to see in a war film. But we had no time to check out the scenery, we had to locate our guys in the middle of the mayhem and extract them as quickly as possible.

The roundabout was surrounded by office blocks, some of them ten or twelve storeys high, with shops at ground level. Although I had seen the roundabout many times, it was a few moments before I realized that several of the buildings on the right hand side of the roundabout were missing; the explosion had turned them into piles of rubble. Wrecked cars were strewn across the road, half hidden in clouds of choking dust. People were running around, some screaming, some crying and some crazy with fear. Others were cradling the injured in their arms, staring at charred and broken bodies scattered across the rubble. (We learnt later that around eight Iraqis were killed and another seventy were injured.) Then there was the cacophony of noise as sirens and car horns mixed with screams, shouts and moans.

But we did not have time to consider the effects of the explosion; we had to push through the traffic to get to our three cars in the middle of it all. We came to Car Three first which would have been at the back of the convoy. The armoured glass was shattered but it had not broken. The guys inside had no visible injuries but they were stunned and speaking incoherently. Car Two was next a short distance in front. The armoured glass had smashed and the guys inside had been injured by flying debris but they were alive. But the worst was to come.

Car One was on its roof on the opposite side of the road and it was burning fiercely. The flames had started to 'cook off' the ammunition stored in the back and rounds were shooting randomly into the air, adding to the chaos and confusion. My first thought was that the entire stack of 1,000 bullets could all go off at any moment. The heat made it impossible to get close to the car but we did not have to. We could see that the five guys inside were dead, killed by the shock of the massive explosion. As much as we hated to we had to concentrate on getting the living to a hospital; we would have to come back later for the bodies.

With no time to lose we started assessing the casualties' injuries. The guys in Car Two were just sat in their seats, eyes glazed over and white from shock. They did not respond to our shouts to get out of the car because their eardrums had been shattered by the blast, leaving them deaf.

The medic found that three of the guys only had cuts and bruises and they were quickly pulled out of the car and pushed into the QRF vehicles. However, the driver's clothes were soaked in blood and the medic soon found out where it was coming from... A piece of metal had shattered the windscreen and hit him in the neck; and it was still there, embedded just below his ear. Any sudden movement could have killed him, so we all gathered round and gently eased him out of his seat and into the QRF vehicle.

We then withdrew to deal with the casualties in Car Three, where again the guys were suffering from cuts and bruises. Although they were in a state of shock, they were able to talk to us. But as we pushed them towards the crowded QRF cars, there was no time for talk; we had another problem to contend with.

Iraqis were coming from all directions to see what had happened and while some helped the injured, others looked on angrily as we rescued our wounded. They had no intention of helping us even though we were the injured party. Instead we were the target for their anger. The chants blamed the casualties and destruction on the Americans and while we knew we were British, we were hardly in a position to explain their error. All that mattered was we were Westerners, making us the focus of their hatred.

The atmosphere was getting ugly and we were in no position to defend ourselves. We might have expected the U.S. military on the scene and they would have been able to deal with the crowds. But there was no sign of them; we were on our own.

It was going to be a hell of a squash getting the eight injured guys inside the two QRF cars and it was going to be even worse when we squeezed on top. But there was no way we could leave anyone behind. But as we eased the injured guys inside, the shout went up that we were in imminent danger. While the majority of the Iraqis jeered and chanted from a safe distance, around 300 or 400 were brave enough to close in on our cars. Then all of a sudden a few ran forward and things looked nasty.

Without thinking I shouted "engage" and the guys instinctively shouldered their weapons, aimed and fired. The crack of the rounds stopped the crowd in their tracks. As we waited for their next move with our rifles to our shoulders, we breathed a sigh as the crowd began to disperse. While they were angrier than ever, they were having second thoughts about taking us on.

Now the Rules of Engagement stated you were allowed to shoot if your life was in imminent danger. In my opinion, a crowd of 400 angry men bearing down on eight able bodied men counted as an imminent danger. Whether the guys fired above the crowd or aimed at individuals, I do not know and we did not discuss it later. I only know what split second decision I took; one taken in the face of danger and one I have thought over many times over the years.

With everyone crammed inside the cars, the two drivers spun them around and headed back across the Tigris to Assassin's Gate. As I looked back I could see a complete state of pandemonium as the crowds screamed at us and jumped on our damaged cars. We could also see the military and the police had started to arrive. While some began cordoning off the scene, others attended to the injured. But the worst thing was, leaving the bodies of our five mates behind. While we aimed to never leave anyone behind, dead or alive, on this occasion, there would have been more bodies to collect if we had not escaped when we did.

We were waved through Assassin's Gate and headed for the hospital where we left two guys to look after the casualties. The rest of us went straight back to the scene to retrieve the bodies. Or that is what we thought. A U.S. military checkpoint would not let us enter Tahir Square and while they listened to our argument, they made it clear that they were still dealing with civilian casualties and crowd control. All they would do was take our phone numbers and promise to call when we could get access to retrieve our bodies.

Although we hated to leave, at least the area had been cordoned off. So we headed back to base.

While we could do nothing at the scene, there was plenty to be done at the villa. The phone never stopped all day. We had to check on the injured guys in the hospital, liaise with the U.S. military over access to Tahir Square and forward the bad news to our London office. We also had the press repeatedly calling for information and they refused to believe that we could not help them. The few sketchy details we did have had been sent to the London office so they could prepare a press release. While we hoped the journalists would let us get on with our job, at least one had managed to get access to the scene and images of the mayhem and carnage at Tahir Square were beaming around the world. Great we thought; we could not retrieve the bodies of our friends, but the press can take photographs of the scene.

The last thing we wanted was the rest of our guys finding out about the attack while they were out working in case it caused them to drop their guard. But some were hanging around offices while their clients were in meetings and they were never far from a television. It only took one to see the news and before long they were calling each other and the office desperate for information about their friends. Rumours travel fast, much faster when everyone had a mobile phone, and we wanted to stamp them out before they got out of hand.

Our operations man was busy calling each team in turn, finding out what they knew. He then confirmed there had been an attack, there had been casualties and that a full report would be given at the evening prayers. In the meantime they had to focus on the job in hand so every man got back to the villa safely. But while we tried to suppress information, the news channels were discussing unconfirmed reports of an attack and it did not take much to put two and two together.

We became increasingly worried about the rest of the teams and we eventually declared a lockdown, ordering everyone to cancel their appointments. Mistakes were going to be made if we did not give ourselves some breathing space so we told everyone to get to a secure place and wait for instructions. It meant that teams were scattered across Baghdad but they were safe.

Back at the hospital the injured guys were coming round slowly and we were able to talk to some of them. While the guys in Car Two would get over their injuries, they would not be able to work again in security. It was a miracle how the driver survived the shrapnel wound in his neck but he did. The four guys in Car Three had whiplash injuries as well as cuts and bruises and while they could be back at work, the question was would they want to?

Between their stories we pieced together what had happened. The three car convoy had driven over the bridge spaced about fifty metres apart. After slowing down, Car One entered Tahir Square roundabout but as it drove around the roundabout, a parked taxi moved off from the road to the right and it pulled alongside. The driver cast one last look at our guys and then detonated the bomb.

The bomber's car disintegrated while the blast blew Car One into the air. The explosion was so ferocious that it flipped the three ton vehicle into the air and it landed ten metres away, on its roof. Cars Two and Three were on the approaches to the roundabout when the blast shattered their windows. Both vehicles skidded to a halt and although the occupants were stunned by the shockwave, they saw the buildings collapse, showering the road with rubble. It had been one hell of a blast.

Now we had a rough idea of what had happened, a detailed report could be sent to the C.P.A. and the U.S. military. It was also time to break the news to our client so they could put their procedures in place. I dreaded breaking the sad news each time I picked up the phone; and there were many times.

While taking statements from the lads in hospital it was clear there was another aspect to the story; and it was an unpleasant one. Our three car convoy had followed a U.S. military convoy out of Assassin's Gate and across the Tigris River. The column of three Humvees left Tahir Square by the first roundabout exit, heading southeast along the river bank. The last Humvee was only a few cars in front of our lead car and the crew had heard the bomb go off; who hadn't? The convoy's Tail End Charlie would have heard the explosion but the column kept going, leaving our guys to fend for themselves. The rest of the team would have seen the effects of the blast but the convoy leader decided to keep driving, leaving our dead and injured guys to the mercy of the mob.

We were furious and called our contact in the American military straight away to give him the information. Initially he denied the revelation but we persisted he checked it out rather than dismiss it. We knew that the convoy would have logged out of Assassin's Gate and made a radio report when they drove through Tahir Square, exactly the same as we had to. We wanted him to check with his communications guys to confirm the convoy's movements.

After tense conversations the U.S. military admitted there had been a patrol nearby. The convoy commander had heard the blast and seen the devastation but had decided to move his troops to a safe area. After all the official line was that the military were not bound to help out a private contractor. If they felt a situation was too dangerous for them to deal with, they would report it and leave. Although we had always known this, it was still very difficult to stomach.

I immediately wrote down my thoughts and forwarded the email to the rest of the security companies in Baghdad. This is what I wrote: "The obvious conclusion here is that it is almost all self help or nothing, as many of you have reported from your own experiences. The Coalition Forces have told me many times to plan on getting nothing and you won't be disappointed. Whilst we sympathize greatly with them and their circumstances to say we were disappointed does not do it justice."

On top of all that we still had to retrieve our mates' bodies. After being turned away five times by the military cordon surrounding Tahir Square, the military finally gave us clearance to return in the evening. There were no frills to the instruction; just "you have permission to retrieve the bodies". So once again we organized a QRF and were back in the cars heading out of Assassin's Gate towards the bomb site, only this time we were accompanied by a hired pickup truck. We also took along an Iraqi doctor who worked for us from time to time, in case we needed to talk to the hospitals.

The soldiers were still manning a cordon but very little had changed since the morning; the area still looked "like something out of a war film". The streets were strewn with rubble, dust and debris and there were still lots of Iraqi sightseers around, some of them shouting anti-Western chants like "America is the enemy of God" and "Death to America". Again we were not in the mood to explain we were British.

The cars were where we had left them but all three had been burnt out by the crowds. We tentatively made our way across to the car on its roof dreading what we would find. Only we found that the bodies had been moved. We were shocked and our first thoughts were, had the Americans taken them or was it the mob? It did not take us long to find out. We found them laid out on a patch of grass in the middle of the roundabout where a group of Iraqis were digging graves. I suppose they intended to bury them before sunset, in accordance with Muslim tradition, but they were burying them in the middle of one of Baghdad's main streets! We were appalled and ran over shouting and screaming, waving our weapons to clear the Iraqis away.

But our horror did not end there; one of the bodies was missing. All we could do was contain our anger, load up the bodies and get the hell out of there. As a military escort led our bizarre convoy back through Assassin's Gate, we felt like everyone's eyes were on us as we drove through the Green Zone.

After visiting the mortuary, we headed back to Tahir Square to look for the missing body. A thorough search of the blast damaged area failed to turn up anything while there were no more signs of digging on the roundabout. We had no idea where else to look and while none of the American soldiers still around knew anything, the crowd were not in the mood for talking to us. However, our Iraqi doctor discovered that a body had been taken to a hospital in a car. The Baghdad emergency services could never cope after traumatic situations and, as often happened, it resulted in a free for all as cars, buses and pickup trucks ferried the injured to hospital.

There was no formal admissions system like you get in a Western hospital and doctors usually worked on patients before asking for personal details. Our doctor called round all the hospitals in Baghdad until he found our missing man but his face told us it was bad news. Although he had been alive when they removed him from the scene, he had been pronounced dead at the hospital. So we had another body to identify, reclaim and escort back to the Green Zone mortuary. Our last little ray of hope had been snuffed out, and it was getting too much to bear all in one day.

But the day was not over. I still had to face the rest of the lads at evening prayers and I knew as we pulled into the villa compound that I was facing the hardest part of what was turning into my worst day in Iraq. The official version stated that "... a contractor convoy was attacked by a suicide car bomb in the Sadun district of central Baghdad during the morning rush hour. Five contractors were killed, five were injured.

According to the Ministry of Health, eight additional Iraqi civilians were killed and 69 injured. Iraqi police have the lead for the investigation and will be supported as required." Abu Musab al-Zarqawi, a Jordanian militant Islamist, also made a statement: "Through the grace of God, members of the Jama'at al-Tawhid wal-Jihad martyrs' brigade were successful in setting a trap for a convoy of mercenaries in the centre of the Iraqi capital." The time was approaching when I had to make my own statement to the friends of those who had been killed and it was not going to be easy.

As we were busy doing all these gruesome tasks, the rest of the teams had returned from their jobs and had assembled in the villa. They were swopping rumours and stories, trying to work out what had happened; it was only natural. More than once, I was asked outright what had happened and each time I told them to wait for prayers when they could all be told together. And that was the question I faced, what was I going to say?

I went into the office, closed the door and sat down; alone for the first time since I had heard the bomb blast over twelve hours earlier. I knew the next few minutes were going to be important for me, the guys and the company and I just thought "what the hell am I going to say". There were five guys in the mortuary and another eight in hospital; four of them unable to work again. Outside the door sixty guys were waiting for an explanation.

When you are running a business like that, you have to spend most of your time in the office, dealing with correspondence, speaking to people, planning and giving out orders. Believe me, when things were all going to plan, it was great being one of the bosses. But on days like this when you were on your own, trying to think of something to say as you stared at the office wall, you wished you were somewhere else.

I was painfully aware my decisions had determined what had happened out on the street and my head was full of unanswered questions about what had happened. Why had we done things the way we had? Why had we not changed our routine? Why had the suicide bomber chosen our convoy? It was crazy what was going on inside my head, I was looking for answers and excuses to all the 'what ifs'. But while they weighed heavily on my mind, I had no time to consider them now because this was not a time for emotion; we all had to go back to work the following morning.

Drawing a deep breath I stood up, opened the office door and walked into the briefing room where there was a sea of solemn faces. By now details of the attack had filtered around and they all knew who had died. They were all looking at me and waiting to see what I had to say and as I looked around, I felt sorry for them because they too had just lost their friends. The day's events were a brutal reminder of what we were up against and they all knew that any one of them could have been lying in the mortuary.

As I stood in front of the lads and explained what had happened, they listened carefully to every word I said. I then went on to tell them that they all had to go back to work tomorrow and pointed out that if we did not, the insurgents would have won their battle and our friends had died for nothing. I had anticipated that they would look at me and say that it was OK for me to say that; I sat in the office while they were out on the road every day.

This was not a time to argue with them or challenge their objections; I had to meet the situation head on. To prove my point, I said I would lead the convoy making the run into the city centre the following morning. That was news to my driver and I could tell that he was not happy, but it had to be done... Those few words changed the mood and the atmosphere relaxed while the lads became more communicative. After those few moments of hostility, I felt they were on my side again. In the frank chat that followed it was clear that they were determined to carry on. We would just have to see what the next few days would bring.

On that day the whole reality of Iraq came home quickly and thoughts of my own mortality loomed large. In the past it had always been another company in the headlines; other guys getting hit. We had probably forgotten how dangerous Baghdad was and we were getting addicted to the adrenaline lifestyle involved with working there. But this time it was our friends and colleagues who had been killed and from now on I questioned everything I did. I bet all the guys did.

Understandably, I did not sleep well that night and I was aroused early next morning by a call from the military authorities confirming the identities of the deceased. We could now notify London and our client so they could inform the next of kin. What a way to start the day and it was going to get worse. My team was due out of the compound at seven o'clock and to say that I was anxious was an understatement. Although I had driven into the city many times before, this time I knew all eyes were on me because I had to show the lads I could do it to get our morale back on track.

There was a lot to do before we left the compound and I threw myself into the full routine of loading up the car and checking the equipment. It was my way of showing a bit of leadership, even if I did not feel like showing any. I did feel a bit sorry for my driver though. He had always followed my instructions without question and I did wonder if I had taken it a step too far this time. Only time would tell.

Then away we went, out of the compound and across the Green Zone to Assassin's Gate. Then it was across the Tigris where the road had been cleared but the debris around Tahir Square was still there; and so were the memories. But there was no time to reminisce; we kept our eyes peeled and headed into the city. In no time at all we were at the Ministry of Finance and once we were inside, my phone started going crazy. And so it continued all day as colleagues and friends called to get the latest news while the press clamoured for statements and exclusive details. It was a complete nightmare.

I could not stay at the Ministry all day because there was too much unfinished business to attend to. Arrangements had been made to relieve me so that I could get back to my work and help organize the repatriation of the bodies. The day was lost in a series of visits to the mortuary and the hospital where there was a mountain of paperwork waiting to be completed. Then it was the military's turn and they wanted to know exactly what our SOPs were to make sure we had followed the rulebook. At times it seemed as if there was no end to the amount of forms we had to fill in.

It was also time to give a couple of reporters an interview. Over the past 24 hours the press had been working on speculation and we had not wanted to add to their rumour mill. Up until then the British press had shown little interest in the security companies working in Iraq, only occasionally referring to us as mercenaries profiting from the spoils of war. But following a double page spread in a popular British daily newspaper we were front page news.

"British ex-Special Forces killed in car bomb disaster" was the sort of headline we were looking at and it ran with an article about the security business in Iraq. The report made the work sound far more exciting and covert than it really was but the press had its job to do, and big headlines got the readers. After that we were in every paper and the rest of the world's press were on our case asking all sorts of probing questions.

We wanted to be under the radar for our own and our clients' safety and we refused to go into details about our work. So as much as the press did not like it, we refused to make further comments and the press blackout stopped information leaking into the news.

It was not over for me though as the bodies had to be escorted out of Iraq. In the Army it is the job of the Royal Army Medical Corps to deal with casualties and their medics and doctors are trained to deal with casualties who they do not know personally. As security contractors we had to do it all ourselves and we had to make it up the best we could, knowing we were doing it for our mates. But it was hard on everyone, myself included.

The difference between serving in the military and working as a security contractor was brought home to us at a difficult time like this. You could see the strain etched across the guys' faces as they loaded the caskets into the vehicles at the mortuary.

Organizing a convoy along Route Irish was not easy at the best of times, but when you are escorting five caskets, the morbid task took on a surreal meaning. We were risking our lives on the most dangerous stretch of road in the country to take our mates' bodies to the airport. It sounded too farfetched for the plot of any horror film. But one thing was for sure though, there was no way our makeshift hearses would be moving at slow speed.

Our sad convoy made it to Baghdad airport without any fuss and we manoeuvred five caskets across the car park and into the terminal building. After getting the caskets and a mountain of baggage through security, it was time to get checked in. The check in clerk asked me if I was checking in any baggage, the same as if I was travelling on a package holiday to Spain. "Yes I do, seventeen pieces" I replied. The sarcastic reply was predictable; "you do realize the maximum number of bags you can check onto the plane is two, sir?" Of course I did, but his tone mellowed as I explained that I worked for the company which had lost five guys the day before. I pointed to the bags and explained I was checking in five coffins and two bags with each coffin; and my own two bags.

The clerk apologized and rushed through my request as quickly as he could. There was no guard of honour or bugler sounding the Last Post as we loaded the coffins into the cavernous hold of the Hercules aircraft, just silence as we piled the bags of personal effects alongside. As luck would have it, no one else was booked on the flight and the four man crew left me alone with my thoughts. Someone had to do it but I just wished it didn't have to be me.

The flight to Kuwait City lasted less than an hour but it was time for a bit of soul searching. It is impossible to describe what goes on in your mind during those quiet moments. For the most part I think it was numb; blank after 24 hours of madness. But the questions kept coming back; could we have done anything different, was it all worth it and could we carry on. I could ask the first question a thousand times and still not come up with a satisfactory answer. The answer to the other two had to wait until I returned to Baghdad.

After what seemed an eternity we were on the runway at Kuwait Airport where I was met by the representatives of our insurance company. Part of the company insurance against death and injury included an international rescue service. It was a sort of bumper holiday insurance and they dealt with the repatriation of bodies and evacuation of injured operatives. The only restriction was that they would not work in a war zone, and they still counted Iraq as one.

They were very professional, providing ambulances, arranging flights and organizing relevant paperwork. All I had to do was organize the hand over, sign the paperwork and they dealt with the rest. It was as simple as that. I was pleased to hear that the British military had organized the plane even though they did not have to do it. It saved us a lot of hassle. At times like this the British military consider you one of their own and they give what help they can, even though they do not have to. And believe me their assistance was always appreciated.

Knowing that the bodies of our colleagues were being looked after was a great relief. But as I flew back to Baghdad airport, I pondered on the fact that there would be no parade through crowds of mourners for our guys; there would be no more mentions on the news and there would be no names on rolls of honour. Nothing despite the many years they had served in the British Army. Many considered us to be paid mercenaries while a few believed we got what we deserved.

I returned to the villa and went straight back to work, because there was a business to run. It was back to the grindstone, as if nothing had happened. Our friends' bodies were still on the plane heading home, when I was back at my desk dealing with the day to day running of the business.

But there was one last thing we had to do for the guys though and that was to deal with their personal effects. As callous as it sounds we broke open each locker and sorted the contents into three piles. The first pile was contraband, like weapons and ammunition, which needed to be disposed of. The second pile was the guy's personnel gear, his boots, clothes and other accoutrements and we followed the British Army tradition of auctioning it off. Although these items were second hand, and probably not worth much, the lads would pay over the odds, knowing that the money would go to the family. The auction was our own remembrance ritual and a form of closure for the lads.

The final pile was heartbreaking; it was the private family items, including photographs, letters and things made by their children. These had to be boxed carefully and sent home to the wives. As we sorted out these personal things it really brought it home to you that you were dealing with a family man who had died suddenly. Back home the people in the photographs were just coming to terms with losing their loved one. It was very hard to do it and it reminded everyone of their own mortality. After all it could be your locker being opened next.

Once the sale was over everyone just got on with their work, showing no emotion and not talking about what had just happened. But you could tell that everyone had their own inner thoughts on the bombing. It also changed how everyone viewed working in Baghdad.

A few of the lads had had enough and one by one they took me quietly to one side and explained that they wanted to hand their notice in. They all knew the risks and although they had enjoyed the work and the money, some had had enough. Although they had always known that working the streets of Baghdad was a deadly game of Russian roulette, the bombing made them realize that it would be their turn soon, and they wanted out.

The bombing had also knocked the stuffing out of me. Personally, that day was my most harrowing in Iraq and the events I had to deal with in the aftermath were some of the most traumatic that I had had to deal with. Although the company had had a good year, the honeymoon period was over and looking back, I reckon that from that day on I wanted a way out. If someone had offered to buy my part of the business I would have sold up on the spot. However, while the guys on the ground could walk away, the bosses like me could not; we had too much tied up in it.

Our relationship with the client changed after that day. Up to that point the guys in the American office had sometimes questioned why we were so cautious in the way we worked. They were probably looking to save money, and why not, they were in business the same as we were. However, when you are in an office half way around the world the risks do not seem as great. After that day they accepted all our security suggestions without question; if we asked for it, there was a good reason for it.

It was becoming widely recognized that the work was becoming more dangerous as the insurgents turned their attentions onto Iraq's infrastructure system and the people who worked on it. The risks had been discussed many times before but they had all of a sudden become frighteningly real.

The increasing threat of suicide attacks also put everyone under a lot of stress because it turned every man, woman and child into a potential threat. Everyone walking close to you could be wearing a suicide vest while every car driver who eyeballed you could be sitting on top of a bomb.

In case you are wondering why I mention women and children, we had reports that women carrying babies had been found walking into hospitals with vests loaded with explosives tied to their bodies. These so called 'black-widow' suicide bombers had also been lured by the financial gain of killing Westerners. The whole concept made you paranoid and no matter how well trained or clued up you were; there was very little you could do to protect yourself.

I flew back to England to attend the funerals of our two guys. Both of them were well known and well liked men with extensive service in the Army and the turnouts were huge. Although the press and the public had not taken much notice, the men's friends and comrades had. Word of their deaths had spread on the military grapevine and there were many old faces there. Only when you saw the wives and families grieving for their lost ones did the impact of their deaths really hit home. After all it could have been any of us.

Chapter Nineteen

Piggy in the Middle

'MONEY MAKES THE WORLD GO AROUND', so the lyrics of an old song go. In the 21st Century it should be changed to 'credit makes the world go around' because the amount of hard cash in circulation diminishes by the day. Virtually all financial transactions today are carried out with the help of computers. Companies use bank transfers and credit loans while the man in the street relies on credit and debit cards to carry out his banking.

Now all this works fine if the banking system is functioning as it should, however, in Iraq it was anything but functioning. While some of the Ministry of Finance buildings in Baghdad had been damaged during the pre-invasion attacks in the spring of 2003, the real damage was done after the Americans occupied the city. Looters went through abandoned government buildings like a horde of locusts, taking anything of value and destroying the rest in the process. Banks were prime targets and while computer equipment was taken away to be sold, wiring was ripped out for scrap. In short, the banking system did not exist.

At the same time the country was awash with money as payments for millions of barrels of oil and construction contracts were being made. Payments for construction projects across the country also totalled millions of dollars a month and contractors had to be paid in cash. Once the computer communications were restored, foreign banks would be able to resume business with Iraq's banks, transferring money electronically. The man in the street also wanted automatic banking restored so that he did not have to be paid his wages in cash. Muggings and house robberies were on the increase and it was a dangerous time to be wandering around the city carrying a lot of money.

While it was a good business for the security companies who had to escort briefcases of cash around the country, it could not go on. I will give you one example of how it could go wrong. At one point we employed four ex-French Foreign Legion guys and after a period of training they began working together as a team. After some time working regular contracts, one of their tasks was to deliver regular cash payments to contractors, driving across the country with a boot full of dollars and then supervising the hand over. They performed well until one day they failed to make their regular call to the operations room. No amount of calls could raise them and even our Quick Reaction Force could not locate them. It was only later that we found out what had happened. They were supposed to deliver around $4 million in hard cash to a construction company working to the west of Baghdad when they went absent without leave. But rather than turn off the motorway as they neared their destination, they turned off their radio and mobile phones and kept driving west, crossing the Syrian border near Al-Bukamel. Although we had put out a call to stop them, they had switched cars; they also used their second passport to cross the border. That is correct, a second passport. Legionnaires are given a new name when they enlist and can apply to get their name back after a year if they wish. They were also entitled to a French passport after five years' service.

Syria had been under French control from the 1920s until the 1940s, giving the two countries a historical connection, and these guys knew their French passports would help them across the border. And blag their way across they did with $4 million. It did not take us long to work out how they had escaped and we informed our American client. They in turn contacted the Syrian Embassy for help in tracking them down; a difficult task because they were on different passports. They also contacted the French embassy for help. They refused point blank on the grounds that France had always opposed the invasion of Iraq.

And so there you had it; they had made a getaway that would have made the Great Train Robbers blush. It was obviously planned from the moment the guys were tasked to move money. As I said before, you never really knew who you were employing once you went outside your close circle of friends.

One of our contracts involved us working for the banking system in Baghdad. A contractor was working to re-establish communications systems between banks and it was our job to look after one of the managers during the four-week commissioning period. We had to escort him between the Green Zone and Baghdad's many banks. But while it was a lucrative job, it was a difficult one to organize.

Our planning made it clear that we could not use our usual team of two 4x4 vehicles. It would soon attract unwelcome attention and become a prime target. Our answer was to go covert, using plain vehicles and disguises. We bought a couple of second hand Mercedes and BMWs with local number plates and kitted them out with armoured plates in our workshop. We did what we could to hide the modifications, trimming Kevlar plates to fit in the foot wells and side panels. We could not make the cars bomb-proof but we had a good try. As a final touch we added all the gear you expected to see in an Iraqi's car, down to the furry dice and the religious icons hanging from the mirror and the box of tissues on the parcel shelf.

The idea was to dress casually and conceal our weapons to keep a low profile. We chose the guys who could grow beards quickly and they worked on their sun tans as they planned their routes. The car's tinted windows would help them look like locals. We just had to keep our heads down and stay alert.

We also recruited a woman from the Intelligence Corps to help us improve our disguise. The whole plan was to make the entourage look like we were escorting a rich businessman and his wife to the bank rather than a top American communications expert. She would dress in local style clothing while a scarf partially concealed her dark skin and dark hair. She would pretend to be our client's wife and they would look like a normal couple to anyone passing by.

We also allocated our battered camper van to the job. The van driver would shadow the convoy, ready to move closer if it came under attack, so the gunner could open the back door and give the bad guys a nasty surprise.

With everything in place we started moving the client around Baghdad and as expected the cars were often stuck in traffic. The three vehicles never drove in convoy but the drivers were always in eye contact and radio contact. They looked like individual vehicles travelling in the same direction to the average bystander. The tinted windows and the disguises also worked a treat and no one took any notice as the team weaved its way across the city.

The approach to the bank involved the first car pulling up and the two guys would get out and mingle with the pedestrians. They would take up 'over watch' positions ready to observe the 'married couple' walk from their car to the entrance of the bank. They kept at a distance with weapons concealed and no evidence of communications on them; everything was done by signals from these stand-off positions. To the untrained eye they would not look like they were associated with the client and, if necessary, even the client did not know who was watching his back. It was what we called protective surveillance.

The client's car could then pull up and the 'happy couple' would walk across to the door of the bank while the over-watchers kept an eye out for unusual movements on the street. They could easily close in if a threat developed while the girl could push the client to the ground if anyone started shooting. From a distance she looked like a dutiful wife but while most women carried makeup in their handbag, this one carried a concealed weapon, spare magazines and a couple of grenades. In other words she was not to be messed with.

While we had a good routine, allowing the client to go about his business across the city, I joined the team one day to make sure everything was going to plan. I went in the first car and we parked outside the bank, taking up over watch positions on the street. The second car arrived and the client stepped out with his female protection officer and walked across to the bank. No one took any notice and there was nothing unusual on the street to note. Our cars moved off and while the client disappeared inside with the girl to attend his meeting, we waited outside observing the street.

An hour later we were warned that our client had finished his meeting and wanted to leave, so I put the call in for our cars to pull up outside. But as the pair emerged from the bank, we noticed two cars driving erratically down the street towards us. As they screeched to a halt in front of the bank, I knew we had a problem but it was all happening so fast...

I put in the radio message "Contact... Wait... Out..." to the operations room, so everybody kept the net clear. We knew then that everyone would be listening in to find out if you needed help. For the moment though, we were fully committed to getting the client behind cover and taking control of the gun battle.

We ran towards the client as the bad guys clambered out of their cars and opened fire from behind them. The girl dragged the client to the floor while our two drivers pulled up in front of them to protect them from the gun fire, and then clambered out to return fire.

It was important that everyone quickly let off one magazine, to keep the bad guys' heads down for a few seconds. That gave us the chance to drag the client to the car, placing him behind the wheel where the axle and the hub would provide some protection. He was stressed out, scared and wondering what was going to happen next. All four of us then started taking aimed shots, hoping that the bad guys did not have the stomach for a fight. But they did, at least for now.

As we engaged in a cops and robbers style gun fight from behind the cars, there was pandemonium across the square and it seemed like everyone in the area was screaming. Some people were lying on the floor, holding their heads, while others were hiding behind whatever cover they could find. The rest were running as fast as they could away from the gun battle.

The Baghdad police were often stationed at all the major road intersections, so they could keep an eye on the traffic and the cops at the nearby junction had heard the commotion. They jumped in their car and headed towards the gunfire to investigate, sirens blazing. As we traded shots, we could hear the approaching sirens but we were keeping our heads down when the police car screeched to a halt close by. The two cops then jumped out, probably expecting to arrest a solitary gunman.

As I glanced across to check out the new arrivals, I saw to my horror that they were running straight towards our line of fire. Although it all seemed to happen in slow motion, it actually happened so fast. So fast that no one had time to warn them off and they ran straight into the crossfire. As they dropped to the ground, riddled with bullets, I sensed the team's shock as they looked at each other as if to say "what the hell happened there".

As we came to terms with the situation, the bad guys realized their opportunity had passed. They were probably running out of ammunition and they definitely did not want to be about when more police arrived so they jumped into their bullet riddled cars and drove off. It left us with a big, big problem.

There were two lifeless policemen lying in the middle of the street and we were the only armed men in the area. We were in line for getting the blame and there were a lot of witnesses who would support that claim. There was no way we were going to get into an argument with the people gathering around the scene and we did not want to be around when the police or the military turned up. If we hung around we would be facing a blame game that we could not win – after all, we were the foreign mercenaries.

So we acted like mercenaries and concentrated on getting our client out of there. We bundled him into the car and drove off, leaving a chaotic scene behind us. We could not do anything about the two lifeless policemen; we had to get back to the safety of the Green Zone and face the music later.

As we raced off out of the square, I looked back in disbelief at the chaos we were leaving behind; it had all happened so fast it was difficult to comprehend. All I could do for now though was to give the all clear over the radio and let the operations room know we were heading home.

As my driver weaved his way through the traffic, there was no time to discuss what we had just been through because my mobile phone was already going crazy. Bad news travelled fast and the word was already out that we had shot two cops and done a runner. Fantastic, I thought; wait until you hear our version first before you start drawing conclusions. Not surprisingly, there were a few people waiting for us outside the villa when our cars pulled into the compound.

There was no time for general chit-chat though, I needed to establish what everyone had seen and the short debriefing confirmed what I suspected – there was nothing we could have done. After dismissing everyone, it was time to sit down and let the adrenaline subside because I needed to be calm ready for when the shit hit the fan.

I did not have to wait long before the American investigators turned up because they were knocking at our door within the hour. They were full of questions and the first was to verify that one of our call signs had been at the scene of an incident in which two Iraqi police officers had died. All security team movements were monitored by AEGIS and they had logged our contact report. The Americans were now faced with having to explain to Baghdad's chief of police why two of his men were in the mortuary. It was a delicate diplomatic situation to say the least.

All we could do was explain our version of events and wait for the investigation team to confirm our story. We believed an examination of the scene and the bodies would show we were telling the truth but things were never that simple in Baghdad. The chief of police had a list of witness statements taken at the scene and he believed a different version of events to what we gave. He was not happy and wanted to question the Baghdad head of the security company involved; and that was me.

When the American investigators returned to the villa they made it clear they intended to hand me over to the police for questioning, so I could make a formal statement. I refused point blank to go to the police headquarters; I might not come back... I knew that while you were subject to American justice and a fair hearing inside the Green Zone, anything could happen when you were in the Red Zone. There was no way I was handing myself in to the Iraqi police.

However, there was a diplomatic incident brewing over the deaths of the two policemen. The rumours on the street were depicting us as the villains and a large group of protesters were gathering outside one of the Green Zone's main gates, demanding justice against the Western mercenaries. Representatives from the Iraqi police were also negotiating my handover with the Americans.

When they finally called to take me to face the police representatives, all I could do was restate our version of events and give our condolences over the deaths. I also reiterated that we could not be held responsible for anyone who ran into the crossfire. They left empty handed, but I knew that that was not the end of it. Now that negotiations had failed, the police representatives headed back to their headquarters to arrange an arrest warrant.

While it was understandable that the police chief wanted justice for his men and the C.P.A. wanted to maintain good relations with him; I was not going into an Iraqi police station to explain our version of events. Once inside, I might not get out and I knew full well that I could easily be handed over as a sacrificial lamb in the interests of diplomacy.

Once back at the villa all I could do was contemplate my fate but whichever way I looked at things it wasn't good. If I stayed I faced getting locked up, and whatever rough treatment followed. If I escaped from Iraq I was out of the business; that is if I made it out. While I mulled over the whys and wherefores, I received a call from an American who refused to give me his details. Intriguing I thought, they usually tell you straight away who they are and what they do. It soon became clear I was being contacted off the record to arrange my escape from Baghdad. I assumed that they were from the C.I.A. or some American spook organization but as I listened to the instructions, I did not care as long as they got me out of there.

I figured the Americans wanted me out of Baghdad at least, and out of the country if possible, to give them time to defuse the situation. Once I was out of the picture, they could tell the police chief that I had disappeared and they were attempting to locate me. So far so good; but how was I going to get out of Baghdad now that I was a marked man?

The plan was simple. I had specific instructions to go to a villa in a different part of the Green Zone early the following morning. I would be given a lift to the airport, escorted onto a plane and flown out of the country. Fantastic, I thought, I can get out of Iraq and wait until the dust settles. After a short holiday I could be back at my desk.

I felt much better after the call but I still had a restless night, going over everything that had happened over the past 24 hours. As I was packing my kit the following morning the phone was constantly ringing as press agencies tried to find out what had happened. Although there had been a press blackout over the incident, it did not take them long to figure out which security company was involved.

I did not have time to put them off, I had an appointment to keep and bang on time I rolled up at the villa to find a guy waiting with a Mercedes car. Excellent I thought, my chauffeur, we just need the rest of the escort team and away we go. Only to my surprise, he handed over the car keys and told me to get going. "Hang on a minute", I said, "I was promised I would be chauffeured to the airport". He told me I was welcome to use the unmarked car to drive to the airport and there was an AK47 and a few magazines on the back seat in case I got into difficulties. However, I had better get a move on if I wanted to catch the plane I was booked onto. Either that or I was going to the police station.

The guy ushered me inside the villa and left me in a dormitory to think over my choices, making it clear I did not have long. As I sat there alone, it dawned on me that it could all be over; my stake in the business and my life as a free man. I also realized that the American authorities could not be seen to be helping me because it would aggravate the situation.

When the guy returned he explained the Iraqi police would be calling at my villa soon and would issue a warrant for my arrest when they found out I was missing. It meant that the Green Zone barricades would become my prison if I did not get moving soon. But the penny had already dropped; I had been suckered into this. I had no choice. I either had to make the drive along Route Irish alone or face the music with the police. Shaking my head in disbelief, I climbed into the car, started the engine and pulled out of the gate as my heart sank into my boots.

It did not take me long to pass through the Green Zone and while no one took any notice; our man in our operations room did when I called him to explain what I had to do. Although they wanted to send backup all they could do was put the QRF team on standby; we both knew if it was scrambled what it would be coming to do was to retrieve my body. All I could do was switch on the GPS and let him log me onto his screen.

The soldiers at the Green Zone's exit gate were also surprised when I rolled up at their checkpoint. They wanted to know where my security detail was and refused to believe me when I said I was travelling alone. I made it clear that I had to get a move on and although the soldiers tried to talk me out of leaving, they had no authority to stop me.

With eyes straining and adrenaline flowing I reported my progress as I headed along Route Irish while the operations room watched on their screen. The journey passed without incident as luck would have it; well that is until I approached the checkpoint at the airport entrance. As normal, the traffic was at a standstill and I had to join the back of the queue.

I looked around nervously and glanced at the AK47 on the seat next to me, wondering if I would have to use it. A mixture of battered cars, pickups and vans surrounded mine and there was no sign of a security team. Just my luck, I thought, that everyone had decided to miss the rush hour traffic on this particular morning of all mornings. I was the only Westerner amongst a crowd of Iraqis and I stuck out like a sore thumb; in fact I felt as if I was ten feet tall and naked with everyone staring at me.

With eyes wide open, I scanned around checking for threats, while trying not to catch anybody's attention. It was too late, I already had. There was a pickup truck in the next lane, just behind my left tail-light, and the eight Iraqi men crouched in the open back were staring at me and pointing. Brilliant I thought, I was trapped and the centre of attention; talk about feeling like a trussed up turkey which had just been delivered for Christmas.

A car is great when it is moving but it is a death trap in a situation like this. Up ahead the traffic was nudging forward towards the checkpoint, one vehicle at a time. The lane to the left was also nose to tail and while the lane to the right was clear; it was clear for a very good reason. It was the emergency lane, the fast-track lane into the airport for emergency vehicles, military vehicles and VIPs, courtesy of the Department of Defence (DoD).

Although I was facing my own little emergency, I knew that it was not what the DoD had in mind. If I drove my unidentified vehicle towards the military checkpoint all that awaited me was an untimely death. The soldiers manning the concrete bunkers at the end were regularly shooting up suicide bombers trying to ram the airport checkpoint with their impressive array of weaponry.

I did not have long to contemplate my dilemma because the Iraqis had jumped off the back of the truck and were banging on my car windows, shouting obscenities and drawing attention to me. Well that made my mind up; I revved the car up and pulled out into the DoD lane, forcing my tormentors to jump out of the way. As I drove away towards the checkpoint with the Iraqis giving chase, a sign threatening the 'Use of lethal force' flashed by; then another saying 'No unauthorized use of this lane'. This was not looking good.

Although I knew I was jumping out of the frying pan and into the fire, I felt it was better to do something than nothing. Looking back in the mirror, I could see the Iraqis had stopped running because they knew they would be shot if they continued to give chase. I also knew there was a good chance my car could be turned into an instant scrapheap if the guards at the checkpoint were having a bad day. I did not want to think what I would be turned into... I stopped at what I thought was a safe distance from the checkpoint, far enough not to pose a threat. I could almost sense the guards' eyes on me and their fingers hovering over their trigger; all it would take would be one to squeeze and it was all over for me.

As I jumped out of the car and waved my arms, I just hoped that they took the time to work out that I was a Westerner and not some mad suicide bomber. To my surprise, and relief, my antics worked and I could see one of the guards cautiously waving me forward. With my heart pounding, I jumped back in the car and drove forward slowly up to the chicane of concrete blocks. The guard gave me a puzzled look as he studied my Department of Defence and Security ID. He also patiently listened to my off the cuff explanation that I was delivering the vehicle and how I had been under threat. Although he was suspicious, my ID was in order and my car checked out OK, so he had no reason to refuse me entry. I was given the all clear to drive through the checkpoint to safety.

News travelled fast that I had made it to the airport because there was an American guy waiting to meet me in the car park. After exchanging pleasantries and checking my name he took the car keys off me and directed me to the check in area. At that time there were no departures boards in Baghdad airport; that was hoping for too much. You went through the same type of security you would expect at any airport and then went to an airline desk to sort out your flight.

No one had explained which flight I was on, so I assumed that it was down to me to get my own ticket. Having done the dangerous part of the journey, I was not going to make a fuss and joined the queue ready to book my ticket. As I stood there wondering what would happen next, I felt a tap on my shoulder and I heard my name mentioned. I spun round to see a smiling face and the guy introduced himself with the words "well I am Tom and I am here to help you".

As he led me away from the queue, he asked how the journey was. "You don't want to know", I laughed; "I only just made it here". After listening to the nightmare journey I had had on Route Irish, he assured me that they were going to sort that out for the future. I did not ask who they were, but I promised him that I was not planning on making the trip again.

We were soon at a side desk which did not appear to be affiliated to any airline and we were both dealt with straight away. Once in the departure hall I decided it was time to ask if we were heading for Kuwait, because I could let our logistics man know that I would be stopping tonight. No he said, we were going in the opposite direction, to Amann in Jordan. By now I knew that this was no normal flight but before I could ask any more questions, his phone rang and without a word, he turned to me and said "it is time to get you out of here my friend".

He led me out of a door and onto the tarmac where a Learjet plane was ready with its steps down waiting to greet us. Two smiling South African air hostesses guided us to our seats on the empty plane and then the tiny plane taxied onto the runway while the pilot went through the pre-flight procedures.

Now this was just a little too surreal and as I sat back with a puzzled look on my face, Tom assured me that everything was going to be OK, he would explain the situation during the flight. I thought, "after the 24 hours I have just had you can tell me anything and I am going to believe you".

As the plane's engines roared into life and the pilot guided it into the skies, I gazed down at Baghdad airport and spotted Route Irish. An hour ago I had been down there trapped between angry Iraqi civilians and twitchy American soldiers; and now I was heading for Jordan.

As we settled into the flight, I started talking to Tom and although he did not tell me who he worked for I assumed he was an agent of the C.I.A. He had a book in his hands and he carefully pointed out one photograph of Henry Kissinger, the U.S. Secretary of State who had been present at all the big Middle East peace deals. Tom then pointed out a younger version of himself; he had been Kissinger's bodyguard. To say I was impressed was an understatement.

He went on to explain that we would chill out for a bit in Amann before flying onto London. Then I could have a break while my future in Iraq was decided. At least someone had a plan I thought, because my head was still spinning from all the excitement. As we touched down at Queen Sofie airport, I could see a presidential style escort waiting on the tarmac and thought that somebody important might be waiting to use our plane. I was wrong; Tom explained that it was our lift, laughing at my shocked reaction. Oh well I thought, in for a penny in for a pound and I jumped in the huge vehicle with my bags.

The car drove us to our hotel and I imagined the Jordanian officials in the car wondered who was this bloke in dusty fatigues in the back while we drove into Amann. The staff at the huge fantastic five star hotel where we stopped wondered as well. They had turned out in force to meet our motorcade and they could not understand what was going on when Tom and I climbed out of the car; they thought it was carrying someone special. Well after the day I had just had, I was starting to feel a bit special, particularly when we were allocated the presidential suite.

After dumping our bags in reception, Tom and I got in the lift to check out our new accommodation. The suite covered the whole floor and had everything you could think of; I think the word he kept hearing me say was "wow". But later as I lay in the presidential style bath of steaming water, I could not get my head around the events of the past twelve hours. This morning I was stuck outside Baghdad Airport and now look at me; the guys back at the villa would never guess and they would not have believed me if I had called them.

The following morning the motorcade took Tom and me back to the airport where we were checked into the first class lounge awaiting a Jordanian Airlines flight back to London. As I settled back into my luxury seat on the plane, the fact I was going home had still not sunk in. Whether I would be going home for good or if I would be able to return to work in Baghdad was still in the air. The main thing for now was that I was about to have a short break, albeit a forced one, and a bit of time with the family which would give me time to take my mind off things for a bit.

After landing at Heathrow Airport and collecting my bags from the carousel, the pair of us walked through customs and into the terminal building. As I was taking in the familiar sights and sounds of a London airport, Tom shook my hand and said "it is time we parted company my friend, I wish you well". And then just as quickly as he had entered my life he was gone, leaving me with my thoughts.

But while I was safe back in London, at the back of my mind I was wondering what was happening in Baghdad, the questions over the business, the lads, the Iraqi police and a host of other things kept me awake at night. I did not have long to find out what my fate was going to be.

Chapter Twenty

Pastures New

AFTER ONLY A FEW DAYS BACK in Mallorca, one of my partners rang me to tell me the good news and the bad news. The bad news was there was no way I could go back into Baghdad, the situation was just too sensitive. If the police found out I was back at my desk again, they would be back demanding my handover. The Americans did not want to answer questions over my assisted departure either.

The good luck was that our main client had been offered extra work in the north of Iraq, in the predominantly Kurdish area around Erbil and Mosul. The engineers would need security teams to protect them and someone had to organize them. I was the ideal man to set up a new regional office alongside other security companies. What a result; I was still in the game and I was so grateful.

My first consideration was where were we going to live? A few calls to the military and other security companies established that Erbil, Kurdistan's largest city, was the best place. The city was 200 miles north of Baghdad and there was an airport and suitable hotel accommodation for the clients. It was a modern city with a good infrastructure and by all accounts it was safe; mind you anywhere would feel safe after Baghdad... That was good news and it got better. I was told that a number of security companies were already in the city and they had clubbed together to form a secure compound, protected by security guards and vehicle checkpoints. It appeared that Erbil had its own little Green Zone; and there was a nice little villa up for rent. So far so good; it was time to get back to Iraq and go and view my new home. Before long I was packing my bags and heading back to northern Iraq for a new adventure.

Arbil in Arabic or Erbil in Turkoman, is the largest city in the Kurdish area of Iraq, with a population of more than 1.3 million people who were a mixture of Christians and Sunni Muslim Kurds. By the time I arrived it had been renamed its Kurdish name, Hawler, and Arabic signs were being replaced as quickly as possible. The city is close to the Turkish and Iranian borders, approximately 50 miles east of Mosul and there is a range of mountains rising to the east. Although it was now a busy commercial and administrative centre, a lot of its money was generated from the local oil industry and agriculture.

That was the Erbil I arrived in, but it was soon clear that it had its roots way back in history. There were ruins of the ancient city in the centre of the city and they had been continuously inhabited for 5,000 years, making it one of the world's oldest towns. The walls sit perched on top of a large 30 metre high mound and the earliest records referring to the settlement date back to the late 3rd Millennium BC.

The Kurds have had a difficult time since Saddam Hussein seized power but following the Kurdish uprising that followed the Gulf war in 1991, Erbil became the capital of the semi-independent Iraqi Kurdistan. A rebel operation backed by the C.I.A. failed to topple Saddam Hussein in March 1996 and while hundreds of Kurds were killed, thousands more escaped, many to the United States. The following August the Kurdistan Democratic Party seized Erbil and most of the region. The Republican Guard reacted violently, bringing Kurdistan's brief semi-independence to an end.

Following the second invasion of Iraq in March 2003, the Kurds once again assumed semi-independence from the rest of Iraq and they set about restoring security across the area. The Armed Forces of Kurdistan or Peshmerga, had been around since the collapse of the Ottoman and Qajar empires in the years following the First World War. The name literally means 'Those Who Face Death' and they had been at the sharp end of all the conflicts with Saddam Hussein's troops. Peshmarga troops also fought alongside U.S. led coalition forces during operations across Kurdistan in the 2003 war and they went on to assume responsibility for the security of the region. When the Iraqi National Guard and the Iraqi Police units failed to control rising insurgent activity in Kurdistan, particularly Mosul, late in 2004, Peshmerga units joined the U.S. military counter-attack.

It was reckoned there were around 250,000 Peshmerga across Kurdistan when I reached the area and they had set up a line of roadblocks and observation points all along its border, to stop insurgents infiltrating. They had also set up a 'Ring of Steel' around Erbil, stopping foreign insurgents wreaking havoc in its streets, like they had done in Baghdad. Other units were stationed in towns and villages to reassure the people and counter attacks. So far it had worked because the amount of terrorist activity to my knowledge was nil.

Our client was a subcontractor for another American company working to bring the power plants across Kurdistan back to life. The main contractor already had people working in Erbil and they had offered to show me the ropes; and it meant for once I would not be driving into uncharted territory. Which was good.

I flew from Dubai to Erbil on one of the small twin propeller planes which served as internal charter flights. Most of the passengers were Iraqi businessmen or families but there were half a dozen Westerners on board. While I avoided a couple of press men, I sat with a couple of security guys. You could always tell the sort, well built, shaved head, goatee, shades and of course, the military style clothing that every security guy seemed to be wearing these days. It had become an unofficial uniform of the private security contractor.

The flight was short, shorter because I had someone in my line of business to talk to, and we were soon coming in to land at Erbil airport. That was the first thing I noticed, the straightforward landing; no manically steep dives to avoid rocket launchers. Getting through security was also far more laid back than Baghdad airport. Erbil airport is five miles northwest of the city centre and by 2006 it was processing 200,000 passengers a year. There were fourteen international destinations, really putting Erbil on the map.

So far so good. In no time at all I had my bag and was having a coffee in the waiting hall. As I settled down to wait for my lift, the two security guys off the plane asked if I wanted a lift because I was heading for the same place they were. I only knew it was in Erbil, not the location and insisted that I waited for my contact to turn up. Before they headed off, they said they would let the camp know I had arrived. My mobile phone had an Iraqi sim card and it would not work up in Erbil, so I could not call ahead. The airport shop did not sell any local ones, so I rang the Baghdad office to pass on a message for me. Even a young Kurdish lad called my contact on his Kurdish phone but there was no reply. Well I had tried everything, all I could do was wait and watch; and watch and wait I did.

I was there for a long time and while the stay was boring, I learnt a lot about the security situation in Kurdistan. The first thing I noticed was that the airport was guarded by Kurdish security personnel and there were no U.S. military around. A number of security teams picked up clients and their routine confirmed the airport was a safe place. Only the police and the security could park outside the terminal building, other cars were not allowed to, they had to be parked in a car park 400 metres away and passengers used a shuttle bus, like they do now in British airports.

Elsewhere people were going about their business and flights were coming and going as they would in any Western airport which fascinated me; I had not seen a civilian flight in Iraq before.

After four hours the call came from Baghdad; my lift would meet me in the car park. I thought to myself what a cock up, it was a good job I was not a client or someone would be in big trouble. We were soon on our way and after only a short drive I was surprised when we stopped by a line of blast walls and a vehicle checkpoint and my driver said "Home Sweet Home". I say surprised because we were in the suburbs and armed Kurdistan guards were checking our ID and our car, rather than U.S. soldiers. As we drove into a street lined with villas and a few shops, I realized that the blast walls surrounded the area.

The companies working in Erbil had rented all the villas to create a mini

Green Zone. By pooling together their money they had created a secure living space midway between the airport and the city centre, with good links to the main roads. While each company looked after their own villa, local Kurds took care of the general security.

We were met by a security guard outside the villa I was due to view and it was not long before the landlord was negotiating the rent in cash. It was a similar set up to the one in Baghdad with its own garden, parking spaces and external wall. The downstairs rooms would serve as the office, operations room, kitchen and armoury. There were plenty of bedrooms upstairs and a roof top terrace for the gym. I could see the airport from the roof and we could always get men up there to fire down on the streets if we came under attack.

The best thing about the villa was that it was fully furnished, meaning I could concentrate on operational matters. The landlord also had a long list of useful contacts and had primed people to visit. In no time at all we had computers, phones and internet. There was a supermarket down the street where we could get everything from food to drink and mobile phones to toiletries. Talk about landing on your feet. If I had known in advance, I would not have bothered with the logistics planning. It was a complete contrast to Basra and Baghdad where we had to beg and bribe everything we needed to get going.

Our Baghdad office and our client were also surprised when I told them the news; it sounded too good to be true. My smooth 'moving in' meant that we were able to get to work straight away and I asked for a four man team to fly up with basic equipment for the office, including a stack of money. Everything, including cars, weapons, ammunition, medical supplies and food had to be bought in cash and, as unsafe as it sounds, we always had a minimum of $10,000 stashed in the house. I guess it was a good job we were always armed.

Once the villa was sorted, I began exploring and found everything we needed in the row of shops at the bottom of the street. There was a bar, so we had no need to build our own. I also saw a restaurant and was pleased to see that it had large television screens; that meant no more moaning about missing the football on a weekend. There were a number of security guys chilling out in the bar and they were keen to talk to the new guy in town. They were only too happy to tell me about what to expect in Kurdistan in exchange for stories about the madness in Baghdad. It was as if they wanted to hear about the bad old days because they wanted reminding how good it was in Erbil.

That night some of the guys introduced me to the local arms dealer and I bought three Tariq 9mm pistols, the Iraq officers' side arm, off him for personal protection. I kept one on me and two in the villa, in case there was a break in. It amused some of the security guys that I wanted to always carry a pistol tucked in my bum bag for self protection. They had only worked in Kurdistan and had never needed to; with me it was just habit and one I was not prepared to break just yet.

That evening I was taken to a restaurant in the city centre and the walk through Erbil's streets was an eye opener. There were families walking around and cars were driving around like normal, it was a surreal experience after the mayhem in Baghdad. After a pleasant evening, I was back at the villa, tucked in my bed. Drifting off to sleep, I thought to myself this is normality; I can get used to this.

The following morning I hired two guys and a couple of cars to take me to pick up the four man team. The short taxi ride with armed drivers was $1,000, and it got me thinking, this is easy money for slack days. I anticipated we were always going to have guys kicking their heels between jobs until we got into the swing of things. The Kurds had made sure that the road to the airport was as safe as any other. A lot of companies were bringing their staff in and they would be in the same position I was when I arrived. All I had to do was get the word out to other clients that we were open for business for small one off jobs or short contracts, and the money would keep our cash flow healthy.

So within 24 hours of my arriving, there were five of us in the villa. The first job for two of the guys was to source our transport from a car dealer on the other side of Kurdistan. Well I say car dealer, the guy was selling armoured cars for a cheap cash price. He could have been legitimate or one of the many local gangsters who were making a living across Kurdistan. I told the guys get me good cars at a good price, no questions asked, and they did. By nightfall there were three second hand armoured cars, a Lincoln, a BMW and a Mercedes, and all in good condition for the grand sum of $40,000; what a bargain. As I said no questions asked, but as there had been a couple of bank robberies in the area recently, maybe they were hot. As we did not have the spare cash to go legitimate, it was a case of beggars could not be choosers. At least we were mobile.

By the afternoon of day two I was back on the phone again to Baghdad, asking for a second four-man team to drive up to Erbil loaded with arms and ammunition. I figured that prices from our established sources around Baghdad would be lower. While the company always promised an AK47 long arm and a side arm for each man, the extra choice would please some of the guys. After all, everyone always had their preference when it came to shoes, clothes, beer and semi-automatic rifles.

The team made the nine-hour drive the following day while I sorted out the operations room with maps, phones and internet. They arrived late that evening and it was good to see them; now we could start work. All four were experienced and the fact that Kurdistan was a secure place made all our jobs easier. I was able to tell our Baghdad office that "we had things squared away".

As well as a cleaner and cook, I also looked at recruiting Kurds to work with our security teams. Starting in 2006 the C.P.A. made it compulsory to employ Iraqi (or Kurdish) nationals on our security teams. It was an unpopular decision with security companies, ours included, because too many things could go wrong; after all we were still responsible for the client's safety. The ruling was brought in because the C.P.A. was anxious to tell everyone that the situation across Iraq had improved. Our guys were out on the streets every day and they could have given plenty of reasons to disagree.

Some companies left Iraq before the law was introduced but those who stayed had to sit down and make contingency plans to limit the security implications. It was a case of working out what jobs the Iraqis could work on to make the best of the situation. We were not looking forward to it because it was going to be a case of damage limitation, both from a security and a financial point of view.

The U.S. military put in stringent checks for each Iraqi applicant and they reckoned the vetting procedure took about six weeks. Each man was checked for terrorist links and because most Iraqis had extended families and networks of friends, the checks nearly always turned up a problem. But after all the hype and all the vetting, we employed about 70 Iraqi employees on the security teams; around 50 in Baghdad and 20 in Kurdistan. We had none in the south because the Iraqi police were already working across the Basra area.

Although many Iraqis were turned away, we were still concerned about the ones cleared to work. Had they slipped through the security net or, more likely, would they be bribed? After all these young men were very poor and even if they did not have a young family to support, they would probably be the chief earner in the household. If it came down to it would they take the money and compromise us or would they remain loyal to us? You just never knew.

We had to introduce new SOPs to minimize the potential security risks, and I think I am safe in saying that no one liked working under them; neither the Westerners nor the Iraqis. The law was that half of the team had to be Iraqi Nationals and we took the decision to put two Westerners in the lead vehicle with the client while the two Iraqis followed in the second car.

The O-Group meeting, where the team leader explained the job for the day to the team had to be changed for starters. While our guys were briefed on where they were going, the Iraqis were not and at no time were they told where they were going. Of course they were always asking "where are we going today boss" out of curiosity but we always refused; no exceptions. They just had to follow the lead car, ask no questions and listen to the radio.

While weapons were issued to the Iraqis the team leader did not hand out magazines until it was time to drive out of the gate. Then he jumped back in the car and away they went. The weapons were confiscated and locked in the armoury as soon as they returned. The Iraqis' mobile phones were also confiscated and they only had short range radios for keeping in touch. The two cars were expected to stay in sight of each other and radio talk was to be as limited as possible.

As you can see we did everything possible to limit the dangers and while we sort of complied with the law, it is doubtful that we were following the spirit of it. While some of the Iraqis disputed our double standards, we stuck to our guns. They kept their job and we had limited the risks. The same fifty-percent nationals rule applied in Kurdistan and we often sent out a three car convoy with four Kurds in one of the cars. These guys were useful translators, particularly as the local dialects were hard to make out, and they were particularly helpful at getting us smoothly through checkpoints manned by Peshmerga fighters.

So within no time at all, we had a good little base set up and as we settled down to work it occurred to me that we had set up four base camps in three years. Starting with five of us and the bit of money we had raised, we had created a large security company with a huge turnover, over 300 employees and a good reputation out of virtually nothing, using the skills we had been taught in the Special Forces; oh and of course a bit of luck thrown in – both good and bad. It was a hell of an achievement by any standards...

Our client had given us a list of places to look up and we had to familiarize ourselves with the geography, the road network and the security situation at each site. I had to price each one up, looking at many different things, some of them straight forward, many of them not. In some cases I had detailed information but sometimes I had to make an educated guess. While the U.S. military could provide intelligence on an area it was always better to see it for yourself.

While we had three weeks to prepare, we had a dozen or more large sites to consider and they ranged from power stations, to hydroelectric dams to new military camps. After amassing a collection of maps, we checked them out and sketched out routes to some pretty remote places. Where possible we planned to do the drive out and back in a day because the chance of finding accommodation in Kurdistan was nil. It did mean, however, that the lads faced some long hard days on the road.

Sites had different start dates and we had to calculate when to install accommodation and security, so we would be ready for the engineers. The security assessment had to consider the size of the compound, the facilities, a suitable defensive system and the surrounding terrain. We also had to estimate the number of local men we needed to find to work on each site, either as security or labourers, so we would be ready to negotiate with the local leaders. Getting information on local threats would have to wait until we got on the ground but the terrain gave us a few clues about what to expect.

The client's needs also had to be considered; their living quarters and logistics requirements, including the long drives we had to take across the country and possible escape routes. Each site needed a security team and manning them took some consideration because it would need a mixture of experienced men from other areas and new men we had to recruit.

And finally I had to work out the logistics for an area over 250 miles from east to west and 100 from north to south. Apart from the handful of cities, this was outback style country; rugged and tribal. We would have to be more self-sufficient than ever. As always we needed to move transport, weapons, ammunition and equipment about, and then we had to feed the men. It was going to be a tough assignment but after Baghdad, anything was a refreshing change. I was looking forward to it because I was heading back into the countryside after months of being cooped up in the Green Zone.

For the next three weeks the teams were busy checking out the routes and the work sites, making route cards and security assessments. There was plenty to do to make sure we were ready for when the client's staff arrived. We could only bill the client at half the operational rate while we were carrying out reconnaissance work so I put my airport run idea into operation. No one else was doing them and after a few conversations in the bar, it was clear that there was a market for a bit of moonlighting. We charged $1,000 a time, topping up both the company's income and the lads' wages for their extra time.

We could see over the blast wall and watch the airport car park from our roof top gym so we relied on an old fashioned method of communications. We set up an observation post and a makeshift flag pole, using a red sheet as our flag. We could not get our hands on a Union Jack to hand and there was no way we were going to use the Stars and Stripes. The routine was to raise the flag when it was safe and take it down when it was not. The team simply stayed at the airport and awaited further instructions if they could not see the flag.

Training still had to go on and we used the local police firing range. All we had to do was call their headquarters to book a slot. Then we could go ahead practising shooting, debussing, driving and good old tyre changing.

Before long the regular routine involved two weekly runs out to a new army camp next to the town of Tal 'Afar on the Syrian border. That involved driving there one morning, stopping over night in the temporary cabins and then driving back the following afternoon. The rest of the week we were doing airport runs and I was quite pleased to say, we had 'a lovely little set up'. The cash was building into a nice little nest egg and I used some of the money to give the lads a bit of a treat. We normally used Tariq pistols as backup weapons but they were heavy and clumsy. This time I acquired some new Glock 17 semi-automatic pistols and while you might be thinking 'boys and their toys', after lugging around an old Tariq, these were the business. The lads were 'creaming themselves' when they got their hands on them. Personally I had always preferred the CZ99 9mm pistol, a Serbian version of a Czech design, which had a reputation for quality and reliability; the grip also fitted snugly into my hand.

When our clients arrived they were settled into Erbil's Sheraton hotel, a new up-to-date place, surrounded by blast walls. All we had to do was flash our passes at security, park up and walk past the fountains to the door. There was no sound of gunfire out on the streets like I remembered all those months ago in Baghdad's Palestine Hotel; this was more like a hotel back in London. Once inside the reception we could sit down with the clients and be served coffee by immaculate waiters while other guests, some locals and some Western contractors, carried on with their business under the watchful eye of the ever present hookers at the bar.

Our workload was expanding, and an old friend from my SF days joined me. We worked back to back in the office, allowing one to run the office while the other one was out checking things were running smoothly. Every evening the pair of us would don our sports gear and go running in the huge park which surrounded Erbil's ancient Citadel. There were armed guards everywhere, but the sense of freedom after the claustrophobia of Baghdad's Green Zone was fantastic.

We also walked down into the town most evenings for food and a touch of normality. Walking was easier than driving because of the roadblocks and the heavy armed presence on the streets. You could see why the people of Erbil called it their 'Ring of Steel'. It was great to be able to mingle with the locals, looking in the markets and shops where there was everything from weapons and clothes to carpets and gifts. You could even get your hair cut at one of the many barber shops, not that I had any to cut. Kurdish men are very particular about their appearance and they loved to have a trim, a proper shave and a manicure while chatting with their friends. I had to make do with having my head shaved while they laughed and joked with me. Then it would be time for a coffee at the Sheraton hotel before heading back to the villa.

Another advantage of working in Erbil was that there was a functioning bank; the 'Emerald Bank' which, as it said on the advertisements was "an independent bank servicing the Kurdish community". For the first time since I had arrived in Iraq, we were able to use normal banking facilities rather than having to dish out wads of cash every time we needed something.

One of the contracts we picked up involved the building of the super camp at Tal 'Afar and an American management team was employing a Kurdish company to carry out the work. There were always hundreds of labourers and dozens of pieces of construction machinery on the site and everyone needed paying. The cost was phenomenal and while the American company was happy to use the Emerald Bank, the Kurdish contractor wanted his money in hard cash; and he wanted it every week.

One of our teams had to escort the American representative to the bank so he could withdraw around half a million dollars at a time. The cash would be stashed in a suitcase and our guys then escorted him through the city to the contactor's villa on the far side of the city. I do not know if the contractor was into any other line of business, but he certainly believed in security because his heavily fortified villa put our Little Green Zone to shame. Once the cash had been handed over, the Kurdish manager would call the camp and tell his supervisors to carry on working. After the discussions over requirements for the following week, it was back to the Sheraton Hotel for the client; another job well done. Of course, it was all unofficial, we were just the middle man in a financial arrangement that we were not party to. Another case of ask no questions, hear no lies...

Our client also had a contract at the Dukan Dam, a huge arch dam where the Lesser Zab River ran through a narrow gorge. The concrete structure had been built back in the 1950s and was in a bad state of repair. However, our client was only interested in the outdated hydroelectric power plant which had to be replaced.

The road east to Dukan followed fantastic mountain ranges along the Iraq-Iran border and the spectacular countryside took your breath away. Again there were few threats apart from breakdowns and for once you could relax a little as you wound your way through the hills. Although the route was 75-miles as the crow flies, the road seemed to go on and on. The longer, but faster, southern route went through the town of Kirkuk, a place dubbed "an absolute nightmare". Like many cities in Iraq the people were a real mixture and in this case the Iraqis and Kurds were fighting for control of it. We did not want to be driving through there and we only sent teams into the town when it was absolutely necessary.

Whenever possible we used an alternative route, courtesy of the U.S. military. There was a heliport at the large AEGIS camp at As Sulaymaniyah, 50 miles to the south and our guys sometimes managed to hitch a lift to Erbil on one of their helicopters.

Another contract was at the Haditha Reservoir on the Euphrates River north of Haditha, 150 miles northwest of Baghdad. The huge concrete wall increased the capacity of Lake Qadasiyah to over eight billion cubic metres of water. The size of the lake is unbelievable and when you looked across the water it reminded you of a sea stretching into the distance; having said that, it was nowhere near as large as some of the other dams across Iraq.

The ageing dam was in a poor condition and the adjacent power station had been hit during both invasions of Iraq. The power station's six turbines were designed to produce 660 MW but water agreements with Turkey and Syria reduced the water flow until it was only producing a third of its maximum. It was still the second largest hydroelectric system contributor to the power system and in desperate need of an overhaul.

A lot of our client's work was inside the reservoir wall where everybody was safely housed inside the abandoned rooms which covered about fourteen storeys. All we needed was a bit of furniture while the guys slept on cots. While that reduced the cost of accommodation, the place was dank and musty and no one liked being inside. The echo of the tomblike rooms and the emergency lighting gave it an eerie feel while the dripping water was a constant reminder that thousands of tons of water were just a few metres away behind the concrete walls.

In quiet moments talk sometimes turned to what we would do if the dam burst. Well we would have had no chance of course and while we tried to talk about anything else, it did prey on your mind at times. It did not help that insurgents occasionally carried out mortar and rocket attacks on the dam and although we were told U.S. Rangers were protecting us, we never felt totally at ease.

No one could stay inside the dam wall for long but climbing out was like being on a treadmill. The musty air made you long for fresh air as you dragged your feet up the stairs. While it was bad enough for us guys who trained every day, it was almost impossible for one of our clients, a twenty-stone American who had not been running since high school. Every time the alarm sounded we had to evacuate and getting him up those fourteen flights of stairs in a hurry was a nightmare.

One of the first contracts we had in Kurdistan was the toughest we had to organize, both from a risk and a logistics point of view; it was the trip to a military super camp at Tal 'Afar 40 miles from the Syrian border. The Iraqi Army was going to use it to control the movement of insurgents entering Iraq around the Rabiah border crossing, northwest of the town.

The camp would take two years to build and it promised to provide us with regular work; we were also tasked with recruiting Ghurkas to work as security during the construction period. A lot of the work involved installing a wall of temporary concrete units to protect the construction site until the permanent walls were ready. Inside contractors were building everything from barracks to garages and from dining halls to cinemas. When it was finished 5,000 troops would live there. In the meantime, our guys had to put up with temporary cabins and a lot of dust.

The military camp had different names at different times (Camp Munsan, Camp Fulda and eventually Camp Sykes) but we did not like the journey whatever it was called. If you look up the camp on the internet you will find that it was described as being in "one of the most dangerous and inaccessible areas of all Iraq; the secular nature of Tal'Afar has only increased the instability of this area". All I will say is that whoever wrote that must have the same sort of fond memories about that forsaken place as I have...

The drive from Erbil to Tal'Afar was about four hours, making a round trip in daylight virtually impossible. The journey started with a one hour drive through open desolate countryside as far as the Great Zab River. The river bridge had been destroyed by the Americans (presumably to stop Iraqi tanks rolling into the Kurdistan capital) leaving the people in the area with a problem. No bridge meant no traffic, which meant no trade, which meant no money, which defeated the object. While the people wanted to be liberated, they did not want to starve.

The problem was high on the agenda of the U.S. military and it did not take too long to install a heavy duty pontoon bridge capable of carrying lorries. The guards would only let one vehicle across at a time, to limit the weight on the pontoons, creating a serious bottleneck. I spent many a nervous hour waiting in the line of traffic for our turn to be waved through the riverside checkpoint.

Once across the bridge, we were in bandit country because the river served as a border between Kurdistan and northern Iraq. Although this part of the world was far safer than the Sunni Triangle, the team leader would always tell his guys "to switch on", as their cars drove up the slope away from the bridge.

Mosul was another 45 minutes west of the Great Zab and the place had bad memories for me because of the ambush a couple of years earlier. The city was a bottleneck of traffic jams with the main choke points at the crossings over the River Tigris. It was also impossible to anticipate where the police and military roadblocks would be. In short, "Mosul was not a place to go and our people did not want to go there."

Our Forward Recon Team had spent some time looking for a way around the sprawling suburbs and their efforts had been rewarded with the discovery of a little bypass around the north side of the city. Well I say bypass, but it was actually a 30 minute drive along a network of country roads and then a quick sprint through the western suburbs so we could cross the River Tigris. While the route was longer, it was quicker than crawling through the city traffic; it was also much safer. The insurgents were too busy stirring up trouble in the city to be worried about what was happening out in the country.

While the city checkpoints were formal affairs which could delay you for hours, we only encountered the occasional makeshift affair on our 'scenic route'. The authorities set them up to check papers but apart from the few stones painted white, all the police officer had for company was a plastic chair and a sunshade. Sometimes the authorities really pushed the boat out and posted two officers in a porta cabin while a pole barrier slung between a couple of concrete filled steel drums staked their claim. Either way they were not going to stop two cars loaded with armed Westerners waving their IDs. We would just do our usual trick and keep moving, keep smiling and keep eyeballing.

The main problem with the scenic route was the poor state of the roads. Apart from the main roads, routes across Kurdistan and northern Iraq were no better than potholed, dirt tracks. They were a nightmare, leaving you bruised and sore at the end of a long uncomfortable bumpy ride, but anything was better than taking our chances in Mosul.

We always had to task one of the 4x4s on rough routes in case one of the civvy cars became stuck and had to be towed out. There were many flat tyres and we carried as many spares as we could. While we strapped them to the roof or the back of the 4x4, we left the spares in their usual place on the civvy style vehicles to try and blend in with the other traffic.

Whenever you had a flat it was into the old routine, and while two of the team changed the tyre, the other two formed the perimeter guard. Changing a wheel was a back breaking job but we had sourced a new device, in the shape of an inflatable jack, which took the strain off the loaded car. You threw the deflated balloon under the car and attached a tube to the exhaust. After revving for couple of minutes the balloon inflated, lifting the wheel off the ground while it was changed; and then you just let the air out. The old fashioned scissor jacks would often sink into mud, especially if you were lifting an armoured car loaded with gear. These inflatable jacks made the drill a lot safer and a little faster.

The road west of Mosul headed almost straight west through undulating countryside and lots of little villages where time had stood still. The only landmark on the route was a huge pipeline which stretched as far as the eye could see across the barren land. It was the Iraq-Turkey pipeline, a massive feat of engineering which carried thousands of barrels a day from the pumping station at Bayji across the border, heading for the Turkish oil terminal at Ceyhan. I often wondered why the insurgents did not blow it up rather than try to kill the likes of us. Surely it would have been easier?

The last structure we saw before getting to Tal 'Afar was a massive jail with huge grim walls surrounding the compound. As we drove past I always used to look up at the hundreds of tiny windows and wonder, "… and we think we have it bad". It just did not bear thinking about what happened inside there. Iraq's judicial system was seriously overloaded since the war ended and many prisoners waited for months before they were charged. They were kept in overcrowded and degrading conditions with no exercise for weeks at a time. However, many Iraqi civilians were living in similar conditions and the Iraqi Interior Ministry could be forgiven for being overwhelmed by problems. It could not be excused for failing to pursue allegations of torture, starvation and abuse which seemed to do the rounds on a regular basis.

After the prison, it was a straight stretch into real bandit country. Tal 'Afar had 200,000 residents under Saddam Hussein's regime and while it was an ethnically diverse mix of people, the main group was the Turkmen. The town had had its problems since the war ended but they peaked in the hot summer months of 2004 when a quarter of the population left, fearing for their lives. The remainder stayed off the streets until the U.S. and Iraqi military worked together to clear the town in September 2004. After the local police chief declared Tal 'Afar insurgent-free, the military began restoring clean water and electricity supplies so the people would return to their homes.

The number of U.S. soldiers in the town had been reduced to 500 by the spring of 2005 and the insurgents began to return. Tal 'Afar's position close to the Syrian border made it an ideal stop off point for foreign insurgents sneaking into Iraq. There were suspicions that the border guards were either incompetent or corrupt and attempts were made to bolster their numbers with U.S. soldiers. But it was too little, too late and the insurgents found many new recruits among the city's disaffected youth. Their work was made easier by the high unemployment levels which rarely fell below 75%.

Disturbances grew into outright challenges and the C.P.A. had to ask the military to restore control. 4,000 American troops joined Iraqi soldiers in a sweep of the town in June. By now the town resembled a battle ground and while Bradley fighting vehicles and Abrahms tanks rolled through the streets, the civilians fled; over 250 insurgents were rounded up in the operation.

With the town secure, steps were taken over the months that followed to restore normality. In March 2006 President George W. Bush declared that Tal 'Afar was a model town where the world could "see the outlines of the Iraq we've been fighting for." Fair enough you might think, but the insurgents took his statement as a challenge. The following day one of them drove a truck into the police station compound and detonated the stack of artillery shells loaded on the back. The explosion demolished the building and killed several policemen, including the senior ranking officer in the area. The 200 strong police force had to relocate to an old Ottoman fortress on the edge of town, the only safe place around.

Bush had really put Tal 'Afar on the insurgents' map and as you might have gathered it was not the sort of place you wanted to hang around – and we did not. Up until Bush's announcement we had been moving clients covertly through the area in standard Lincolns and Mercedes. But we could not afford to do that anymore; we needed as much protection as we could get and we switched to armoured 4x4s.

After passing through two police checkpoints on the outskirts of the town, the first thing you saw was the demolished police station with its flattened walls and collapsed concrete roof. It was a stark reminder of what lay ahead and no one in their right mind went into the town.

A roundabout marked the start of Tal 'Afar bypass, codenamed Route Santa Fe, and the start of one of the most dangerous stretches of road in Iraq at the time. The team leader would announce over the radio 'every man for himself' as the lead car approached the roundabout. Everyone braced themselves for the ride of their life as the drivers put their foot down and drove as fast as they could.

While there was open desert to the right, there was a line of deserted houses riddled with bullet holes along the left side. Someone was always watching and if they did not do anything this time you could be sure they were watching, getting a feel for your tactics. The insurgents had plenty of volunteers wanting to 'dick' us for money and we viewed anyone loitering near the road with suspicion. No one hung around there for fun, it was too dangerous.

We often came under fire from the buildings and a few braver guys jumped out of one of the alleys to spray us with automatic fire. While these guys tested your nerves, the worst that could happen would be the sound of bullets hitting the Kevlar panels and the occasional cracked windscreen. The route was also riddled with IEDs and we were constantly on the lookout for markers. Every now and again one detonated but we always drove fast enough to avoid the blast.

A second roundabout at the far end of the town marked the end of the rat run and once we were through the final two police checkpoints, we could breathe a sigh of relief as we 'legged it' down to the camp.

The client usually had plenty to do at the camp and we always planned to camp down in one of the porta-cabins for the night. The following morning the client would finish off his work and then it was time to head back to Erbil. The team started their journey with the mad dash along Route Santa Fe and then faced the four hour drive across the desolation that was Kurdistan.

Chapter Twenty One

Nothing is What it Seems

I TRIED TO GET OUT OF THE ERBIL OFFICE when I could, and while nobody relished making the long drive to Tal 'Afar it was time to see how things were getting on. The convoy consisted of the usual two car, four man, security team and a third car with four Kurdistan locals. The journey there was uneventful and for once the client finished his work much earlier than expected. So I decided to check if we could drive back that evening. The U.S. Army intelligence officer had not heard of any unusual insurgent activity and we had time to cross into Kurdistan before it was dark. While travelling in Iraq after dusk was too dangerous, it was never a problem in Kurdistan.

Having been given the all clear to leave, the lads agreed to get moving. On occasions like these we held what we call a 'Chinese Parliament'. The plan would be explained and then put to the vote with everyone having an equal say. It was then down to the team leader to make the final decision. This democratic form of decision making works in circumstances like these and everyone was up for 'cutting away' rather than stopping over night, the client more than anyone. He was staying at the Sheraton hotel in Erbil and who could blame him for preferring a luxury hotel room to an army camp bed.

So as the sun was going down on the horizon, we drove out of the gate with my vehicle in the lead. It was only a couple of miles to the first police checkpoint, a ramshackle affair of concrete units across the road. Next to the chicane was a small guard hut protected by more concrete units. Usually, the policemen came out of the hut when they heard a car approaching but this time we saw no one. My driver slowed the car down and put the side lights and hazard lights on to get the guards' attention. I also dropped the sun visor to flash the Union Jack taped to the back.

As we crawled closer there was still no sign of movement so we kept moving. There had been seven suicide bomb attacks in the last two weeks in the area and we did not want to be the target of number eight; the sooner we were past it the better.

I called over the radio to let the others know we were going to go through and the other two waited at a safe distance while we moved slowly forward. As soon as I called "checkpoint clear" the second car headed for the chicane. All the time I was scanning the area for signs of life, thinking "this is just crazy..." Then as we pulled away, we heard two shots behind us and a fraction of a second later, bang, bang, at the rear of the car.

I called "Contact… drive, drive, drive" over the radio, so the rest of the team knew we were under fire and we had to break contact. The driver flicked off the car lights as we pulled away from the checkpoint, so we were harder to see. I reached around to pull the client down to the floor for safety. I also wanted to try and see who was shooting at us. As we sped away tracer lit up the darkening sky behind us and it was coming from the checkpoint. I thought "where the hell have they come from" but there was no time for answers: it was time to get out of there.

But as my driver hit the accelerator, the radio crackled into life as car two reported; "We have been stopped… we have all been stopped". After telling my driver to stop, I replied "What do you mean you have been stopped?" It did not take long to find out what had happened. As car two drove through the checkpoint, several police appeared out of the darkness behind the guard hut. While some of the cops had opened fire on us, the rest had surrounded cars two and three brandishing their guns.

Looking back it is easy to understand what had happened. There had been so many suicide bombs over the past few days that the police had taken to camping out in the shadows rather than sitting in the hut. When they heard three unmarked vehicles with darkened windows driving slowly towards the checkpoint, they assumed they were up to no good and had decided to stay out the way. As soon as my car had driven through the checkpoint they decided to put in an appearance. For once our attempts to travel covertly had backfired; you just couldn't win sometimes in Iraq.

So we faced a dangerous situation due to a simple misunderstanding and I had to make a tough decision. We could either make a run for it or go back to the checkpoint and explain who we were. My main concern was, were the cops genuine or not? It would not be the first time a security team had been taken hostage by bogus cops.

So we faced a Catch 22 situation. If they were genuine police, they were annoyed; they would have also alerted the checkpoints ahead that a suspicious car was on its way. If they were fake police, then we were really in trouble and the world news would be reporting the discovery of our bodies in the morning. It was my call and I decided we had to turn around and see if we could clear up the confusion or try and blag our way out of it.

Everything now started to happen at once. As my driver turned around in the road, red and blue lights flickered on in the distance. Checkpoint one had told checkpoint two that a car of bad guys was heading for them. So they climbed in their two police cars and were heading towards us. Brilliant, I thought. As I told the lads over the radio that we were heading back, they gave us some bad news. They had been manhandled out of the cars, forced to stand spread eagled against the cars and were being stripped of their weapons. Then the radio went dead.

Now I was faced with a real dilemma. The client was our number one priority and I briefly considered making a run for it. But that would have left the rest of the team at the mercy of the police. While they might have pursued us, they were more likely to turn on the rest of the team. If they were real cops, our four Kurdistan guys would not stand a chance because of the bitter history between Kurdistan and Iraqi. They would probably be executed on the spot and the report would read "shot while trying to make their escape". Our lads would have been roughed up and thrown into jail while their release was negotiated. If they were fake cops then the Kurds were probably already dead and our guys were looking at being paraded on the television in the orange jumpsuits.

As we came to terms with the situation, the radio crackled into life once more. The cops had ordered one of our guys to convince us to return. I replied "If they stop firing at me I will come back but you can forget it otherwise." After hearing repeated shouts of "cease fire" over the radio, the tracer stopped. While it was against all the SOPs to put the client in danger, I had made my mind up; we were heading back.

So why did I do it? Well there were several reasons. Firstly, the cops at checkpoint one must have spoken to checkpoint two to alert them, which meant there was a good chance they were genuine. They had also let our guy speak on the radio, so they were thinking rashly. It also helped that they had stopped firing.

If we kept driving we faced three checkpoints manned by armed police waiting to shoot at us. The only other option was to drive into the desert, maybe abandon the car and then go on foot. Escape and Evasion in hostile territory with a twenty stone civilian in tow is inadvisable under the best of circumstances; it is suicidal when you have dozens of armed police on your trail.

All those thoughts went through my mind in a few moments and were enough to convince me to go back. As the driver swung the car round, the client started to protest fiercely, but there was no time to argue. After all I was convinced it was not a trap and we had a chance of talking our way out. Of course I did not know what to expect but he was just going to have to trust my judgement. Only no one could have guessed what happened next, not even me.

The two police vehicles from checkpoint two saw us turn around and decided we were making our escape. As the drivers put their foot on the gas, their passengers hung out of the windows and turned their AK47s on us. The client was going crazy, my driver was wondering which way we were going to turn next and I was getting fed up of being shot at.

Fortunately, their aim was poor and they were missing us. Unfortunately they were hitting checkpoint one, causing pandemonium. Checkpoint one thought we were shooting at them, not their colleagues so not to be outdone, they returned fire. We were in the middle of some pretty hot crossfire. The client was moaning "get me out of here" on the floor of the car and while I was thinking the same, I knew it was going to take some serious talking before he saw his hotel room again.

As tracer bullets lit up the sky, I confirmed over the radio that we were not firing. I also asked if everybody would please stop shooting, or choice words to that effect. The whole situation was rapidly turning into one of those final gunfight moments in a gangster film. Well either that or a moment from a Keystone Cops movie, only the stakes were much higher.

My message must have got through because the firing suddenly stopped. The police cars also stopped chasing us. But as we drove up to checkpoint one, it did not look good. We could see our guys standing with their hands behind their heads surrounded by lots of twitchy police brandishing weapons. I guessed they had come from the nearby police headquarters as soon as they had heard the shooting. This was going to take some talking out of.

As I climbed out of the car, a cop pulled my semi-automatic rifle out of hands while a nervous young lad, who looked about sixteen, pulled my pistol out of my holster. While the older guy had no difficulty clearing my M21, the kid could not clear the pistol. I offered to help him, and believe it or not, he gave it to me to clear. He did not notice the rounds fall into the palm of my hand and nodded his approval as I handed the pistol back. Talk about inexperience.

Two cops then shoved me against the car and held me there, while others dragged the client and the driver out of the car. This was looking bad. While all the guys were wearing uniforms they looked too young and untidy to be real cops. For one horrible moment I thought I had made a fatal mistake. As my heart sank into my boots, one of the older cops stepped forward and started speaking in English.

I could smell his breath as he shoved his face in front of mine and shouted; "You broke the checkpoint... you opened fire on us... we had to return fire..."

So that was it; he was making up a story to cover his backside. I tried to explain that we had not, after all how could we shoot without stopping and getting out of the cars? He repeatedly claimed that we had fired first and was adamant we were to blame. To prove his point, he told us we had to explain the situation to his boss. I could feel dozens of pairs of eyes looking at me, particularly from my own team; but there was no time for a Chinese Parliament now. The client had been silent since he had been pulled from the car and he looked petrified. Having said that, he was not on his own, only some of us were doing a better job of hiding it than others. As I calmly agreed to meet the head man, I thought to myself; if I am wrong here, it could be game over for us all tonight.

We were all allowed to climb back into our cars and the cops escorted us slowly towards Tal 'Afar. Our convoy must have been an odd sight, our three cars surrounded by six police cars crammed with Iraqi cops, flashing lights illuminating the night sky. Just before checkpoint two the cop cars at the head of the convoy took a sudden right onto a dirt road and we were forced to follow them. It was one of those 'uh oh' moments as I looked across at my driver, I could see he was thinking the same as me; this is it.

After a few hundred metres, the police cars pulled up outside a scruffy two storey building. Our head lights lit up the white walls surrounding the place but there was no sign of life. As we were ordered out of the cars, the only illumination came from a small light inside the compound. Although I knew the insurgents had destroyed the original police station, this place did not look like the replacement.

The police sergeant singled me out and told me I had to speak to his boss inside. This was nothing unusual, because no one had the courage to make decisions in Iraq, one of the legacies of Saddam Hussein's regime. You always had to speak to the top man, who was also usually the one with the biggest moustache, another Saddam legacy.

I had to go inside and speak to their officer, and although my driver was allowed to join me, everyone else had to stay outside. I did not want to split up our team but it looked like there was no option. But before heading inside, I snatched a few moments with the rest of the guys. I made it clear that I was still unsure about the cops and told them to make a break if we were not out in 20 minutes. I reckoned any longer and we had had it.

Here goes I thought, as the huge steel gate swung open and the two of us were ushered inside the yard. As the gate clanged shut behind us, it was clear that we had walked into a lion's den. There were dozens of police waiting inside and they milled around us, pulling at our clothes and hitting us as we were half shoved and half dragged towards the building. Once inside, we were manhandled down a dimly lit corridor and a door swung open at the end. We were pushed into a room where an officer was sat waiting for us behind a desk. He told us to sit down and introduced himself in perfect English.

After all the pushing and shoving by the mob out in the yard, this guy's calm attitude and well groomed uniform was just what we wanted to see. He looked the real thing, unlike his men. The three pips on his shoulder were also reassuring. You never saw a captain's uniform for sale on the market; no one wanted the responsibility.

He started by apologizing for bringing us to the station but he had reports that we had refused to stop at the checkpoint. Then he explained how his men had been forced to fire a warning shot and how we had returned fire, alerting the second checkpoint. It was clear that his men had conjured up a different version of events to cover their backsides, landing us in a whole load of trouble.

Eventually the captain looked up and signalled me to give my version. I told him how I had been in Iraq for over three years doing the job and knew the drill at checkpoints. The sergeant shifted uncomfortably when I explained how we had found it deserted and he protested when I explained how we had come under fire. I put the question, why would we stop to return fire once we had passed the checkpoint, we would have carried on. As I finished, I invited the captain to go and look at the bullet holes in the back of our car to collaborate my story. I was also anxious to get back outside because my 20 minute time limit was nearly up.

The sergeant was fuming because I had accused him of lying in front of his boss. However, the captain stood up and gestured to his men to escort us out to the car; he wanted to see the evidence for himself. I was hoping that the rest of our guys had not tried to do a runner, because we would be in big trouble if they had.

As the compound gates were thrown open, I gave a sigh of relief to see the rest of the team still there. In turn they were looking at me to see if I knew what was going on. It was too early I gestured, as the captain walked around my car, inspecting the damage. I asked if he would check our weapons too.

It did not take him long to work out that they had not been fired upon and he spun round and started shouting at his sergeant. As he was now on the defensive, I felt it was time to reiterate how we had followed procedures and that we had not done anything wrong. As the captain's fury increased, the sergeant eventually confessed what had happened.

He hesitantly explained that the recent spate of suicide car bombs in the area had made his team nervous. The sight of three unmarked cars approaching the checkpoint at dusk had looked suspicious, especially when two stopped at a distance while the lead one drove up to the chicane. He assumed that the leading car was carrying a bomb while the other two were filled with armed gunmen, waiting to finish them off. Rather than tempt fate, he had withdrawn his men to a safe distance to see what happened.

When our first car had headed off, he assumed that the 'suicide bomber' had decided against detonating his explosives at the deserted checkpoint. After warning checkpoint two what was heading their way, he had ordered his men to open fire on us. And the rest was history. Charming I thought, he thought I wanted to blow myself up. But while I could see it from his point of view; it did not help us.

By now the captain was furious. Not only had his sergeant failed to follow his orders, he had told a few lies to save his skin. As the captain ordered two of his guys to manhandle me back inside, everyone wanted to get involved. Arguments broke everywhere as I was pushed down the corridor to his office and made to sit in front of the captain. But we were not alone; everyone wanted to get involved.

The Iraqi way of sorting out issues sometimes involves everybody and I suppose you could call it their version of a Chinese Parliament. Only theirs is far from civilized. There seemed to be no order as everyone in the room shouted their opinion. Some were angry that I had exposed their sergeant as a liar. The sergeant was repeatedly shouting that I am a foreign mercenary and how can anyone believe me over him? What had started so well out in the car park had turned nasty very quickly. After a while I seemed to have been forgotten entirely as everyone shouted at each other and waved their arms. And this time I had not made any plans for the rest of the guys to get away.

In the middle of all this, the door opened and two guys in U.S. military fatigues walked in. I gasped as one said in an American accent "Hey man we heard all the gunshots, what's happening?" The first thing I noticed was their full beards, which were not allowed in the regular army. "Hello" I thought, "are the U.S. Special Forces operating around here?" With a puzzled look I asked them "don't tell me you two are Americans", as they nodded, I laughed and said "well I have never been so glad to see Americans..." They too laughed as I explained that I thought we were done for.

They assured us we would be OK and one calmed the situation down in fluent Arabic. The captain's attitude mellowed quickly and a handshake changed the mood in the room. We were the best of friends in the time it took to boil the kettle and chatting away as one of the cops placed a tray of their best china and a huge tea pot on the table. Sipping tea together was another Iraq tradition used to soothe over any discussion.

As the rest of my team were ushered in for a cuppa it was smiles all round and the Special Forces guys explained what we had stumbled upon. It turned out the Americans had established a small Special Forces camp close to the police station but nobody was supposed to know about it. They kept an eye on activities in Tal 'Afar, sharing intelligence with the police. They never got involved in the checkpoints but the sound of gunfire had alerted them and, fortunately for us, they had decided to investigate.

The Special Forces guys invited us to stay in their camp for the night and promised to escort us out of the area in the morning. Although their camp was a rough and ready affair inside an abandoned warehouse, anywhere would have done after all the excitement. After coffee and food we were happy to settle down anywhere safe.

We were saddled up ready to go when the sun came up over the horizon, anxious to head back to Erbil. The police also wanted to see us off their patch and we had to wait for their escorts before we were given the all clear to move out. They led us past the town, far too slowly for our liking, but for once no one took any notice of our little convoy. Our escorts made a U-turn at the roundabout marking the eastern end of the bypass and we split right, watching the ruins of Tal 'Afar disappear in our wing mirrors. Only one more checkpoint to go and we were out of that horrible place.

Up ahead we could see the concrete chicane across the road when our Tail End Charlie reported a small convoy of trucks closing in behind. As the trucks loomed up in my wing mirror, it was clear they belonged to the Iraqi Army and as the lead driver started blowing his horn, a horrible thought went into my mind; the Iraqis had changed their mind, they wanted to escort us back into the town for further questioning.

I did not want another misunderstanding so I came on the radio, "Pull right... pull right... let them past." As our three cars came to a halt, they were showered in dust as three trucks filled with troops drove past. They pulled up, nose to tail, at the checkpoint about 300m ahead. I did not want to join their queue, so I told the team we would wait until they had cleared the checkpoint.

We watched as the policeman came out of his hut and shouted up to the driver and we watched as the two of them exchanged pleasantries. Then our jaws dropped as the checkpoint erupted in a cloud of smoke, dust and flames. Three IEDs had been hidden in the scrub either side of the road, positioned to crossfire shrapnel into the chicane. The explosions destroyed two vehicles, and while the soldiers started jumping off the third, several dozen insurgents rose out of the scrub to the side of the road and opened fire.

As the surviving Iraqis scrambled for cover and tried to return fire, I called over the radio, "About turn... about turn"; it was time to get out of there, although I wasn't sure where we were going to go... As we made a U turn in the road, the squeal of tyres turned a few heads and the rounds started coming in. As my driver spun the steering wheel and hit the gas, I pulled the client to the floor and not a moment too soon. My car was now at the back of the convoy and it attracted most of the fire. We all ducked down as the windows started shattering and although none broke, the splintering glass scared the hell out of us. We did not sit up straight in our seats until the sound of bullets thudding against the armoured panels stopped. We later counted over fifty holes in the car, all made in a matter of seconds.

Talk about out of the frying pan and into the fire. We were now caught in a trap and it looked like there was no way out of there. We are heading back towards Tal 'Afar in bullet riddled cars... The police would be on their way to investigate the explosions and guess who was speeding away from the scene? Yes... we were... The questions raised by our situation did not bear thinking out. Were the IEDs planned for us; did we lure the Iraqis into a trap; was this incident linked to the one the night before; and who knows what else. Only one thing was certain; it did not look good.

As Tal 'Afar loomed on the horizon I thought we needed an escape route and fast; so it was time to improvise. A quick glance at the GPS showed nothing but open land either side of the road. However, the map showed a small side road which headed through a couple of small villages before stopping at the edge of a wadi. The main road was just beyond and we would join it beyond the checkpoint. The question was could we get across the wadi? Well it was worth trying and after ordering my driver to overtake the rest of the team, I called over the radio "follow me right onto a dirt track, 500 metres".

Driving down a road that had never been checked was against our procedures but on this occasion I was prepared to take a chance. We followed the dirt track through the villages and the noise of our cars brought the locals running to see what all the commotion was. They stood open mouthed as we raced past in a cloud of dust and I doubted any of them had seen a car before, never mind three bullet riddled ones filled with Westerners. I bet they are still talking about us today.

The sweat was rolling off me as I strained to catch a glimpse of the wadi ahead, but for once the map was bang on and I called a halt as it loomed up in front of us. The good news was that we could see the main road on the far side but it definitely was a case of so near yet so far. The dirt track ended in a fording point used by the locals to get their animals across. While the ramp down was gentle and the mud in the bottom looked fairly dry, there was one hell of a steep climb out. But it was worth a shot.

As I called over the radio for everyone to stand by, my driver nudged the car forward down into the wadi. Everyone held their breath as the tyres dug into the muddy streambed, but there were enough rocks to grip on as we edged across. Now for the difficult part and I shouted back to the client, "hold on tight, we are nearly home". My driver hit the gas, slipped the clutch and the car lurched forward, the engine groaning as we climbed up the slope. And then we jumped over the crest, like a cork popping out of a champagne bottle. And if I had had a bottle I would have opened it there and then because the main road was right in front of us.

Five minutes later all three cars were across the wadi and after a short drive across country, we skidded onto the tarmac and away we went. The first building we saw was the prison and you can bet that we have never been so pleased to see a prison. However, the biggest cheer went up when we crossed the Great Zab River into Kurdistan. Only then did I feel brave enough to call up the villa on the satellite phone and tell them that we were finally heading home.

By the time we dropped our client off at his hotel in Erbil, he was a changed man. His nerves had been shaken after coming under crossfire at the checkpoints while the attitude of the Iraqi police had not helped. He had not slept much in the SF camp but I think the IEDs were the final straw.

Although he had a lot of praise for us, he made it clear that the job was not for him and I understand he put in for a transfer soon afterwards.

Most of the guys were out working when we pulled back into the villa compound in our bullet riddled cars. The stories would have to wait until later because I still had an office to run while the guys had to prepare for the next run.

If you are wondering what I learnt from Tal 'Afar, I would say it was just one of those days when you have to grit your teeth and keep calm to get through. There were several occasions when I could have taken a different decision and things could have been a little easier; alternatively things could have gone horribly wrong. It is all too easy to reflect on bad situations with hindsight and draw the wrong decisions.

Chapter Twenty Two

The End Game

AFTER WE HAD BEEN IN IRAQ for a couple of years, we all realized that the situation across the country was changing and that our contract could not last forever. We were successful but that was part of the problem. We were employed by one of the largest American companies working for the C.P.A. and our company name was cropping up in many circles. We were getting involved in larger contracts, some for our own client and some for others. Our problem was that we were a British company and while that went down well in the British sector around Basra, it was upsetting a few people in the American sector.

One contract which raised a few eyebrows involved escorting two huge electricity generators from the Jordan border to Baghdad South power station, a distance of 300 miles. They would replace worn out generators neglected under Saddam's regime and provide electricity for large parts of the capital. Now that might sound straight forward but the logistics involved moving them across the country were one big headache. Each generator was worth around $250 million and while a lucky RPG or mortar round would cause catastrophic damage, even a single bullet could cause $10,000s of dollars worth of damage. Any damage would be the jackpot for an insurgent and we had to protect it.

The generators had to be moved by massive tractors hauling large trailers, each around fifty metres long, with hundreds of small wheels to distribute the weight. They had a top speed of around five kilometres an hour and we faced a nine-day journey escorting them through some of the most hostile territory in the world at the time.

After crossing the Jordan-Iraq border at Turaybil we would drive east across Al Anbar. Then came the dangerous section, the Sunni triangle, where the road passed through Al Ramadi and Al Fallujah, the hotbed of insurgency. 1st Marine Division had recently ended a campaign to clear the area of insurgents but Abu Musab Al-Zarqawi led hundreds of insurgents into the area as soon as they withdrew. They were digging in for a last stand battle and we just had to hope that they did not turn their attentions to our generators. After passing through the Sunni Triangle, it was a simple case of getting them past Baghdad and to the power station.

During the planning stage the U.S. military made us a bizarre offer; they put a list of 300 assets at our disposal to use along the route. An asset had a value rated at a number of tanks, aeroplanes or helicopters. Each one could cover only parts of the route, as they could not transfer from division to division. So we had to plan carefully, deciding what asset would work where, like some crazy computer strategy game. Only this game was for real and our lives were at stake; not to mention the $500 million of equipment. If the insurgents took them out we would be front page news; and for all the wrong reasons.

We reckoned that the effective mortar range was around 3,800 metres and one lucky strike could make a whole lot of money go up in smoke. So we asked the military to organize a five kilometre exclusion zone. Our personnel would travel in nine armoured 4x4 vehicles and they would drive up and down the convoy at slow speed, giving the drivers reassurance. They could also stop any crazy fool who slipped through the military net armed with a grenade or suicide vest.

As dangerous as it sounds, the job was one of the most boring, yet surreal experiences we had ever undertaken in Iraq. All day long we drove up and down the crawling convoy, giving regular thumbs up to the lorry drivers and trying desperately not to get on each other's nerves. The military did what they promised, creating a safe bubble around us, dropping by regularly to check on us. We stayed in the cars soaking up the cool air from the air conditioning during the day and slept under them at night. And hour by hour, and day by day, we edged closer to the Sunni Triangle.

The map indicated four over bridges at road intersections up ahead and we guessed they were too low for the generators to pass under. We considered driving around them but there were concerns that the trailers would bog down in the mud if they left the road. As it turned out we need not have bothered worrying.

As we approached the first intersection we could see, to our surprise, that the bridge had gone. The U.S. military engineers demolished it with controlled demolitions, collapsing the bridge deck onto the road below. Excavators then moved the rubble to the verges, leaving the road clear for us. The missing bridge was a bit of a shock but it made sense when we thought about it. The cost of a replacement generator far outweighed the cost a new bridge. Only the engineers did not do it just once; they did it four times.

After Al Hambar we drove through the Sunni Triangle, the hotbed of insurgents. As we crawled along, we occasionally saw glimpses of tanks or Humvees moving in the distance and sometimes we could hear shooting. Planes and helicopters flying overhead were also a constant reminder that we had a precious piece of cargo on our hands. However, apart from the military in the distance we rarely saw or heard anything suspicious around the generator. The bubble was certainly complete around and above us; a completely surreal experience.

The journey felt like it lasted a lifetime and the only break in the boredom was the occasional visit by a senior officer as we entered his unit's sector. It was a case of look interested, see if there was anything different in his briefing and then continue along the way. After nine endless days on the road we were relieved to pass through the gate of Baghdad South Power Station. Two huge expensive bits of kit delivered in one piece and one healthy pay cheque for us.

However, there had been a lot of controversy when the contract was awarded to our company. Many in the Green Zone believed that American companies should be protecting such important pieces of equipment. So did some people in the United States and complaints were aired in the American press that one of the star contracts had been awarded to a British company. In hindsight we may have been awarded the contract to avoid any arguments over choosing one American company against another. Who knows? While it raised the company profile, it also made it a target for a takeover...

We met our client every three months for a review of progress and, more importantly, to discuss what the future held for us, so we could plan ahead. Our clients' faces said it all when we sat down for our quarterly meeting in the autumn of 2007. We knew they had bad news. Their contract was up for renewal at the end of the year and word on the street was that clients who employed American security contractors would be favoured. It was a case of jobs for the boys and it stemmed all the way back to political pressure coming from Washington D.C. More than once we heard that pressure was being put on our client to watch where its money was going. Our client explained that two American security contractors were already looking at the new contract, with a view to bidding for it. But there was no point complaining because senior American politicians had connections with the reconstruction and security industries in Iraq. And the money involved was billions of dollars a year.

Believe it or not, our turnover had climbed from nothing to around $30 million a year in less than four years. Not bad for a few ex-Army lads and less than $1 million investment. There was $120 million for the new four-year contract up for grabs at the current turnover but it could easily double if the client continued to increase his workload. There was also a good chance that the successful company would be offered work with other infrastructure companies.

We already had around 270 employees and from a personal point of view it was starting to get too big for my liking. Although we tried giving our contracts as much personal attention as possible, the company had grown much larger than we could have imagined. We also prided ourselves on using as many ex-Special Forces guys as possible but the rapid expansion of security work around the world was making it difficult to find them.

It was also getting harder to please everyone, be it the military, the C.P.A., the Iraqi police, the client; you name it, they all had an opinion on how we should conduct our business. In the early days in Iraq we had been given a free rein, which was the Special Forces way of doing things. We were used to being given an objective and then being left to accomplish it, no questions asked. The new regulations and laws were stifling the initiative which we thrived on and, more importantly, the initiative which made us successful. It was getting harder to do our work and it was going to get harder.

Some of the larger American companies were drawing unwelcome attention to the work of the security contractor due to unfortunate incidents. While we had avoided the limelight and worked hard to stay below the radar, it was becoming increasingly difficult to stay out of the media spotlight. Sometimes in life you just have to walk away from a situation and it looked as though this was one of them.

One American security company was very keen to get the contract and we understood that their bid was likely to be much less than ours. The company was one of the big players in the world of security, with thousands of personnel and hundreds of armoured vehicles working on contracts across the Middle East. It had the infrastructure in Iraq and could easily pick up where we left off. And with that sort of worldwide backup, it could afford to be cheaper.

During the meeting our client dropped the bombshell; our contract was going to the American company. Four and a half years of building up a security company on the back of rebuilding Iraq was going to end. It was over as far as the company was concerned because we had no assets to sell; just a contract which was about to be terminated. We hired the vehicles from our client, rented our premises from Iraqi landlords or the U.S. and British military, and most of what we earned went on wages. To put it bluntly, without the contract, there were no assets to sell and no good will to pass on, just a good name, and we could not sell that on.

When the meeting was over I discussed the outcome of the meeting with the four other guys who had started the company with me. We all felt pretty much the same; it was time to move on. Two had already been contacted by other companies and they had jobs to walk into. The other two were looking to have a break before planning a new future outside of Iraq. I felt the same. I had made a few dollars, had one hell of an experience and had learnt a lot. I had lost some good friends along the way though.

So with the contract signed over, I was asked to attend a handover meeting with the client and the new contractor. It seemed strange to be back in Kuwait City, where our journey had started; just five of us and a couple of hire cars. Thoughts about what had happened since then, some good memories and some bad, flashed through my mind as I was driven through the city streets to the hotel. But the main one which stuck in my mind was, would I do it all again if knew then what I knew now. I am still stuck on that one.

I did not know what to expect as I entered the hotel and made my way up to the executive suite where the meeting was scheduled. I had to forget thoughts of the past and get my business head on ready to focus on what lay ahead. The client had to explain the terms and conditions of the handover while I had to explain the business to the new contractor. It was not something I was looking forward to. Imagine spending lots of time and effort building a classic car with your friends and then having to hand the keys over to a stranger and explain the controls to them so they can drive it away. Well that is the closest analogy I can give.

As I walked into the room, I was surprised to see a face from the past waiting to shake my hand. It was the guy we had escorted to Mosul two years earlier when we lost two good guys in the ambush. That was a bit of a turn up I thought, but the introductions did not last long because there was a lot of business to get through.

As we sat around the table the meeting started grimly with details of our contract termination. I knew them all already and while I did not want to hear them again, it had to be done. The new contract made sure we could not just walk away from the business though, no matter what we thought of the situation. It stated we had to work through a handover period of one month during which our guys would work side by side with their guys. This allowed them to pick over the bones of our operation, seeing what we did and how we did it. It would limit the amount of hitches and make it a smooth transfer in which the client's work would not suffer.

The new company would also have to employ anyone who wanted to stay on and they would continue to work under the existing contract until it was renegotiated after twelve months. The idea was not to put anyone out of work, after all the client wanted as many experienced men as possible to stay on for as long as possible. Well that was the guys sorted but there was no such grace for the partners. We were out... The new company had its own directors waiting to take over and start implementing the new regime.

As the meeting drew to a close it was time for the exchange of the contracts; the final signing on the dotted line which would bring it all to the end. Shuffling the papers before him, the client looked at me and said "I told you that I would never forget what your guys did for me in Mosul". All I could do was nod my head, waiting for it all to be over. "Well I meant it then and I still mean it now", he said smiling and slid the contract across the table to me. I looked puzzled, wondering what to say. The client then looked across the table at the new contractor's director and in a firm voice said "you have to buy the contract from them."

Looking back at me, he said "now, tell him how much you want for it". My mouth dropped as his words sank in, it was unbelievable. I was taken aback and, for once, lost for words, as the concept sunk in. I was not expecting this at all. The client could see that I was stumped and he broke the silent tension. "I will tell you what I will do. I will give each of the partners a sum of money. If you pass that contract over now," he said.

As I said earlier, my partners had already planned our futures, believing that we were walking away with what we had already saved. We had not been expecting anything else. I was not going to argue, so I said it was a deal. We thought we were going to get nothing and this was a big bonus. The new contractor then asked if two of the partners would stay on to maintain contacts in the British military.

I was stunned as I signed and passed the contract back across the table. I never thought we would walk away with a lump sum. After all we had gone in there and built a security company out of nothing. The whole idea was still sinking in when I called my partners to explain the deal. If we signed now we would all get different things. The other two had been offered posts by the new company, and again that is what they wanted. 'I was out of the game' and so was another; it suited us because we had both had enough of Iraq. Part of the deal was I had to leave Iraq immediately, and I could not return because I knew too much about the workings of the company. Maybe they thought I might have unsettled the guys if I went around saying my goodbyes; I was also banned from corresponding with them for the foreseeable future. All in all they had it well tied up and there was no way I was going to influence what they were doing in Iraq.

Within 45 minutes of landing at Kuwait the deal was done and we all knew what we were doing. It all happened that fast. All that was left to do was to sort out contractual matters with our respective lawyers in London. And of course it was time to have a little party to celebrate getting something out of the contract. And party I did, all night at the Sheraton Hotel where I was staying. The relief of getting out of the business, both alive and with a few dollars, was immense.

After that everything went very smoothly because the new company had organized everything in advance. Their personnel had already been booked on flights and they were flying in to take over our three offices in Shaibah, Baghdad and Erbil. After a brief handover period it was all theirs.

We also had to put out messages to all the employers stating that a new company had taken over. They still had their job and the work would continue as before but different guys were running the offices and the paperwork had a different heading. And that was that, no party with the lads, no time to shake hands or say thanks to them all. Just get on the plane and leave. After over four and a half years it was over...

I flew to England the following day and after an overnight stop in London it was time to go through the fine print with both teams of lawyers. It was clear that the payments would be made in three instalments and my bank confirmed that the first was already in my account. The remainder would be released when the new company was sure it had what they expected; the men, the equipment and the weapons we were handing over.

The next thing was to forward money to the families of each of the guys killed working for the company. We had made a collective decision to divide 20% of the money equally between them. We all felt that we had done well out of the business and wanted to do something for the families. Although each one would receive a sizeable sum, it was no compensation for losing a loved one. Payment plans were organized over the next few days and the phone calls followed because we had not warned the families. Each call went the same as they asked why had a lump of money just appeared in my bank account, what's happened? We explained it was the least we could do – and yes, if you are wondering, it did ease our conscience a little. After living off an army wage for years, it felt strange to be in a position to give money away.

As for my future, employment possibilities were limited. There was an exclusivity clause, stopping me from getting involved in security work in Iraq or Afghanistan for the next three years. They also stated that any job offers in that line of work had to be approved by the new company before I could start work.

And that was that. In just over a week I had gone from facing the end of the contract to coming out with a chunk of money and a lot of memories, some good and some bad. Many of them I have shared with you. And that was the end game – it was over. It was time to pick up where I had left off after that fateful day, September 11, 2001; the day which had changed my life. It was time to catch up with my family, spend some time with the children who were growing so fast and time to reflect on my experiences. And it was also time to decide what to do next.

You are probably wondering what happened to the lads that had worked for us for two or three years? Although we could not contact them while they were working for the company, they were straight on the phone or email as soon as they left. Over the months that followed it was possible to work out what had happened after the new company took over at the beginning of 2008.

A lot of American personnel moved in and along with them came the American way of working. The old system had promoted individuality and leadership while the new system stifled both. A regime of meetings and committees was installed and many of the original guys did not like it. After being used to being given an objective and the freedom to work out how to complete it, they did not like being told how to do things. Many of the original guys who had worked their way up to be project managers and team leaders, walked away soon after we left. But many of the regular army lads were happy to continue under the new regime. It was all a matter of personal choice. One day soon they too would be facing the same choices I was facing having survived more than a few cheeky moments in Iraq.

Postscript

Still Living the Dream

IN MARCH 2013 IT WILL BE TEN YEARS since the Allies invaded Iraq and only a short time later we made our first covert drive up to Baghdad. We were in the country until the end of 2007, losing seventeen guys in three and a half years. Looking back I do not know how we lost so few... I guess our training helped us on many occasions while luck intervened on many more.

The non-competition clause in the termination contract prohibited me from returning to Iraq to work for three years, so I was effectively redundant. That was unless I found completely different security work which had been approved by the new company. Either way, a holiday was required and I returned to Mallorca to spend time with the family. I also needed a blow out to wind down; and there were many.

But after a few months of enjoying life, it was time to find something new to do. Old friends had been in contact and offers of lighter work started to come my way. It usually involved close protection work, the sort we had excelled in around Iraq, only London was far safer than Baghdad. As part of a team I was involved in looking after a few high profile people, including a few bankers who were rather unpopular in the wake of the Credit Crunch. It was popular at the time to 'bash a banker' and we had to make sure our client could get from A to B without getting harassed by the mob or hassled by the media.

Some of our clients were rich people from the Middle East who had chosen to live in London and they wanted a security team living with them, protecting their family and their home. We also had to escort them around the capital and sometimes to other places. I was also on teams who looked after film stars and working at places like the Cannes Film Festival and the Monaco Grand Prix was a far cry from the Green Zone and Route Irish. I guess the craziest client we looked after was the Crystal Skull at Cannes as part of the publicity for the 2008 film 'Indiana Jones and the Kingdom of the Crystal Skull'. Although it was the quietest thing I had looked after, it was certainly the creepiest.

Construction site security was also becoming important, particularly in the build up to the 2012 Olympics. Some groups did not want the Games to be a success and they hoped to plan a security incident to raise their profile. I found myself up against Eco-Warriors at Weymouth as they battled to stop the bypass for the Olympic regatta site. Then for two years I worked as a security consultant to the Olympic committee when it was clear that both al-Qaeda and the Real IRA would have liked to stage an attack. Fortunately, we all know they did not.

While engaged in these part time jobs, I had also become involved in a couple of new ventures based out in Mallorca; a nightclub and an energy drink. Both were risky investments and they both tied up my time and money. But I had a lot of fun, met some interesting people and learnt a lot of lessons.

But by 2012 I was getting itchy feet and needed to get involved in something more up my street. The non-competition clause had expired so I could talk to who I wanted and it did not take me long to get involved in a new venture; the gold business. The price of gold has rocketed since the financial crash and so has the desire for it, both at a personal and national level as people lose confidence in cash. So yet again it was time to take advantage of the situation and put my skills to the test once more.

After taking over six months to get the right team together I am back into the breach so to speak. Our skills are being used to secure gold from some of the deadliest places in Africa. Just think about the film 'Wild Geese' with Richard Burton, Roger Moore, Richard Harris and Hardy Krüger, and you are not far from the truth. They were just better looking and had more hair than we do.

Best Wishes

JG